ERNEST HEMINGWAY

A Reconsideration

ERNEST HEMINGWAY

A RECONSIDERATION

Philip Young

THE PENNSYLVANIA STATE
UNIVERSITY PRESS

 1966
University Park and London

ACKNOWLEDGMENTS AND A NOTE ON THE TEXT

The present volume is based on the text published in London by G. Bell and Sons in 1952, which incorporated a very few changes in the text originally brought out by Rinehart and Company, New York, also 1952. The original volume has been revised extensively in minor ways —by changes of tense, deletion of old footnotes and substitution of others, the addition of several details and the striking of a few. The Foreword and the Afterword are new.

The critic would like to express again his gratitude to the memory of Ernest Hemingway who, despite the deepest misgivings, eventually granted permission to quote without reservation from his work—as well as to Charles Scribner's Sons, publishers of most of it.

He also thanks the *Kenyon Review,* in which both the section on *A Moveable Feast,* substantially in its present form, and the new Foreword, here somewhat expanded, first appeared.

Library of Congress Catalog Card Number 65–26101
Copyright © 1966 by Philip Young
All rights reserved
Printed in the United States of America

Designed by Marilyn Shobaken

"Giving style" to one's character—a great and rare art! It is exercised by those who see all the strengths and weaknesses of their own natures and then comprehend them in an artistic plan until everything appears as art and reason and even weakness delights the eye.

ALSO SPRACH ZARATHUSTRA

PREFACE

Jake Barnes, principal character of Hemingway's *The Sun Also Rises,* was reading Turgenev very early one morning while drunk on brandy in Spain, and he speculated that one day somewhere he would remember it all, and what he read would seem really to have happened to him. There must be a good many people, sober, evening readers, who will remember Hemingway somewhere. And if they do not feel that it all happened to them, exactly, at least they remember it. People who read modern fiction at all can generally bring to mind a few of his stories and two or three of the novels. Things like the "Hemingway style," the "Hemingway hero," the "manner" and "attitude" of Hemingway are very widely recognized. Back in the minds of all literate Americans there is a place where this man etched a few lines. He is a part of our reading past, and the cleavage between what has happened to us directly, and what has happened to us in books, is not so deep as some think.

Hemingway made a difference. There are people who do not admire his work, but even these are perfectly ready to admit—if only that they may deplore the fact—that he is "important." It is hard to think of a contemporary American who had more influence on modern writing, or on whom both general readers and literary critics are more likely to agree that the experience of his fiction is worth having, or, in his own time, of a writer more widely publicized. And yet despite all the attention, Hemingway's work, which is what we should ultimately remember him for, is still by no means as well understood as it might be. The purpose of this book is to help increase the understanding of a limited yet unmistakably major American writer.

P.Y.

University Park, Pennsylvania
January, 1966

CONTENTS

FOREWORD | AUTHOR AND CRITIC: A RATHER LONG STORY

Wherefore do I take my flesh in my teeth. . . .

JOB

July 2, 1961, it was, late of a hot bright Sunday morning, when the phone rang with the news of Hemingway's sudden departure from the living. All the instruments agreed: the day of his death was a hot bright day, and the shock of it ran the whole world round. His scorn for the "cowardice" of self-destruction, especially as he had planted it in the thoughts of the protagonist of *For Whom the Bell Tolls,* seemed to rule it out for him—on the entirely foolish assumption that a man who had expressed his bitter distaste for suicide could not in another country, condition, and era commit it.

We were conditioned to expect that Hemingway's death would come with a bang

1

when it came; following the airplane crashes in Uganda in 1954 there had already been obituaries. Most important I had recently learned through an unusually direct and accurate operation of the literary grapevine that the author was a great deal sicker than the press, on his two hospitalizations, had announced or been in a position to know. But the news hurt anyway.

After great pain, claims the poet, a formal feeling comes. What came instead were more phone calls—later a couple of telegrams, later still letters—all excited and to the same effect: You called it, Young! These messages belong to a rare species of the genus Congratulation, but the recipient was not gratified. Nor was the remark particularly accurate, as anyone who reads this book will see, unless by extrapolation from it. But there is more to this than first appears, and it is fortunate that an objective statement of the problem already exists.

In a preface to the new edition of his *Art of Ernest Hemingway* the British critic, John Atkins, provides a sort of "Coming Attraction" for the present volume:

> ... shortly after my own book appeared there came an extremely interesting study by Philip Young. I understand that Hemingway tried to prevent the publication of this book. Its treatment was very intimate ... and if its diagnosis was accurate it was a brilliant piece of work. If, on the other hand, the diagnosis was specious and only apparently consistent, it was a piece of impudence. According to Hemingway, it was a collection of mistaken conclusions based upon partial information. . . .

Fair enough, as a statement of a difference of opinion; and understandable enough the "irritation of Hemingway and his widow" toward Young that Atkins mentions later

on. But then, with reference to Hemingway's first protagonist, Nick Adams, comes the trouble:

> Many of us had been puzzled by our own reaction
> to those early stories. . . . We felt they contained
> some deep significance. It is to Young's credit, I
> think, that he revealed this significance by showing
> the subject-matter to be the aftermath of fear. . . .
> All his life he had exposed himself (overexposed
> himself, claims Young) to things he feared. It may
> be a distasteful thing to discover, but I cannot
> help feeling that Young virtually foretold self-
> destruction.

"Distasteful" is not entirely adequate. But the question
is, if the diagnosis were specious and mistaken, how could
Young have "virtually foretold" suicide on the basis of it?
It is important first to get the picture hung straight.
Move number one is to repeat that Young did not predict
suicide. He described a situation, a pattern, a process in
Hemingway's life and work in which the act of suicide
would not be altogether inconsistent. Second move is to
state that nobody I know of recognized such a prediction,
nor was I ever aware of it, except by hindsight. But I
think—I feel?—that there is a deeper problem only a very
few have been tactless enough to raise.
Suppose, as is the case, the author had in advance
warned his literary analyst of the enormous damage a
psychological working over could do him. Suppose further
he had mentioned a very long letter, almost certainly to
the same effect, that he had composed but, since it could
only, he said, give the critic worry, he was not going to
mail. (To tell a writer he has a neurosis, Hemingway did
write me, is as bad as telling him he has cancer: you can
put a writer permanently out of business this way.) Suppose then that critic, critic's critic, editor, and publisher

all believed that Hemingway was needlessly and irrationally alarmed about the matter and so went ahead and produced a book which contains, among other things, a description of a syndrome the critic thought he had found in the author's work, which he believed the author's experience had caused him to delineate carefully there, and from which an after-the-fact prediction of death by his own hand could be, and was, imaginatively inferred. Could a head-on collision with such material conceivably have anything at all to do with the destructive way in which the syndrome worked itself out? If a diagnosis implies a prognosis can the diagnosis operate so as to induce the prognosis? Or help prevent it? Or have no effect at all?

Before questions of such complexity the critic is understandably mute. He does not know enough about the places and how the weather was to make even an impudent guess. Among the countless events that crowd a man's life, and this was a very crowded one, it is utterly beyond him to measure the effect of any single event. All he can know certainly is that for a year or two the "threat" of his book had an unmistakable effect on Hemingway and that in subsequent recorded interviews, right down to the last one, Hemingway was mindful of it.

But worry the critic has had—letter mailed or no. However his full discomfort, like his alleged prediction, came only after the fact. At the time of his struggle with the author, which developed into a struggle with himself as well, he simply could not get it into his head that a totally obscure $3,100-per-year instructor at the Washington Square College of New York University could actually hurt the most confident (apparently) American novelist of his age—and, next only to Faulkner, the best one. Neither could any of the others involved. Save only Hemingway.

In short, the critic is not as sure as he once was

(once he felt quite sufficiently sure) that in his eventual "victory" a greater degree of right triumphed over a lesser degree. This is no matter of *mea culpa,* which would constitute an act of impudence to pass all men's believing. (Anyway, much of the tale is less morality play than farce.) And the critic will still defend the thinking according to which he and others, not knowing their own infernal strength, if Hemingway was right, built the case for publishing the book. Nor would he hesitate to make the case for bringing it out again. But it helps to admit at the start that like the ancient subterranean brook which is flowing still under Washington Square something is running under his reasoning, silently tugging at the foundations of it.

*   *   *

I had liked this writer for a long time, and had even ported a *Portable Hemingway,* along with a very few other books, half way across Europe during World War II. But the story really starts later, with some well-remembered moments of a postwar afternoon in one of Iowa City's most wretched apartments for young-marrieds when the pieces of my fragmentary reading of him began to fall into place—and, simultaneously, to align themselves with a recent and then-heterodox rereading of *Huckleberry Finn.* What I knew I had, if it would flesh-out, was the argument for the subject of the doctoral dissertation I had to write. Flesh-out it did, as things went along, in all kinds of ways.

The story consists more of endings than starts, however, and the first one came in 1948 when I first finished the job—the first book-length study of Hemingway, I believe—and lurched off with the degree. There are two arguments among several to be found in that strenuous effort, as in this book, which are necessary to an understanding of subsequent events. First: the notion that the so-called "Hemingway hero" as I defined him was pretty close to being Hemingway himself. Second: that one fact about this recurrent protagonist, as about the man who created him, is necessary to any real understanding of either figure, and that is the fact of the "wound," a severe injury suffered in World War I which left permanent scars, visible and otherwise. I should also put it down for later relevance that in the beginning I answered a frequent question—what does *he* say about all this?—by explaining that since I knew roughly how he felt about critics and academics I was pretty certain he would not reply and hadn't asked him. When the question became oppressive I did write to ask if he wanted to comment and I was correct in the first place; he didn't answer. (At least I can take satisfaction in knowing that I did not start the procession of "these damn students" who "call me up in the middle of the night to get something to hang on me so they can get a Ph.D.") (Or, as he metaphorically looked at it, did I?)

The first of an impressive number of celebrations attended this ending; as for my work, it was supposed to pass and be forgotten with the rest. And, except for doing a nice little piece of business on the inter-library loan circuit, it had begun that process even as my wife and I made our way to New York. But that first finish was undone when I was conned by some generous and well-intentioned people into a tedious interchange with a couple of university presses. And that misadventure ended when after eight months one unmentionable editor (he had once shot an antelope or something and was a great fan of *Green Hills of Africa*) returned the volume with the explanation that he was going to publish instead a work which would pretty much upset it. (Just how I was not to learn, since if that book appeared the secret never leaked.) Meanwhile, however, a good friend and colleague at

N.Y.U., William M. Gibson, had read a copy and had sent it to a trade publisher with a college department, Rinehart and Company, where was employed a friend of his named Thomas A. Bledsoe.

Mr. Bledsoe was soon to figure largely in this story. He in turn became a friend and also established himself as the best all-round editor I ever encountered. He compounded at least one spectacular mistake of mine; he was forever on the road when we should have been in action back at 232 Madison Avenue; when he was there he was badly overburdened with all sorts of other books. But he worked with energy, intelligence, taste, and understanding from start of this to finish and I am still in his debt— especially for a couple of organizational and strategic ideas that worked.

The first smart thing Tom did was make a prompt offer, which was that if I would clean the thing up so as to get the Ph.D. out of it (largely because the subject resisted the same there was less of that than is normal), and if I would arrange things so that Hemingway shared less of the stage with Huck Finn, then Rinehart would publish it. Astonished and delighted with a new dimension to things, I attended my first of those let's-get-together-soon-I-mean-it New York luncheons, and became quite looped in a happy, expansive sort of way.

Thus for several months, exercising in the still night when only the moon raged, and the lovers lay abed, I remorselessly did the job over, chapter by chapter, adding one and junking another, until it was finally finished. But we only thought it was done, because right then, as if out of nowhere, came the announcement of Hemingway's first book in exactly a decade. This novel appeared initially in some improbable magazine; once each month I minutely observed the current idiosyncracies of Col. Richard Cantwell, protagonist of *Across the River and Into the Trees*.

Of all living readers only John O'Hara and Carlos Baker, I believe, have refused to call this near-parody of Hemingway a bad book. But I wonder when a critic-errant ever had a more astonishing adventure with a new work; it was precisely as if the author had got hold of my manuscript, incomprehensibly had determined to prove its notions to the hilt, and had brilliantly succeeded. For without pretending otherwise the Colonel was about as close to his author as it is possible to get and still be called fictional, and now it was *Hemingway* who was demonstrating how his life had centered on that violent World War I misfortune. Here was staggering evidence for my argument, and nothing to do but put it in. Put it in I did. And finished again.

Even at this time I knew that when critic and editor have done all they can for a manuscript a common practice is to send it out to an Independent Expert. So I said if you're going to do this, how about Malcolm Cowley? He had been a friend of Hemingway's for many years, had himself written well and substantially on the subject, and was rumored to be available for such assignments. I had never met him at this point, but Tom knew him and thought he was a good if obvious choice. So the critic's critic was employed.

Cowley was to become the unintentional agent of a great deal of trouble but at first he certainly earned his money. In April of 1951 he sent me directly a detailed interim report, which was a thoughtful thing to do, as I could begin considering changes at once. He related as well a good deal of factual information which I couldn't put in the book but which was reassuring anyway. In particular he brought up places where I had given impressions I hadn't intended and places where I had made bad guesses, and he objected to several things that I felt I wanted to leave the way they were. A month later he submitted his formal report, and I profited once more. He was gratifyingly enthusiastic about the first two and last two chapters, less so about the three in between, which I had already tediously reworked. But he had some solid objections, and I did a few things yet once more, finally in late May winding it up again.

The subsequent celebration took a nasty turn and became a wake. After reading the study Cowley had sent an informal account of it to Hemingway, commending much of it to him, and Hemingway had unaccountably got a very odd impression of what I had done. He proposed at once to stop it; and when Cowley had the letter to this effect, he reported it, with his hair on end, to Bledsoe, who had said nothing to me while I was still at work on this book of criticism. The letter was from Ernest to Malcolm and dated 22 May 1951.*

What Cowley reported in horror I read in shock. About this book of Young's, Hemingway wrote. He was absolutely determined that no biography of him was going to appear while he was alive to stop it. All he had to do was refuse to grant permission for quotation from his work, and then if the project went ahead all he had to do was turn it over to the lawyers. He was sorry, but every single time he had tried to be polite or helpful or

* Not even that date is a quotation (Hemingway didn't write dates in that fashion), and it may be necessary to make clear why it is not. In May of 1958 Hemingway wrote out an edict, with his wife as witness of it, to the effect that his letters, or even parts of them, were never to be published. One comes to understand his reasons. His letters are typically open and free-wheeling (and often very funny); he took few pains with the composition of them; he wanted to be remembered for his work, not his biography. But no one knows what "never" to be published, in this case, means. One thing it almost surely does not mean is "never." It certainly, however, does not mean "now." In savage retaliation to this policy I hereby refuse myself permission to quote from my own letters, or from Cowley's or Bledsoe's either.

frank to someone who was trying to make money out of his life it had gone badly. Thus if Mr. Young planned to publish his life while he was still in it, he would block him. He had no desire to be rude to Mr. Young or Mr. Bledsoe, but this was his considered stand and he did not intend to budge.

Perhaps this looks easy. I had most assuredly not written his biography—nor have ever wished to—and as for making money no one was more surprised than I, except the publisher, when the book did turn a profit. But to me it looked more than a little ominous. The book was criticism. But maybe you could call it "biographical criticism"; it did unfashionably contain enough biography to demonstrate that the experience of the hero was typically a refraction or projection of the author's. A sense of foreboding I couldn't account for distracted me even as words for a message of clarification began to form in my mind. But it was instantly decided that Rinehart would do the straightening out, and I acquiesced. Thus began what I still think of as The Year (it was really longer than that) of the Great Mess.

The struggle that followed was in large part real enough, but some of it was unreal and some of it was ridiculous. The real questions were, first: what are the rights of living authors, and what the rights of critics? Second: at what point can criticism become an invasion of an author's privacy? And how much privacy can a writer expect when he has allowed himself to become an internationally public figure, or even, according to some, had worked very hard at promoting the image? Lastly, and this was much the toughest of the lot: given a respect for the author, which grew as the struggle progressed, how far is the critic willing to venture, even in defense of the author against many other critics, in violation of the author's deepest wishes that certain theories about him not be published? (As I said, much of the debate was then as now as much with myself as with Hemingway.)

As for the false part: in addition to being no biography written to cash in on his life the book was in no way, as he warily seemed to feel, an attack on him. Quite the contrary. And as for invading privacy, I had from the start been careful to include absolutely nothing of a factual nature that I had not already seen in print, although I knew a great many other things. Only my organization of the facts, which was really a perception of how I thought and think *he* had, not far beneath the surface, organized them, was new. And as frustrating as anything was that the single impediment to publishing the book when it was ready was the pre-announced refusal to grant permission to quote from his work and, if I quoted anyway, to take legal action. The joker in this pack was that nobody but Hemingway thought he would have a case. Despite his confident belief, which without any appreciable effect first Cowley, then Bledsoe, patiently explained to him to be almost certainly unsound, the considered opinion of the literary-legal experts like Morris Ernst was that if a case came to court in which a critic had without permission quoted for legitimate purposes and was not trying to sell the author's work as his own, the court would almost certainly find for the critic. (This was, however, a useless opinion in this instance, and Hemingway simply ignored it, probably figuring as I did that it didn't matter, since no reputable publisher at that time was likely to go to press without having satisfied the convention.)

In the light of the reality of central problems, however, it is remarkable how much of what happened was farcical. In the first place nobody, but nobody, except Hemingway answered his mail promptly. (When this eventually dawned on him he cut it out.) Indeed Bledsoe, who was in the naval reserve, went off at one critical point on an extended sea venture, having stowed away in his gear a letter that he thought he'd left behind for his immediate superior, Ranny Hobbs, to deal with. There was nothing to be done; I didn't even find out which ocean he was on.

Second is the fact that at this time Hemingway was living in San Francisco de Paula, which is a hamlet near Havana, Cuba. Now the mail clerk at Rinehart, whom I once or twice encountered on the elevator, appeared to be a nice enough girl. But I don't believe she ever did really master what I came to think of as the Cuba Concept. This had nothing whatever to do with politics, Castro not having yet been heard of. It was made up of the notion that Cuba lies outside the territorial limits of the United States. Thus mail journeying there by plane required three cents, I think it was, in extra postage to make the trip successfully, clear customs, and get unpacked. As a result of the clerk's failure to comprehend this, our letters, already long overdue, would typically wing south only to float back as it seemed on the trade winds, covered with blurred purple lettering which when deciphered and translated always turned out to signify Returned for Insufficient Postage, and had to wing it again. (The misconception must have been contagious; toward the end even Hemingway, in reverse, picked it up.) Then a fit of petty jealousy brought in the United States Post Office; two of our most winning bits of diplomacy touched base first at San Francisco, California, only later to take off, somewhat dispirited, in a proper direction.

And, Lord help us, there were the lawyers. Hypersensitive to Hemingway's pithy references to law and lawsuits, Official Rinehart (but never Bledsoe) ran scared all the way. I may not have all of it exactly straight, because much of this specialized activity, or inactivity, was not deemed suitable for my observation. But if the reports I got were accurate *three* firms had the manuscript to check out for libel—of which of course there wasn't any. One lawyer broke his hip, became intensely irritable, and refused to do any work during a lengthy stay at the hospital. After another long delay another lawyer announced, under some pressure, an Imminent Opinion ("by Monday"), whereupon he expired over the weekend. Then I heard that Stanley Rinehart and Charles Scribner appeared to have the thing about patched up on the front-office level when Mr. Scribner died. And all that time— it was nearly a year—until Hemingway wrote to ask why in hell he never heard from the *author* of the damned book, my hands were tied (and sweating).

Obviously things moved very slowly in this adventure-by-mail, which needs only a little cleaning up for family consumption and a little care in correcting the spelling (else one would be quoting).* We had not even got started with the correspondence when, six full months after Cowley's original shocker, he wrote Tom again. By this time the situation had become so miserable for him he wished he'd never heard of the wretched book. Word of it had apparently reached Hemingway from some additional source; anyway, we learned that by now the author

* Hemingway had, to use his wife's phrase for it, "this crazy thing about spelling," which was chiefly that he usually inserted an "e" in words that do not conventionally retain it— e.g., liveing, writeing; the extra vowel in his *Moveable Feast* exists in honor of the practice. It is possible that he had some subtle purpose in mind here, but that would not account for the various ways in which the word "psychoanalytic" was later to appear; nor does it make his position impregnable when in the *Feast* he kids Fitzgerald for having known him "two years before he could spell my name" (which usually came out "Hemminway"). (But truth to tell it is doubtful that Fitzgerald could have survived the first cut in a fourth-grade spelling bee, while Hemingway, if he put his mind to it, could.)

was so disturbed that he had written his own publisher a whole *series* of letters on the subject. Since Cowley had commended the project to him in large part, he now seemed to Hemingway vaguely aligned with the enemy. Understandably the critic's critic wanted to take his leave of the affair at this point—which only made Hemingway all the angrier at the man he referred to in one letter as an old, close friend (the same man who had done a good, honest job on the manuscript, and whose offer to return his check for it Bledsoe naturally refused). It is not pleasant to recall the time many years later when Cowley told me that following this mix-up he never once heard from Hemingway again. But I also know that Hemingway subsequently praised one of Cowley's books, and I remind myself that he has a compensatory privilege in being one of the very, very few who are going through all the manuscript Hemingway left behind.

Up to this point neither Tom nor I had written Hemingway, nor had we heard directly from him. On 3 December 1951, however, Tom did write, as Cowley had done and as we should have done six months before, in an attempt to bring the whole matter into focus. Some time later (due to insufficient postage our letter had only just arrived) the author replied at great length. And an open, rambling and friendly letter it was. But it boiled down to his insistence that too much had already been written about his life. First there had recently been Cowley's own long biographical study in *Life* which, well-meaning as it was, had the effect of moving attention from his work to himself. Then there was the notorious *New Yorker* "profile" by Lillian Ross, another good friend. Despite her complacence this had horrified him when he read it in proof, but he had done nothing to interfere with it. The result of all this (and much more), he felt, was that his writing was being judged from the standpoint of these widely-read biographical impressions and not on its own merits. He had not discouraged any of these people (they had all needed the money) but by now he had had bloody-well enough. Although he had been a very long time hearing from us and wondered why and intended to be firm, he did not wish to seem rude or intractable, he said. He predicted that pretty soon there would be no writers, only critics, who would go off to Hollywood and be wrecked by the movies. What did we want to bet that Arthur Mizener wouldn't soon be on TV? All we had to do was get him another Scott Fitzgerald. I have nothing against Professor Mizener, but it was a most ingratiating letter, which ended wishing us a good holiday.

The holiday was Christmas, and better than a month was to elapse before Hemingway was to get a response to his most friendly overture. But it should not be assumed that Bledsoe and I were idle all that time. Indeed not; we were busy making things infinitely more difficult. Christmas time, for all healthy-minded college and university English teachers, is also Modern Language Association time, when we stage our own peculiar version of a plumbers' convention. The proceedings that winter were in Detroit, and I had been invited to read a short paper on Hemingway. I did, it was a mistake, and when Bledsoe finally answered Hemingway's letter (he'd been extensively on the road again), he enforced the error, proudly describing the reception of the talk, which he had attended.

Tom's letter, again returned for more stamping, arrived on the evening of January 16. The next morning Hemingway replied to it and by now his patience was tiring. He pointed out that in a frank and friendly way he had spelled out his position only to wait a month for a response to it. If Mr. Bledsoe was too busy, why didn't he hear from Mr. Young? Was it true that Mr. Young was corresponding with a critic in the Sudan? * He couldn't understand why, if Mr. Young had time to be traveling about giving papers on his work, he couldn't find time to write the author about it. *And* send along a copy of the talk. He closed, but on January 31 added a postscript explaining that he had put the letter aside for two weeks so that he would not be the only person involved who answered his mail. He also stressed his eagerness to read my paper: he felt it might help him in his present efforts.

The trouble was that, as assigned, my effort (restricted to something like twelve minutes) was a critique of three Hemingway papers that preceded it. Two of those papers were by chance psychoanalytic in approach—John Aldridge's "Jungian," and Frederick Hoffman's "Freudian." To establish the widest possible area of agreement among us I followed the lead, voted for Freud, and, carrying the tendency of Hoffman's remarks to what seemed a logical conclusion, ended with what I still take to be the appropriate psychoanalytic terminology. Hemingway's sense of indignation at this vocabulary did not surprise anyone. My position is what needs explaining.

There were two lines of defense at this dreadful juncture. One is that I stumbled on the psychoanalytic theory and its terminology *after* I had completed my own analysis of the wounding process and its results, which I felt Hemingway had delineated carefully only to have the whole matter ignored by his swarming critics. I remember this clearly. As part of my General Education, back in Iowa, I was reading *Beyond the Pleasure Principle* when it suddenly broke over me that Freud was writing about precisely the kind of thing I had constructed out of

* Probably a reference to Atkins who was, I believe, in the Foreign Service.

Hemingway's scattered descriptions of it. Told that Freud had undergone a lot of modification, I got hold of Fenichel, recommended to me as the most authoritative of the post-Freudian Freudians, and there I found a more detailed account of the same business. What I had called, in a very special sense, "primitivism," Fenichel called "primitivation"; I had written "shell shock," he called it "traumatic neurosis." All I had done in the paper was to supply these and other terms, and to remark how skillfully Hemingway had illustrated them in fiction.

The second point is that for the MLA there was no need to waste even thirty seconds acknowledging the obvious fact that the critic was no trained analyst. I have a recent anthology called *Psychoanalysis and American Fiction,* which has fifteen contributors; all of them, including myself (but not on Hemingway), are English professors or literary critics or both, and not one of them felt the need to point out that he has no medical license to practice. It might have been unreasonable to have expected Hemingway to know this, but in our branch of service, as the saying goes, it goes without saying.

Rinehart clearly was betting no money at all on my diplomatic talents; before my first letter to Hemingway had passed a board of review Bledsoe had written again, and on February 12 received an eloquent reply. First noting that for once sufficient postage had been supplied only to have the letter go to California (he enclosed the envelope), Hemingway gritted his teeth and remarked once more how much he looked forward to hearing from me in person and reading my paper. But he said he had a real objection to people who won't leave writers alone to do their work (precisely why, except for my reluctant, unanswered letter of years before he had not been aware of my existence until hearing from Cowley). And people don't wish writers luck. They annoy them and worry them instead of simply hoping they will be healthy, live a long time, escape financial and female difficulties, and most of all go on writing. Writing is very tough work, he said, yet it requires mechanisms as delicate as the most delicate mechanisms imaginable. If someone comes along, not himself an expert, and takes the machine apart for his own benefit, it's all very well to say that he has a right to take any old machine apart, but Hemingway did not feel the right existed while the mechanisms were still in good running order. And that was what he meant when he said some criticism constitutes an invasion of privacy.

A man who cannot, first shot, put down two English sentences in a row that are nowhere barbarous did not need telling that writing is an extremely difficult way to pass the time. But the important fact to me was that on February 6 I had the first chance to present the case myself—which, despite the cogency of Bledsoe's and Cowley's letters, I probably should not have relinquished in the first place. I explained my previous silence, pointed out that the connection between himself and his recurrent protagonist was not in my mind the central idea of the study, and tried to salvage what I could from the Detroit debacle. I expressed my admiration for his work, noted that my own book had come to mean quite a bit to me, too, and closed.

At this point Hemingway went on a fishing trip, and it was one month to the day of my first effort when he sent the most memorable reply I ever got from anyone. It began with a simple offer: if I would give him my word that my book was not a biography disguised as criticism, further that I was not psychoanalyzing him alive, then he had no objection to my publishing it. He was not going to go over the whole business again, he said. But then he wondered if I really understood how damaging it could be to a practicing writer to tell him he has a neurosis. It damages him with all his readers and could so injure the writer himself that he could no longer write. He said he had found my Detroit paper, which I had so kindly sent him, very interesting; but he was shocked by my use of serious medical language. He repeated it: the paper he thought interesting, and likewise the conclusions of it, but he was shocked by the terminology when there were no medical qualifications for employing it.

What followed, as he tried to explain the amount of trouble I had caused him over the past ten months, shocked me. It surely seemed to him, he said, that there were enough dead writers to work on to allow the living to work in peace. So far I had caused him serious worry, hence a serious interruption in his work. First there was Cowley, who had disturbed him with that first report, and next, leaving a mystery, had washed his hands of the thing. Then there was all the rest. The disturbance caused by me, he said, had been very bad for a man who was trying to keep his mind peaceful during a year which had already seen the death of his first grandson, the serious illness (cancer) of his father-in-law, the death of his mother, the death of a former wife (mother of two of his three children), the suicide of the maidservant of his house on the heels of a previous attempt, the death of his last old friend in Africa, and then the death of his very dear friend and publisher, Charles Scribner. On top of everything were piled the menace of my book and then the neurosis or neuroses charges made in Detroit. Out of all this he said he sincerely hoped my luck had been good; his assuredly had not. (Many of his letters had been composed on an obviously decrepit typewriter but this one was hand written, three pages of it, and he explained that the lines were askew because of the hot day, which made his forearm sweat on the paper.)

The effect of seeing myself in the company of such events was nearly catatonic, so that, although I thought of little else, two weeks elapsed before I was able to respond and to clear the response again with the board. I had begun to think my initial sense of doom was profoundly justified. There did not seem much point in explaining that I had studied a good many writers, most of them dead, without coming up with a set of ideas that would support the like of my doctor's thesis and the consequent book. What I said instead was that the easy way would be to give the word he asked for. I could satisfy the letter of his conditions. But I was less sure about the spirit of them. He had been so decent throughout this business that I couldn't tell him less than the truth. The biography part was simple but not the psychoanalytic; perhaps I should have offered simply to remove what little I had got from the analysts. I was glad to read, eventually, Mark Schorer's judgment that this material was handled with "great sensitivity," but a couple of other reviewers were to remark that my case would stand without it, and as already noted there had been a time when it had not been around to cut. But the shoe I handed readers to put on if they wished seemed to fit so well I could not resist offering it, and I tried instead to explain: there were only a few hundred words of offensive matter; it dealt with *nothing* but the wound; *I* had not done the psychoanalyzing—had, rather, quoted from two analysts and called their theories plausible and incomplete. One thing I was trying to show, I wrote him, was the remarkable resemblance between a psychiatrist's description of how a man acts who has been badly hit and his own account of, say, Nick Adams fishing the Big Two-Hearted River (which he had complained no one had ever understood). I also told him that however much things had gone astray I had surely never intended to injure him in any fashion. If a critic could hurt a writer with his readers then it must follow that he could help; I hadn't wasted the better part of the last few years trying to knock anybody down. I said I felt badly about having caused him so much trouble, and that I did, very much, wish him well.

It was not surprising when at this point Hemingway lapsed into a complete silence. As the weeks went by, it became clear that we were on dead center. Ranny Hobbs sent a cable asking for a favorable decision on my letter; a few days passed; then he received a cable from Hemingway saying that he was thinking my letter over as I had done his. He would write soon. But he did not, for a long time. The situation had ceased to be bad and had become desperate; conceivably the whole project should have been dumped at this point. But that did not really seem an option to me, because of a scarcely less serious situation that had developed simultaneously with these events.

Following the postwar G.I. bulge of students, enrollments at N.Y.U. dropped precipitously, and as an untenured instructor in 1951 who had not published anything breathtaking I was perishing fast. Although no one had told Hemingway this, I was, by the time now reached in the story, unemployed for a whole year. Except for the mercies of the American Council of Learned Societies, which paid a small wage to keep me from leaving the profession (as I had come near doing in Detroit), and for the fact that Carolyn, my wife, had a part-time job as hostess in a tea-roomy sort of restaurant, I don't know what we would have been eating. Further I had no job for the next year, and when I eventually landed one it was strictly a temporary appointment so that I faced unemployment again for the following year. Lastly, since the book had long ago been announced all over the place I was receiving a certain amount of static from the wrong quarters about not being able to deliver.

Thus I felt that if I was unable to get Hemingway's go-ahead for what I thought the right reasons I had very little choice but to try to get it for the wrong, and so on 23 May 1952 I wrote again, explaining very briefly my predicament. I also said that, although it was none of my business, it was hard for me to understand why, because she needed the money, he had assented to Miss Ross's "murderous" *New Yorker* profile but would not permit a book which made the strongest case it could for his importance. Anyway, I felt now there was only one thing I could do. If he would not grant the conventional permission then I was quite prepared to rewrite the book paraphrasing all the quotations. I was positive he would prefer his own language to mine but it was up to him how it went. Bledsoe wrote to confirm it: Rinehart would publish the book that way. Five days later I had a cable from Hemingway telling me to inform his editor that permission to quote was granted. He said he hoped I was happy.

Over the years I had accumulated a good deal of circumstantial evidence of Hemingway's generosity. He liked very much to be generous; perhaps for some reason he needed to be. I thought then that however much he deplored what he thought I was doing to him he seemed now to want to be generous with me, and I wrote to thank him. I remarked that I could scarcely be happy when it was so clear he was not, but that I was grateful and accepted his kindness not only because I needed it but because I thought—as Cowley had thought—that he would be pleased with much, not all, of the book.

The insufficient postage problem originated with Hemingway this time, so that two weeks later I got a letter that had been written before the cable was sent. It was a warm letter. He said that as a matter of principle he would maintain his stand with Mr. Bledsoe forever, but that however mistaken he thought my book he felt badly at its being held up and my chances for making a living impaired. Since he was granting the permission, it would only worry me to have a very long letter he had written me, so he was not mailing it. Then it was as if all his skies cleared and the sun poured down. He would tell Scribner's, he said, to pay to me instead of him his share of my permission-costs (this was done), and if I had practiced economy in quotation to hold down expenses, he would be pleased if I would quote more extensively. (I hadn't realized the quotes were to be paid for, so there was no need of this.) Lastly he wrote that he was real sorry, buddy, if I was in crummy shape financially. He could let me have a couple of hundred and I could still feel free to call him a bastard if I wanted. If I was broke I couldn't be sued.

I did call on the Scribner editor, Wallace Meyer, who gave every appearance of having expected a man with at least two heads. Settling down we went over the principal quotations I was going to make; I seemed again to have passed some sort of examination; then I wrote Hemingway at once (no board of review any more) accepting his generosity with the permissions-fees and declining with thanks the two hundred dollars. I listed each and every quotation, including bits from things not published by Scribner's, and assured him that there had never been a moment when I felt like calling him a bastard.

There followed a rapid exchange of entirely coopera-tive and cheerful letters. After discovering precisely and down to the tiniest detail what words of his I was using, and commenting on several passages of them, he approved them without protest, exception, or change. Habitually he would extend the friendliest of best wishes, remark the heat, and include some little diversion such as an anecdote. I did what I could to reply in kind.

Negotiations had been going on for over a year now but the end was once more in sight; the manuscript, all tattered and torn, was once again at Rinehart ready to go. And then publication of *The Old Man and the Sea* was announced. I had known "a new book" was in the works. Hemingway had written that he hoped I would like it— that although he had gone through it over two hundred times it still did something to him. Mr. Meyer had predicted I would like it: there was not, he said, a single four-letter word anywhere in it. (Not even, I thought, "this" or "that" or "fish"?) But I had not known publication was imminent. So back from the printer came all my pages. I read an advance copy on its arrival, and did at that time like it, and wrote a new rousing climax to the chapter on the novels which (hopefully) had already climaxed twice. Then a few months later my book, officially dated 1952, unbelievably did appear—on the twenty-sixth day of February in the year of our Lord nineteen hundred and fifty-three.

I remember little of that celebration except driving back late from Tom's house on Long Island, with a knowing but now silent and vicariously exhausted Carolyn beside me, and finding myself irrevocably committed to the George Washington Bridge, hence to New Jersey— which would not have been absolutely unacceptable but for the fact that we were then living in the Bronx. I remember too the morning after, when of all books published that day the *Times* reviewed mine, and Charles Poore offered me a medal for composing the atrocity of the year. (February was pretty early in the year for that, but then it turned out he was editing a Hemingway omnibus for Scribner's.) I stifled an immediate response to the gist of his attack: he must be crazy to say that I had said Hemingway was crazy, thereby proving that I was crazy. And that was the last bad review I saw.

*   *   *

Partly because I had not realized in how many out-of-the-way places book reviews are made I was astonished by the number that appeared. (For instance there was the *Public Spirit* of Hatboro, Pennsylvania—"highly recommended"—which metropolis I had never heard of.) The book came out shortly afterward in England, where reviews were equally generous, and then, translated, in Germany, where sales were excellent. It was published as well in Spanish and has long been postponed to appear with Hemingway's *Collected Works* in Italian. A substantial piece of it was in a French journal, and bits of it came out in such unlikely tongues as Telugu, Bengali, and Marathi. Best of all it was pirated in the Argentine, and when Rinehart went to collect it was discovered that the publisher, a Peronista, was both bankrupt and in jail, which is the start of a saga the reader is to be spared.

From feature stories in the papers to solemn academic exercises, several writers paid the honor of plagiarism. (If imitation is the sincerest flattery then what's plagiarism?) (Almost as good as piracy.) There were television plays, at least two movies, and one live play (which happily closed before it ever got to Broadway) that revealed a bungling study of the book. So much of this went on that I finally decided to crib myself, and by invitation wrote another *Ernest Hemingway,* the first pamphlet in the flourishing Minnesota series on American writers. This has now appeared in three English versions, three in Japan, two in Spanish, and one each in Italian, Portugese, Japanese, Arabic, Korean, and Pushtu (which, according to my *Britannica,* is the language of the Afghans,

90% of whom are, it says, illiterate). The book itself, reverting to type, went out of print the very week it was selected for the new White House Library, and it took nearly three months of real effort to locate a fresh copy for Washington.

Mindful of this run the original question left unanswered becomes central: what did Hemingway say? Several reviewers had wondered about this; the *Times Literary Supplement* had asked it, and more, with a vengeance: "Though simple and at first sight devastating, the argument is solidly based on a thorough analysis. . . . What will happen to Hemingway when he has read this book?" Curious to find out about this myself I mailed him the first advance copy I got hands on, and in view of his great alarm, followed by the enthusiasm, I was surprised at the speed with which he returned it—the wrapping reversed, my name and address carefully lettered in. Very well, I thought; it can't hurt him a whole lot if he doesn't read it. That returned parcel was the last contact.

Before long, however, I began hearing from people who knew him, and it became clear he had read the book all right. Then when he took the Nobel Prize, *Time* ran a cover story on him, and the anonymous interviewer who went to Cuba asked him what he thought of it. "How would you like it," he asked, "if someone said that everything you've done in your life was because of some trauma?" Also, with reference to the amazing list of his physical injuries I had compiled, he objected that he didn't "want to go down as the Legs Diamond of Letters."

Many years later, in August of 1965, *The Atlantic Monthly* ran some free verse of doubtful quality by the author and along with it an interview by Robert Manning, which seemed to have been conducted in the same period as *Time*'s and remarkably resembled it. On this occasion Hemingway is reported as saying of the book: "If you haven't read it, don't bother. How would you like it if someone said that everything you've done in your life was done because of some trauma? Young had a theory that was like—you know—the Procrustean bed, and he had to cut me to fit into it." (The mystery of the similarities is cleared up by our man in Havana, who submits intelligence to the effect that there was only one interview—and some correspondence: the *Time* reporter was Robert Manning too.) *

An indecisive but somewhat different exchange took place later in the *Paris Review*. Editor Plimpton:

> Philip Young in his book on you suggests that the traumatic shock of your severe 1918 mortar wound had a great influence on you as a writer. I remember in Madrid you talked briefly about his thesis, finding little in it, and going on to say that you thought the artist's equipment was not an acquired characteristic, but inherited, in the Mendelian sense.

Ernest Hemingway:

> Evidently in Madrid that year my mind could not be called very sound. The only thing to recommend it would be that I spoke only briefly about Mr. Young's book and his trauma theory of literature. Perhaps the two concussions and a skull fracture of that year made me irresponsible. . . . I do remember telling you that I believed imagination

---

* Mr. Manning had added a little to the record by noting in a letter the great care with which Hemingway had obviously read the book and the good-humored way in which he rejected it, so that his remarks, Manning says, look more hostile in print than they sounded in conversation. In a subsequent and only mildly obscene letter to his interviewer Hemingway rewrote my list of his wounds so as to make it hilarious. He also added to the reference to Legs Diamond his disinclination to enter literary history as a clay pigeon.

could be the result of inherited racial experience. It sounds all right in good jolly post-concussion talk, but I think that is more or less where it belongs. . . . On the question you raised, the effects of wounds vary greatly. . . . Wounds that do extensive bone and nerve damage are not good for writers, nor anybody else.

The only other reports received on the subject of the author's reaction to the critic's book have come from old acquaintances unforgot, and the last one reliably described came not long before Hemingway's death. Professors Leslie Fiedler and Seymour Betsky, both then of Montana, had called on the author in his Sun Valley home. A short time later Fiedler was in my house, where he briefed me on the shocking, unpublicized condition of the writer's physical and mental health—which is why I was not as startled as many with the news of his explosive end while at the same time being perhaps more moved by it. Fiedler was unable to recall what had been said about the book, but Betsky did remember and wrote me that to the best of his recollection Hemingway's exact words were: "Mr. Young is a good man and he is certainly entitled to his opinion of my work. But I think in his book he was riding a thesis and I think the thesis distorts the work somewhat."

I wish I had expressed that second sentence myself. All theses distort the work in some degree. In trying to get at the figure in the carpet, the man who thinks he has found the essential pattern ignores at least for the time it takes him to demonstrate it the whole of the rug for the figure in it. But when he is done, he hopes that the pattern will sink back into the carpet, and the carpet none the worse for wear. Even, maybe, if the revelation was truly new and sufficiently convincing, all the more to be valued.

1 | ADVENTURES OF NICK ADAMS

Maria: "You were too young. . . . You were too young for such things."
Pilar: "Don't speak of such things. It is unhealthy."

FOR WHOM THE BELL TOLLS

On the Place Contrescarpe at the summit of the rue Cardinal Lemoine, Harry remembered, there was a room at the top of a tall hotel, and it was in this room that he had written "the start of all he was to do." Harry, dying of gangrene in a story called "The Snows of Kilimanjaro," can easily be connected with Ernest Hemingway, who wrote the story, and Hemingway had in mind some prose which finally went into his first significant book. This posed as a book of short stories, and was published in New York in 1925 with the title *In Our Time*. After Horace Liveright had bowdlerized one story (an amusing but rather nasty piece called "Mr. and Mrs. Elliot") and had cut out another completely ("Up in Michigan"), it consisted of thirteen short

29

stories and several interchapter sketches. And it was as germinal a book for Hemingway as ever a book for a writer. It was truly the start of everything he was ever going to do.

The title *In Our Time* may simply have been meant to indicate, as is commonly thought, that the material was contemporary, and to some extent representative of early twentieth-century experience. But Hemingway delighted in irony and in titles that are quotations; it is almost certain that he intended here a sardonic allusion to that phrase from the Book of Common Prayer which Neville Chamberlain was later to make notorious: "Give peace in our time, O Lord," for the stories are mainly of violence or evil in one form or another. It is that there is no peace in them.

These stories alternate in the book with sixteen short "sketches," which are of contemporary scenes and for the most part are of sickening violence. These are arranged at least roughly according to the order in which their author experienced them. With one very notable exception, however, they have no other apparent relation to the stories. Moreover, half of the stories are unrelated to the main interest of the book, which is the spotty but careful development of an important but little-understood character named Nick Adams.

The stories about Nick are subtly, even obscurely, organized and presented. It is not always obvious that Nick is any more than an observer of the events they relate, and his age is never mentioned. But the book cannot really be understood at all without the clear perception that the stories are arranged in the chronological order of his boyhood and young manhood, and that the volume is in large part devoted to a scrupulously planned account of his character, and the reasons for it. The well-known "Big Two-Hearted River," for example, cannot possibly be read with comprehension unless one understands the earlier stories. One would think it no more than it pretends to be —a story about a man fishing—and it would be, as readers often used to complain, quite pointless. So the unrelated sketches and the stories not about Nick are to be more or less put aside for the moment in order that an obscure but meaningful pattern may emerge.

In Our Time opens with an "Introduction by the Author"—"Introduction" in the sense that it sets the tone for the whole collection; "by the Author" in that the events were particularly significant for him. This piece describes Turks and Greeks at a quai at Smyrna, where there are women who will not give up their dead babies, and soldiers who dispose of their baggage mules by breaking their legs and dumping them into the shallow water of the port to drown. And there is the harbor itself with "plenty of nice things floating around in it." "I got so I dreamed about things," says the "I" of the sketch in an apparently unimportant remark which actually looks very far ahead.

The first of the seven Nick stories, and a "typical" one, is "Indian Camp." A typical Nick Adams story is of an initiation, is the telling of an event which is violent or evil, or both, or at the very least is the description of an incident which brings the boy into contact with something that is perplexing and unpleasant. One of the reasons why these stories were once not generally understood is that it is not at first apparent that they are about Nick at all; they seem to be about other people, and it simply seems to happen that Nick is around. "Indian Camp," for example, tells about a doctor, Nick's father, who delivers an Indian woman of a baby by Caesarean section, with a jackknife and without anesthetic. The woman's invalid husband lies in a bunk above his screaming wife, Nick— a young boy—holds a basin for his father, and four men hold the mother down until the child is successfully born.

When it is over the doctor looks in the bunk above and discovers that the husband, who has been through two days of screaming, had found the operation on his wife more than he could take, and had cut his head nearly off with a razor.

> "Take Nick out of the shanty, George," the doctor said.
> There was no need of that. Nick, standing in the door of the kitchen, had a good view of the upper bunk when his father, the lamp in one hand, tipped the Indian's head back.

This is Nick's initiation to pain, and to the violence of birth and death. The story ends (with Nick and his father rowing off from the camp) so "objectively," so completely without comment, that it is easy to understand why readers failed to see that Nick is the central character in a book of short stories that is nearly a novel about him, so closely related are the seven stories in which he appears. Here as elsewhere Nick is not recognized as protagonist unless one perceives that the last page of the five-page piece would be irrelevant if the story were about Indians or the doctor, and also unless one looks back later to see that Hemingway has begun with his first story a pattern of contacts with violence and evil for Nick that he develops in the rest of the stories until he has built what is actually a plot. Like the later and more famous "Killers," "Indian Camp" is Nick's story, with Indians and gangsters only devices for offering him some direct experience of peace in our time.

The next two stories of the collection are called "The Doctor and the Doctor's Wife" and "The End of Something," and they give the boy's first contacts with things that are not violent, but which complicate his young life considerably because they deeply perplex. They are prefaced with two very short examples of contemporary serenity. One is of a military evacuation with a girl holding a blanket over the head of an otherwise unattended woman who is having a baby; the other is about shooting Austrians to death, one after another. The two Nick stories which follow are somewhat more placid, but they are in the nature of early lessons which can be just as unsettling to a boy as violence. "The Doctor and the Doctor's Wife" teaches Nick something about the solidarity of the male sex; more precisely, it presents him with the conclusion that he is completely dissatisfied with his mother. A workman tries to pick a fight with Doctor Adams so that he can more easily avoid paying a large bill he owes for treatment of his wife. The doctor refuses to fight, and Nick's mother, who is a Christian Scientist and will not believe that a man would do what the workman has just done, quotes Scripture. When the doctor tells Nick that his mother wants him, and Nick wants to go hunting with his father instead, the doctor says, "All right. Come on, then," and they go squirrel hunting, leaving the doctor's wife to wonder where Nick is. Nick is still a small boy, apparently (he calls his father "Daddy"), but even so it is clear that he cannot stomach his mother's naïve refusal to face facts.*

"The End of Something" is the end of a sort of love affair that an adolescent Nick has had with a girl named Marjorie. For some reason, possibly because he feels he has an unpleasant task to perform, Nick is "out of sorts." He takes the girl trolling for trout, demonstrates some knowledge of fish and fishing, and finally gets the girl to leave, perhaps for good. These two stories make up the beginning of a somewhat peculiar attitude toward women

* Hemingway remarked once that this story was about the time he discovered his father was a coward. A writer's intention is not necessarily the same as his accomplishment.

which the Hemingway hero is going to have when he is grown—grown, for example, into Robert Jordan of *For Whom the Bell Tolls*. "The End of Something" is also one of the stories of which people complain that it has no "point." This is partly because what point it does have is subtle and slight. The "Old Lady" of *Death in the Afternoon* was not alone when she objected to Hemingway, after he told her another story that ended rather mysteriously:

> And is that all of the story? Is there not to be what we called in my youth a wow at the end?
> Ah, Madame, it is years since I added the wow to the end of a story.

When the old lady insists, however, on hearing the "point," and the author gives it to her, she complains:

> This seems to me a very feeble wow.
> Madame, the whole subject is feeble and too hearty a wow would overbalance it.

The end of "The End of Something," too, is rather less of a bang than a whimper: things can suddenly go all wrong with the pleasantest of love affairs. But the real difficulty in finding the meaning of this story of *In Our Time* is the same difficulty that has been encountered with "Indian Camp": the story is like a chapter of a novel (the book has Roman numeral chapter headings in addition to the usual story titles); it is like a chapter of a novel in that it by no means has all of its meaning when taken in isolation.

The next story, which follows a peaceful one-paragraph sketch describing more shooting of soldiers who are this time coming over a "simply priceless" barricade, is called "The Three-Day Blow," and relates among other things how "The End of Something" felt to Nick: the end of his affair with Marjorie felt like the autumnal three-day wind storm that is blowing: "All of a sudden everything was over. . . . Just like when the three-day blows come and rip all the leaves off the trees." The story extends the pattern of the previous ones and reveals the lesson Nick learned from the preceding episode. The lesson was not pleasant at the time, and it was also disturbing. Nick accomplished his purpose in "The End of Something," and got rid of the girl, but he was not at all happy about it. It is Nick's friend Bill who reveals the lesson, remarking that after all Nick might get back into the affair again. This thought is surprising to Nick: the end "had seemed so absolute. . . . He felt happy now. There was not anything that was irrevocable." And that is about all the "point" there is to this story; Nick is learning things. And now *we* learn—learn why it was that Nick forced that break with Marjorie: she was of the "wrong" class for a doctor's son. It is again Bill who brings this out. You just can't mix oil and water, he says; it's just like it was with Bill and "Ida that works for Strattons." Here is more perplexity for Nick, and the whole business makes him extremely uncomfortable. He did it, but he doesn't want to talk about it, as he says, and it is not until this point that we can really understand why he was "out of sorts" in "The End of Something."

"The Three-Day Blow"—a many-sided story—is also a kind of tour de force, a skillful representation of the conversation of adolescent boys. Nick and Bill discuss sports, drinking, women, and literature while with affected nonchalance they get drunk on Bill's father's whisky. Thus the story also effectively documents Nick's introduction to drunkenness, a condition which is to become important for the Hemingway protagonist and is therefore worth recording.

But these are not the primary issues of the book, and

with the next one-paragraph sketch called Chapter V we are abruptly taken back from the experiences which perplex to the pattern of violence, pain and evil which began with the introduction to the book and the first story in it. This sketch describes the execution by firing squad of six cabinet ministers, and commences a crescendo which continues through the story that follows and then is climaxed by the next sketch to come, in which Nick is wounded in the war. After that event, the going is all down hill.

The center of attraction in the Chapter V sketch is a cabinet minister who is sick with typhoid. He presents a difficulty to his captors because he is too weak to support himself against the wall where he is to be executed. Finally he has to be shot separately, sitting in a puddle of water before the wall with his head on his knees.

This scene serves to introduce the story of Chapter V, called "The Battler." People who complain about the sordid nature of many of Hemingway's stories seldom if ever cite this one, perhaps because the unpleasantness is more in the undertones and in things not said than in the outer events which, though not happy, are not entirely extraordinary in our time. But if the subtleties are drawn out and examined, "The Battler" is as unpleasant as anything its author ever wrote.

It opens with an adolescent Nick who has left home and is out on his own for the first time. He has been "riding the rods" and has just been knocked off a moving freight by a brakeman. He is limping up the tracks, heading for the next town on foot, when in crossing a bridge he sees below him in the darkness a campfire with a man sitting beside it. Nick, in answer to the man's question, reveals that he got his black eye from the brakeman:

> "It must have made him feel good to bust you," the man said seriously.

In the firelight Nick makes out the stranger's face, which was queerly formed and mutilated. "It was like putty in color. Dead looking in the firelight." The man notices how the boy is staring and obligingly exhibits one cauli-flower ear and a stump where the other ear should have been. This makes the boy "a little sick." The small man reveals then that he is Ad Francis, an ex-prizefighter Nick has heard of, and that he is "not quite right" in the head, is "crazy." * He also demonstrates that his heart thumps only forty times a minute. A Negro named Bugs then appears with some ham and eggs, which he fries in the fire. This is a very large Negro who is extremely soft-spoken and polite to his punch-drunk companion, and to Nick, whom he addresses with oppressive deference as "Mister Adams." He makes sandwiches:

> "Just close that sandwich, will you, please, and give it to Mister Francis."
> Ad took the sandwich and started eating.
> "Watch out how that egg runs," the negro warned. "This is for you, Mister Adams. The re-mainder for myself. . . . May I offer you a slice of bread dipped right in the hot ham fat?" Bugs said.

The men and the boy are eating when suddenly the situation, which has been growing somewhat uneasy, be-comes extremely uncomfortable. Ad, who has been sitting in complete silence for some time, starts without provoca-tion to pick a fight with Nick.

> "You're a hot sketch. Who the hell asked you to butt in here?"

* Hemingway surely had in mind Ad Wolgast, the "Michigan Wildcat," who became lightweight champion of the world in 1910 but lost most of his mind in the process, spent away a fortune and was declared legally incompetent in 1917. Blind but still shadow-boxing, he died in the psychopathic ward of the Stockton (California) State Hospital in 1955.

"Nobody."

"You're damn right nobody did. Nobody asked you to stay either. You come in here and act snotty about my face and smoke my cigars and drink my liquor. . . . You're going to get your can knocked off. Do you get that?"

The battler approaches the boy and the situation all of a sudden is saved by the Negro, who creeps up behind Ad, sets himself, and taps him across the base of the skull with a cloth-wrapped blackjack. Bugs then tenderly treats the unconscious man with water until his eyes close; while he lies there still unconscious the boy and the Negro talk by the fire. This, Bugs explains smiling, is the way he has to "change" Ad from time to time—"he won't remember nothing of it." As they drink coffee the Negro sketches in Ad's past, the unpalatable decline of his career and intellect, and reveals that the two men met in jail, and have been together ever since, "seeing the country."

"Right away I liked him and when I got out I looked him up. . . . I like to be with him. . . ."

After this conversation the story draws to a close. Bugs says that he should wake Ad now, and with a graceful apology he tells Nick that he'd better move along so that it won't be necessary to tap Ad again. He gives the boy directions and another sandwich to take along—"all this in a low, smooth, polite nigger voice." Nick walks out of the firelight and back to the tracks where he stops to listen:

The low soft voice of the negro was talking. Nick could not hear the words. Then he heard the little man say, "I got an awful headache, Bugs."

"You'll feel better, Mister Francis," the negro's voice soothed. "Just you drink a cup of this
coffee."

The story ends with Nick starting away up the tracks. For
the first time in the book we get an obvious word about
what the *effect* of what he has seen, done and heard has
had on him: Nick has been so stunned by this twosome
that he walked quite a distance before he "found he had
a ham sandwich in his hand and put it in his pocket."

Clearly, like "Indian Camp," this is a story of a boy
coming in contact with violence and evil, and here for a
moment the force of the impression has been registered.
The story is also, however, among the most suggestive of
Hemingway's; there is more that is sinister and unpleasant
about this gentle, large, courteous and thoughtful blackjacking colored man than may at first meet the eye, and it
can have only one very probable interpretation. The
tender, motherly, male-nursing Bugs is too comfortable
in the relationship with the little, demented ex-fighter.
The companionship which started as a prison friendship
and which is self-sufficient financially (the couple is sent
money by Ad's ex-manager and wife) seems self-sufficient
in other ways. Although Nick understands no more than
that something is very wrong here, the reader may get the
never-stated but potently suggested notion that it is not
only Ad who is queer. This theme, which crops up in five
other stories, in all but one of the novels, and violently,
obsessively, in his posthumously published recollections of
Paris, is normally used by Hemingway as it is used here
—a kind of ultimate in evil. When this atmosphere is
added to the violence of getting punched off a moving
train at night, and nearly being beaten by an ex-champion,
and meeting a highly polished Negro hobo who habitually
blackjacks his companion in sweet good humor and then
nurses him back to consciousness with a love that was

present even in the blow, it is not difficult to see that here is another nice thing that the Author, as in his Introduction, may get to dream about.

The sketch, Chapter VI, which immediately follows "The Battler" is the only place in the book where the interchapter material meets with the stories, and this crossing unmistakably signals the climax of *In Our Time:* X marks the spot, as a short paragraph reveals that Nick is in the war, tells us that he has been hit in the spine, and that he has made a "separate peace" with the enemy, is no longer fighting the war for democracy. It would be quite impossible to exaggerate the importance of this short scene, which is to be duplicated by a new protagonist named Frederic Henry in *A Farewell to Arms,* and to serve as climax for all of Hemingway's heroes for at least the next twenty-five years.

This event, Nick's serious injuring, does two things for *In Our Time* and for the development of the character of the Hemingway hero. First the wound culminates, climaxes and epitomizes the wounds he has been getting as a growing boy. Life—as we have already partly seen—was really like this up in Michigan, where Nick was already well on the way to becoming a casualty. The effect of the wounds Nick Adams has been suffering (and will suffer more of when Hemingway later goes back, with more Nick stories, to fill in) is just beginning to be hinted at: this shell that has caught Nick in the spine is of a piece with the blows he took when he saw the jackknife Caesarean, the nearly decapitated Indian, the battler and the blackjacking Negro, when he felt himself forced to repudiate his mother and his girl friend, when he hit the cinders after a blow in the face on a freight train. This wound, which is to be the same wound which "emasculates" Jake Barnes in *The Sun Also Rises* and is to hospitalize Lt. Henry in *A Farewell to Arms,* and whose scar Col. Cantwell bears more than thirty years later in *Across the River and Into the Trees,* is significant even beyond these facts.

From here on in the Hemingway hero is to be a wounded man, wounded not only physically but—as soon becomes clear—psychically as well. The pattern of Nick Adams' development, which exists so far only in sketchiest outline, is of a boy who, while with his father up in Michigan, and without him on his own as a hobo or with friends, has been learning some lessons about life. These lessons have more often than not proved to be the sort of experiences which could very well cripple an impressionable and sensitive boy. This is the kind of boy Nick is, as the author was shortly to make clear, and his experiences have indeed crippled him, as Hemingway was also to show, as surely as his initiation to shrapnel has done. This culminating blow in the spine is symbol and climax for a process that has been going on since we first met Nick; it is an outward and visible sign of an inward and spiritual dis-grace.

If there were no more to the event than this, it would be crucial for the development of the Hemingway protagonist, who will show the effects of his physical and psychical injuries right up to his most recent appearance. But in addition the injury has an immediate result that is nearly as important as the wound itself. Nick's first reaction, as he waits in the hot sun for a stretcher, is to turn to his friend Rinaldi who is also hit and say: "You and me we've made a separate peace. . . . Not patriots." Of course this could be taken to mean simply that for these two the war is over. But "not patriots" implies much more than that. When Lt. Henry in *A Farewell to Arms* (whose friend is also named Rinaldi) is wounded and has recovered, he is not patriotic to the point of deserting the army and society as a whole. This sketch sharply adumbrates the novel. A "good soldier" would still be fighting the war in spirit if no longer in body, but Nick has decided to hell with it: at this precise point begins the long break with society that is to take the Hemingway protagonist into his expatriation in *The Sun Also Rises,* is to be repeated in *A Farewell to Arms,* is to take Hemingway himself big game hunting in the *Green Hills of Africa* and to the bull-fights in *Death in the Afternoon,* and is to help him make Harry Morgan in *To Have and Have Not* an outlaw up until the moment of his death, when he mends the break and decides that he was wrong. The wound itself the hero will never lose, either as an outward or an inward scar, as long as he lives.

All of this, of course, remained to be shown. It took Hemingway several books and many years to deal with the implications of this short paragraph, and—to make the pattern clearer—he had also to fill in many of the gaps in the sketchy outline we have of Nick. Even before he patched up Nick's biographical framework, however, he added one more important story dealing with Nick's adventures *In Our Time,* and before that a less significant and transitional one called "Cross Country Snow."

This latter story is prefaced with a paragraph, Chapter XII, which describes a fatally struck bull who is looking straight at his conqueror in the bullfight, "roaring blood . . . and his legs caving." The story itself finds Nick recuperated from his injury, except that he cannot "telemark." The war is over, and Nick and a friend are skiing in Switzerland. Skiing (like fishing and hunting and bullfight-ing and drinking) is one of the things that become very important personal indulgences for the Hemingway protagonist now that he is outside society. The trouble here is that by now he is also married. What is more his wife Helen is pregnant, and they have to return to America. Nick doesn't particularly want to go, although he approves the idea of the baby. He says, somewhat hysterically, that if you can't ski, life "isn't worth while." However, he must go back, and the opposition between the fellowship and freedom of the slopes, and the mixed blessings of the United States and parenthood, is about all the meaning the story has.

But "Big Two-Hearted River" gets us back to the main show. This is a long, two-part tale which finds Nick back up in Michigan fishing. It is extraordinary for the often-remarked brilliance of the description of the fishing trip, which Nick takes alone, but there is a lot more to it than that. Yet of all the critics who struggled with it for twenty-five years only Malcolm Cowley discussed it perceptively, and no one really understood it. Cowley saw that some of Hemingway's stories are "nightmares at noonday." "Big Two-Hearted River" is apparently a collection of sharp sensory details, he says, but if it is read closely one realizes that actually it is a kind of "waking dream." There are shadows in the story that one does not see at first; the thing goes on several levels. The fishing is an escape "from a nightmare or from realities that have become a nightmare"; it is for Nick a kind of rite, an incantation, "a spell to banish evil spirits."

Edmund Wilson, who is usually a perceptive critic too, and who wrote an introduction for an edition of *In Our Time,* refers to the Nick we see in this story as a "boy." This slip is only apparently trivial, for to fail to see that the boy Nick is by now a man is to fail to see the development that has been taking place in his character, and how the stories are related to each other; it is to miss seeing what *kind* of man he is, and therefore, of course, what made him that way, and thus it is to read the whole piece wrong. In order to read it right one must place it firmly in the evolution of the hero Hemingway has been tracing, and see how it is the unhappy result of the quiet and sketchy but meaningful pattern the author has been building up. The story is crucial for all of Hemingway because here and for the first time we get a sustained look at the remarkable effects of what has happened to the boy who innocently accompanied his father into the Indian camp so many years before.

At the outset of the story we are told that Nick has returned to country that had been burned out a year ago, though he hadn't known about it. He is excited over the trip because "it was a long time since Nick had looked into a stream and seen trout." Later he remembers that he and a friend of his, who is very wealthy and owns a yacht, were once going to cruise the northern shore of Lake Superior, but "that was a long time ago. . . ." Obviously, Nick is a grown man now, who has been away. He has been abroad, as we have seen, and in a war.

The opening page of the fishing trip establishes the atmosphere of shadows and tensions Cowley is conscious of. When Nick first sees the river he is going to work he sees trout "keeping themselves steady in the current with wavering fins" and others "in deep, fast moving water, slightly distorted," and at the bottom of the pool he finally can make out the big ones. The whole trip is seen as these first fish are seen. Nick goes about his business exactly as if he were a trout keeping himself steady in the current, the whole affair is seen sharply but is slightly distorted, and there are now several deep pools in Nick's personality—where in the shadows lurk the "big ones." Nick is clearly in escape from something: as he walked along he "felt happy. He felt that he had left everything behind. . . . It was all back of him." He walks to where he is going to camp, pausing to catch grasshoppers for bait along the way, and then he finds a level piece of ground and pitches his tent. Each step of the process—smoothing the ground, arranging the blankets, cutting the tent pegs and raising the canvas—is related in a regular and monotonous sequence unrelieved by even a phrase of comment or a break in the rhythm. The action goes along against a backdrop of something only dimly seen; Nick goes through the motions now in a dead-pan, one-two-three-four routine which is rather new to him, and which suggests much less that he is the mindless primitive the Hemingway hero was so often thought to be than that he is desperately protecting his mind against whatever it is that he is escaping. Finally he gets the tent up, and crawls in to test it:

> Nick was happy as he crawled inside the tent. He had not been unhappy all day. This was different though. Now things were done. There had been this to do. Now it was done.

Then why it is that he is happy becomes a little clearer:

> He was settled. Nothing could touch him. It was a good place to camp. He was there, in the good place.

Next Nick came out of the tent and, with the same deliberateness with which he made camp, he cooked supper. He ate, and everything was going well until suddenly "his mind was starting to work." This was all right, however, for here was a night when he could stop it (later on there will be nights when he cannot): "He knew he could choke it because he was tired enough." He falls asleep at once, and Part I of the story ends.

Part II opens on the following morning and takes Nick through a day of fishing. This fishing (and the breakfast he eats before it and the lunch he puts up for himself) is again described in terms of chronologically ordered, mechanical, deliberate movements which begin to wear on one's nervous system. But here at least there can be, with proper understanding, no objection to the pulsing monotony of the sentence-cadence: He did this. And then he did that. And then he did that, and this—and so on, paragraphs together. There can be no objection because the tense, exasperating effect of this rhythm on the reader is extraordinarily appropriate to the state of Nick's nerves, which is above all what Hemingway is trying to convey. A terrible panic is just barely under control, and the style —this is the "Hemingway style" at its most extreme—is the perfect expression of the content of the story. Nick's mechanical movements—of cooking, casting, baiting his hook and the rest—are the mindless movements of, say, a woman who all alone busies herself with a thorough housecleaning on the morning after the sudden death of her husband, or the movements of the hands of a badly shell-shocked veteran who, while he can control himself, is performing simple jobs over and over in a factory: this, and then that. And then that and this. When the extreme excitement of a big strike from a trout intervenes the style changes abruptly. The pressure is off the man, he is nowhere but right there playing the fish, and then the sentences lengthen greatly and become appropriately graceful:

> With the core of the reel showing, his heart feeling stopped with the excitement, leaning back against the current that mounted icily his thighs, Nick thumbed the reel hard with his left hand.

He loses this large one, and the excitement has been so great that he feels sick and has to sit down. He does not dare "to rush his sensations any." He tries to smoke, and when a baby trout strikes at the match he throws into the current he laughs. This tells him that everything is all right; he can sit there a while: "He would finish the cigarette."

Nick fishes all day, and in the course of following him around we see that he is very frightened by the something that is lurking in the back of his mind and that he is escaping. Also we get a picture of a man who has a great deal in the way of outdoor "know-how" and is superstitious as well. He knows precisely how to disengage and throw back a small trout so it will not suffer from the experience, and he spits on his bait for luck. Nothing much ever really happens. We learn that there is a place where "the river narrowed and went into a swamp," and that he doesn't want to go downstream into it today (this region has some connotation for him that is unpleasant but enigmatic, for the time being), and the story ends with him returning to his camp encouraged but thinking that he has gone as far with himself as is best for one day—"there were plenty of days coming when he could fish the swamp."

Clearly, "Big Two-Hearted River" presents a picture of a sick man, and of a man who is in escape from whatever it is that made him sick. And Nick obviously knows what is the matter and what he must do about it and must not do. He must keep physically occupied, keep his hands busy; he must not think or he will be unable to sleep, he must not get too excited or he will get sick, and he must not go into the swamp, which unlike the tent, "the good place," is the bad place. It is as though he were on a doctor's prescription, and indeed he is on the strictest sort of emotional diet but is his own nutritionist.

By now the cause of this condition should be equally clear. Fragmentary as the outline is so far it can already be seen that the causes of the difficulties which "Big Two-Hearted River" gives symptoms of are the experience, already partly related, of the man's past: the blows which he has suffered—physical, psychical, moral, spiritual and emotional—have damaged him. He has been complicated and wounded by what he has seen, done and been through. This is the whole "point" of an otherwise pointless story and with it Hemingway brought his book to a close. When one extracts from it as we have done the stories in which

Nick appears one sees that actually Hemingway has plotted a story which covers perhaps as much as twenty years in the life of Nick Adams, first leading actor in a coherent drama to which he dedicated nearly four decades of his life.

*   *   *

To fill in some of the gaps in Nick's development Hemingway included two more stories about him in *Men without Women* (1927) and three more in *Winner Take Nothing* (1933). The first four of these are relevant here; the fifth fits in better later. The two stories which appeared in the 1927 volume, "Ten Indians" and "The Killers," take us first to Nick's early boyhood up in Michigan, and secondly to the trip, very likely, he was on in "The Battler."

In the Indian story we find "Nickie" a young boy who is being kidded about having an Indian girl friend named Prudence Mitchell. He is pleased about this until his father, who had walked that afternoon up to the Indian camp of the story of that name, tells the boy that he saw Prudie and Frank Washburn "threshing around" in the woods. When the father comes back we learn that Nick has been crying, and he tells himself "If I feel this way my heart must be broken." He goes to bed, and in the morning he is awake a long time before he remembers this tragic fact; he has learned another lesson.

"The Killers" is a more significant story. The scene is laid in a lunchroom where the boy—a guess would be that he is in his teens—watches and listens to two gangsters who are waiting for an ex-prizefighter, whom they are going to kill. Nick and a colored cook are bound and gagged in the kitchen, but when the victim does not appear the "killers" release them and leave. Nick knows where the fighter, Ole Andreson, lives, and he goes to warn him. He finds that the man is aware that he is going to be murdered and will do nothing to escape his fate. He is "an awfully nice man" who thanks Nick for his interest, and declines again to do anything to protect himself; Nick leaves. Back at the lunchroom we get the "point" of the story, which clearly consists of the boy's reaction to this somewhat sickening situation. Hemingway delineated three distinct responses: the cook (who, being colored and a short-order cook to boot, presumably has trouble enough of his own) wants nothing whatsoever to do with it—" 'I don't even listen to it,' he said and shut the door." George, the counterman in the diner, is more affected: "It's a hell of a thing." But it is of course the effect the incident has had on Nick that Hemingway was interested in:

> "I'm going to get out of this town," Nick said. . . . "I can't stand to think about him waiting in the room and knowing he's going to get it. It's too damned awful."

George then gives him the advice which Nick is later to give himself: "Well . . . you better not think about it."

It is obvious here that Nick, far from being calloused, is an extremely sensitive, even an abnormally sensitive, human being. Of the three reactions here it is George's which is probably "average": Nick's is roughly as excessive as the cook's is deficient. Nick cannot "stand to think about him waiting in the room and knowing he's going to get it," and he has got to clear the town completely. If the Hemingway hero were the "bovine," "dull-witted," "wooden-headed," "heavy-footed," "village idiot" that Wyndham Lewis to much applause once made him out then such a story as this one would be unthinkable. The contact Nick has made here with impending violence and horrifying inertia has made its mark on him, and in "The Killers" the whole pattern of Hemingway's method of dealing with his boy is suggested in the space of a few sentences.

"The Light of the World" fills in more of this period "on the bum," and although the tale is not violent it does, like the two other incidents recording the trip Nick made, indicate that life up in Michigan might provide a boy with no better training for a proper middle-class existence in America than a war in Europe, especially if he got off on his own and saw some of it. Nick and an older friend called Tom, whom he is now traveling with, come into a small town in the evening, experience a little difficulty with a man in a bar who say that as "punks" they "stink," and go down to hang around the railroad station. The story is mainly taken up with the conversation in the waiting room, where there are five very fat prostitutes, six white men (of whom one is homosexual) and four silent Indians. This talk is fairly tough; two of the whores get into an argument ("you dried up old hot-water bottle," "you big mountain of pus"); the homosexual tries to pick up the boys; Nick is considering a woman of 350 pounds when the older Tom gets him to leave and the story ends. Nothing much has happened, except that Nick has been in close contact with things a young boy who had stayed at home would nor- mally not meet—with things that the conventions governing the average boyhood do not define or present answers for, and that raise problems which the Scripture-quoting Mrs. Adams would not even admit let alone deal with. In the course of the piece the boy has been in on a discussion of adultery, fornication, homosexual and heterosexual "per- versions," has conversed somewhat professionally with a grotesque prostitute and has been attracted to her, and has successfully escaped the advances of what one of the men calls a "sister." One gets the idea that this little vacation spent riding freights from town to town is bringing him into contact with more than may be "good for him."

That the experience of the war was not good for him is made patent by "A Way You'll Never Be" (in *Winner*

Take Nothing, 1933). This can be placed, in time of action, between the Chapter VI sketch in which Nick was wounded in a visible way, and "Cross Country Snow," where he was about to return to the United States after the war. In this story one learns a good deal more about what made Nick the sick man he was when, back in America, he fished the Big Two-Hearted. One also finds that the Chapter VI paragraph telescoped the relation of the wounding to quitting the war and society somewhat: after Nick was hurt he did return for a time to a very peculiar kind of action before he finally walked out. This development also fits the experience of Lt. Henry in *A Farewell to Arms.*

"A Way You'll Never Be" (one depends on it) finds Nick in a simulated American uniform making his way by bicycle through the Austrian dead to an Italian infantry battalion, where he seeks out a captain who was a friend of his before Nick got hit. It seems that it is his job (or at least he believes this is so) to be seen in this uniform, the hope being that it will help the Italian troops to feel that the Yanks are coming. Before Paravicini, the captain, discovers something is wrong with Nick they talk about various things, including drinking; Nick reveals that during attacks he used to get drunk on a mixture of Grappa and ether. Para says:

> "You're much braver in an attack than I am."
> "No," Nick said. "I know how I am and I prefer to get stinking. . . ."

But Nick doesn't want to talk about this. Paravicini asks him if he is really all right and Nick says that he is, except that he cannot sleep without a light in the room. And then, suddenly:

> "What's the matter? I don't seem crazy to you, do I?"

"You seem in top-hole shape."

"It's a hell of a nuisance once they've had you certified as nutty," Nick said.

He finally agrees to lie down for a while, his trouble starts, and now we learn what it was that he was so closely guarding himself against on the fishing trip. Para has gone, and Nick pictures a night when he was in Para's outfit; a bombardment before an attack is taking place, and the captain has him lead a hysterical platoon two at a time out into the shelling to show them that it can be done. Nick has his chin strap bound tight across his mouth. Then, in a crazy way, he sees himself becoming a casualty, and then his mind goes completely:

> And there was Gaby Delys, oddly enough, with feathers on; you called me baby doll a year ago tadada you said that I was rather nice to know tadada with feathers on, with feathers off, the great Gaby . . .

He comes out of this after a time, and is ashamed to see that various soldiers at the Command Post have been watching him. He begins to talk to them, explains that he is now "reformed out of the war" and is simply "demonstrating an American uniform" (see photograph opposite page 54, taken four months after Hemingway's own serious wounding). But then he begins to deliver a disquisition on grasshoppers and locusts, about which he is very erudite. An adjutant sends for the captain and Nick goes on with his speech. He jabbers along, a second runner goes to get Paravicini and finally the captain comes. Nick improves somewhat, though he complains of his helmet, the like of which he has seen "full of brains too many times," and then he must lie down again.

He sees in his mind a bad place—a house and a long stable and a river, which imagery is customary for him during these spells, and so meaningful to him that almost twenty years later under the name of Dick Cantwell he will make a personal pilgrimage to this very place in reality. "Every night" he had this vision, in "A Way You'll Never Be," and "what frightened him so that he could not get rid of it was that long yellow house and the different width of the river." Nearly two decades were to elapse before Hemingway was to reveal, in *Across the River and Into the Trees,* that this scenery comes to Nick because this is the place where he was wounded. Furthermore, nearly one decade had already elapsed since he had described another bad place, an entrance to a swamp which Nick feared unaccountably on the Big Two-Hearted River. And now Hemingway gives a clue to that mystery. In the story of Nick's actual insanity, where in terror he relives the event of being badly shot up, it is something about "the different width of the river" which terrifies him. Later when he is fishing the Big Two-Hearted he dreads and is unable to go past the spot where "the river narrowed' and went into the swamp: the geography of the place where he was blown up is naturally, and deeply, associated in his mind with the blow itself; it was, as we suggested at the time, the re-experience of shrapnel that he avoided by fishing. A change in the width of the river was what made the swamp horrible: it is in such a way that Hemingway's work extends backward and forward, is enigmatic and then clearer, and is integrated, and bound tight about a core of shock.

"A Way You'll Never Be" is a discomforting as well as a revealing story. One never knows what is going on—why the half-crazy soldier is allowed to go about on the loose, or if he really is permitted to, or whether or not he is actually supposed to be demonstrating this bogus uniform, or what. But one thing is obvious: there are many things Nick Adams cannot stand to think about at all.

And this is the end, for the moment, of the stories about him. To assemble them chronologically and look at them very briefly makes the pattern Hemingway arranged for his protagonist clear; the nature of Nick's character can also be made out. Here is a boy, and after that a man, who both in his early environment and later out on his own has been coming in contact with "life" in our time. Each of these contacts has been in some way violent, evil, or unsettling in that no ready answers are available. The effect of these episodes is equally apparent. They have complicated and damaged the man who, when an ex-infantryman, is a very unwell soldier. He cannot sleep at night; when he can sleep he has nightmares. He has seen a great deal of unpleasantness, not only in the war but earlier up in Michigan as well; and he has been wounded by these experiences in a physical way, and—since the spine blow is both fact and symbol—also in a psychical way. What has happened to Nick, in short, has made him sick.

This pattern is climaxed by rebellion, by two desertions which can already be dimly seen. One is of the respectable home Nick has left, and later—when the damage begun at Indian Camp is epitomized with a shell fragment —he deserts the whole of organized society.

Nick's character, too, has emerged. Here is a sensitive, humorless, honest, rather passive male. He is the outdoor man, who revels in the life of the senses, loves to hunt and fish and takes pride in his knowledge of how to do such things. He is virile even as an adolescent, and very conscious of his nerve; maturity has forced a reckoning with his nerves as well. Once grown he is a man who knows his way around but he is superstitious too, and is

Milan: November, 1918

Up in Michigan: *ca.* 1913

developing a complex ritual whereby thinking can be stopped, the evil spirits placated and warded off.

This pattern, this process and this figure, with whatever distortions seen, were going to be known half the world over, for the relationship of this Nick to what is called the "Hemingway hero" is intimate, to put it mildly: Nick *is* the Hemingway hero, the first one. The drawing of him is very sketchy as yet, but it is true and Hemingway never takes it back to cancel half a line: the experiences of childhood, adolescence and young manhood which shape Nick Adams shaped as well Lt. Henry, Jake Barnes, Col. Cantwell, and several other heroes. They all have had Nick's childhood, Nick's adolescence, Nick's young manhood. It is obvious that this man is not the simple primitive he was mistaken for, and it is equally clear that a good deal of what there is of the primitive in him is a defense, which trembles and cracks, against a terror which he cannot face head on. The "escapes" are escapes from horror; the Hemingway hero, the big, tough, outdoor man, is also the wounded man, and descriptions of certain scenes in the life of Nick Adams have explained how he got that way. The man will die a thousand times before his death, but from his wounds he would never recover so long as Hemingway lived and recorded his adventures.

2 | THE HERO
AND THE CODE

*I did not care what it was all about. All
I wanted to know was how to live in it.*

THE SUN ALSO RISES

" 'Ayee!' suddenly screamed the lieutenant"
in a story of Hemingway's called "A Natural
History of the Dead."

> "You have blinded me! You
> have blinded me!"
> "Hold him tight," said the doc-
> tor. "He is in much pain. Hold him
> very tight."

As doctors are not always available, and are
often of little use, holding tight against pain
is an exercise which was to become important to the Hemingway hero. Considerably broadened and elaborated, the effort
to hold tight developed into what is known
as the Hemingway "code." But the hero is
still only a sketch, and before one is in the
best position to understand the code there
are some more stories in Hemingway's "first
forty-nine"—in addition to the Nick ones—

which fill out the main body of that man a good deal. These are "I"-stories, written in the first person. None of them contains anything that basically conflicts with the outline already given of Adams; several of them do deepen, broaden, and clarify the pattern that has been working itself out. We have already seen one of these, for the "Author's Introduction" to *In Our Time* appears in Hemingway's collected stories as "On the Quai at Smyrna." This was the sketch in which appear the women who will not give up their dead babies, and, among other things, the mules with broken forelegs drowning in the shallow water—pictures hard for the author to get rid of, apparently, since he used them twice again in *Death in the Afternoon*. This brief piece was already significant as a forecast, because "I got so I dreamed about things," which is of course what was to happen to Nick.

That this "I" *is* Nick becomes perfectly apparent in the war story called "Now I Lay Me" which appeared in *Men without Women*. Here the "I" says he cannot sleep unless he has a light, as Nick could not in "A Way You'll Never Be," and although still in uniform he is not in the fighting, as before. If there is any doubt that this is Nick it disappears when, remembering his parents as he tries to occupy himself on a sleepless night, he hears his father call him by that name.

The story itself presents the picture of the man who cannot sleep "for thinking," and Nick tells of the many ways he has of occupying his mind harmlessly on these bad nights, the principal one of which is to reconstruct trout streams he has fished. In terms which clearly identify this part of the story with the trip to "Big Two-Hearted River," Hemingway tells how he pictures this fishing. And thus we suspect again that we were right when we saw that fishing trip as conducted against a background of escape and terror, that it was taken as a device to keep

Nick from going crazy, for here that is its clearly stated function. The swamp he could not enter is present again, too; this time it is a place where he runs out of bait and has to cut up one of the trout he caught, to use pieces of it to catch other trout with. This, like the wounded hyena in *Green Hills of Africa* which eats its own intestines, is a cannibalism which Hemingway did not approve: the swamp is a "bad place" again.

Then Nick remembers scenes from his childhood (in which the doctor's wife comes off poorly again) and he tries to pray for his parents. When he is very badly off he fails at this. Then he has a conversation with an Italo-American named John; we learn that Nick has been wounded twice and that he is now a lieutenant. John decides that it is "worry" that keeps Nick awake all night: "You ought to get married, Signor Tenente. Then you wouldn't worry." Signor Tenente suspects that the problem is not so simple and he ends thinking somewhat wryly of John: "He was very certain about marriage and knew it would fix up everything."

"In Another Country," also from *Men without Women,* is another first-person-Nick story. It is moving as a story, and is interesting for the way in which it points two directions in the development of the hero. Looking backward, it deals with his physical recuperation in Milan from the second of what have now become two separate woundings. The story has to do with a fellow patient in a hospital, a wounded major whose young wife has just died suddenly. The major gives the hero the reverse of the advice he got from John just above: "A man must not marry. . . . If he is to lose everything, he should not place himself in a position to lose that." Nick is still unwell but —and here the story points forward—for once Hemingway is not concerned so much with Nick. It is the major's pain that the story is about; the hero's wounds have been established, and there are now two casualties. This points to *The Sun Also Rises,* where a whole "lost generation" is wounded as Jake (Nick) is wounded, and even to *A Farewell to Arms* where Catherine Barkley is, just as Brett Ashley was in the former novel, a woman completely unsettled by the fact that a former lover died in the war under terrible circumstances. The pattern thus is broadening for a while, and what was the history of Nick becomes —loosely speaking—the history of a war generation. This story presents, too, the same picture of Milan to be found in *A Farewell to Arms—In Einem Andern Land* was the title for the German edition of that novel. Unless one knows the origin of this title its point is lost. In the story it is a brutal allusion to the major's bereavement, and in the novel it was—in the German—an even more terrible commentary. Catherine Barkley, everyone remembers, had an idyllic love affair with Lt. Henry in the novel; they lived together in Italy and in Switzerland, out of wedlock, until she died in childbirth. The allusion is to Marlowe's *Jew of Malta:*

> Thou hast committed—
> Fornication: but that was in another country,
> And, besides, the wench is dead.

Another new development turns up in a story from the same *Men without Women* called "An Alpine Idyll." The tale is again told in the first person and returns, very likely, to the skiing trip Nick was on in "Cross Country Snow." Again the story is utterly without a "point" if not seen in the context of the other stories. Nick and a friend named John are drinking before dinner in a Swiss inn and they hear the tale of a Swiss peasant whose wife (whom he loved) had died some months before. The peasant kept her body in his woodshed all winter, waiting for the earth to thaw before digging her grave. Every night he cut wood in this shed, and

> "When I started to use the big wood she was stiff and I put her up against the wall. Her mouth was open and when I came into the shed at night to cut up the big wood, I hung the lantern from it."

This is the pattern of "The Killers" again, and again the rest of the story—and its focus—centers on the responses of the listeners. A change in these responses is the point: Nick is hardening a little. When the story is over he is silent. John says, "How about eating?" Nick says, "You order," and talks on for a moment with the innkeeper about the peasant. Where his reaction to the incident in "The Killers" was a horrified inability even "to think about it," and a desire to get completely out of town, he is now not so sensitive. John repeats impatiently, "Say . . . how about eating?" Nick replies, "All right," and the story ends. A shell is growing over the wound to protect it a little; by 1940 the defense will be nearly—if temporarily—impenetrable.

The "I" of these stories is Nick Adams; it is also possible to see correspondences between Nick Adams and Ernest Hemingway, the man who for a long time after his wounding in Italy in 1917 could not sleep with the light out. A glance at the briefest paragraph biographies of the author would convince most people of this; the last of the Nick stories, "Fathers and Sons" from *Winner Take Nothing,* is itself convincing enough. This story, with its title presumably from Turgenev, presents to us a relatively placid thirty-eight-year-old Nick who is driving in a car with his son. Nick is thinking about his father, the doctor (who is described precisely as photographs represent Dr. Hemingway), and specifically he is thinking about the man's death. (Hemingway's father died suddenly in 1928.) This death is very troubling to Nick; it was violent and unpleasant, and "he could not write about it yet, although he would." We now get our first real insight into how Hemingway wrote, and why—among other reasons—he was a writer:

> Nick had loved him very much and for a long time. Now, knowing how it had all been, even remembering the earliest times before things had gone badly was not good remembering.

Here then is another instance of violence that is "not good remembering"—"the handsome job the undertaker had done on his father's face had not blurred in his mind." Such scars are permanent, and if time will not take the soreness from them, writing "fiction" may, and it is the only way, apparently, he could purge himself of the image that bothered him. Literature, thought to be in some way cathartic for its audience, becomes here supreme catharsis for its creator:

> If he wrote it he could get rid of it. He had gotten rid of many things by writing them. But it was still too early for that.

Readers had to wait until *For Whom the Bell Tolls* (where Robert Jordan is to explain carefully and at length what is the matter here) for it to be no longer too early for Hemingway to get rid of this unpleasant piece of his past, but his method is already apparent: the things which have happened to Nick which are "not good remembering" he was writing away in his stories. That he had some success with this treatment is suggested by the composure which—most of the time—the hero as Jordan is able to maintain.

In the "Fathers and Sons" story the author played

subtly with the complexities of the relationships between generations—Nick's relationship to his father and to his son. Just as the doctor taught his son to hunt so Nick is teaching his; and just as the doctor was not much help with other problems, Nick cannot communicate either. Nick remembers what he learned from an Indian girl named Trudy—a reasonable change from the "Prudie" of "Ten Indians," which would have inappropriate connotations now:

"You think we make a baby?"
"I don't think so," he said.
"Make plenty baby what the hell."

But when Nick's son wants to know what the Ojibway Indians were like Nick can only tell him "It's hard to say." ("Could you say she did first what no one has ever done better?") Also the boy causes trouble by wanting to visit his grandfather's grave, a place he has never been. This is precisely what Nick does not want to think about, but his son is insistent and the story ends with the father giving in: "I can see we'll have to go." There is the merest suggestion of defeat in this; Nick is failing as his father had failed, and the present must acknowledge the past.

It is pretty clear, then, that Nick Adams has much in common with Ernest Hemingway. This is not to say that he "is" Hemingway. He is, rather, a projection of certain kinds of problems Hemingway was deeply concerned to write about, and write out. Nick is a special kind of mask.

But there are masks which do not disguise or conceal very much and some of them, like the theatrical masks of ancient Greece, actually serve to identify character and even to reveal it. These are odd distortions indeed in that they are really clarifications. By selection among the possibilities of personality, and by emphasis of some few of its features, they expose as well as hide, disclose as well as cover. Nick Adams is such a mask, for while he presents to the world a face that is not exactly Hemingway's, he also projects chiefly that one set of problems revolving around the wound that is the best aid in our recognition of Hemingway. Thus Nick is a simplification, and to that extent a distortion, of the actual complex personality, but is also a kind of revelation.

In much the same way, the adventures which Hemingway related were not always wholly and strictly autobiographical, for literature does not work with life in quite that way. But investigation shows that actually many of the stories about Nick are very literal translations of some of the most important events in Hemingway's own life, and that remarkably little has been changed in the telling. Indeed it would be hard to think of even an "autobiographical writer" (Thomas Wolfe, for instance) who gave a more exact account of his own experience and of his own personality in the guise of prose fiction.

Obviously something was needed to bind the wounds these experiences had made in that personality, and for that reason there is another "I" in the Hemingway short stories, a minor figure who is a kind of spectator or reporter. This man is not Hemingway, is not the hero, and is not even a center of interest. Instead he observes a man, not the hero either, who in importance rates second only to the hero himself. This man changes form—his profession and even his nationality—much more than the hero ever will, but he is still a consistent character in that he always introduces and exemplifies a theme in the author's work that has rightly been made a good deal of. This is the Hemingway "code"—a "grace under pressure." It is made of the controls of honor and courage which in a life of tension and pain make a man a man and distinguish him from the people who follow random impulses, let down their hair, and are generally messy, perhaps cowardly, and without inviolable rules for how to live holding tight.

This code is very important because the "code hero,"

as he is usually called, presents a solution to the problems of Nick Adams, of the true "Hemingway hero," * and for Hemingway it was about the only solution. He found this code operating among various sporting figures, and he wrote several short stories the intention of which is to formulate the basic principles of the code by illustrating it in action. These stories deal, as is logical for a man broken from respectability, with such persons of disrepute as a fixed prizefighter and a crooked gambler who, since they have the code, are admired by the man who created them.

As Hemingway once put it, "There is honor among pickpockets and honor among whores. It is simply that the standards differ." What Hemingway is thinking of becomes most clear in a story like "Fifty Grand," which presents this honor-and-courage-among-thieves concept in near-pristine form. Here, as in some other stories, the reportorial "I" is part of the retinue which surrounds a prizefighter named Jack. This welterweight (who has passed his prime, knows he is going to lose his championship, does not want to fight any more, is lonesome for his wife and daughters, and needs money) bets fifty thousand dollars on his opponent. But he has been double-crossed by some gamblers who were party to this arrangement, and in the fight, as he is well on his way to successful defeat, he is viciously fouled by his opponent. If he succumbs to the low blow, which has him in debilitating pain, he will win the fight on the basis of the obvious misdeed of the challenger. This would be to lose fifty thousand dollars and to go back on his part in the swindle; it would be dishonorable. And so he denies he has been fouled, makes

---

* Though now in wide usage the terms are cumbersome and infelicitous. It may be that substitutions employed by Earl Rovit in his *Ernest Hemingway* (1963)—of "tutor" for code hero and "tyro" for Hemingway hero—are preferable.

the supreme effort, and sticks it out until he has fouled the challenger into writhing submission. Thus he loses the fight, wins his bet, establishes his courage and maintains his honor.

Here is the reverse of the wealthy homosexual fighter in "Mother of a Queen" (who lets the bones of his mother be thrown into the public bone heap, and will not take offense when "I" insults him in every manner he can think of). This, Hemingway seems to be saying with considerable irony in "Fifty Grand," is life and the way to live in it. These are the conditions of life, which is a highly compromising affair, and a man can be a man only by making a deal with it, and then sticking to his bargain if it kills him.

But it is a bad mistake to think of this man as the "Hemingway hero"; he is rather an illustration of qualities which are essential to that legend. It is a mistake because it confuses and blurs the clear picture Hemingway has been presenting. This is the same confusion that mistakes the hero, as practically all readers once did, for the outlaw Harry Morgan of *To Have and Have Not*. Actually both this fighter and Morgan represent the man with the code, who is another man entirely. Sometimes the real hero talks like the code hero, but the distinction between them can always be made, and to consider this prizefighter, or Manuel ("The Undefeated" bullfighter), or the pirate Morgan as the Hemingway hero not only blurs and confuses what Hemingway made quite clear, but also and directly brings about a thoroughly erroneous misconception of that man. Further it is to fail to see that actually Hemingway had, since 1924, been writing out the story of one man who was based on himself. The real hero is the protagonist who was up in Michigan and was wounded while fighting as an American in the Italian army, who lived and wrote fiction in Paris; he is the generic Nick

Adams. All the proper parts fit this single story; the hero is—with each successive appearance—the sum of what has happened to him. And psychically it all happened to Hemingway, who was never a bullfighter (although he tried it), or a prizefighter (although he tried that too), or a one-armed, two-daughtered smuggler of rum and China-men (which he apparently never tried at all). The hero is a twentieth-century American, born, raised and hurt in the Middle West, who like all of us has been going through life with the marks his experiences have made on him. The outlaws and professional sportsmen who have appeared along the way have taught the man to try to live by a code, but they are not the man himself. What is more, the lessons have not always been of the sort the hero can immediately master.

This becomes clear in a story called "The Gambler, the Nun and the Radio" (1933), which presents in one place both the hero and the man who exemplifies the code, and presents them as two quite different people. The generic Nick is here called Mr. Frazer; he is having a "bad time" again, and he is also, once more, to be associated with the man who wrote the story. The man whom the hero admires and studies is this time an unlucky gambler.

In 1930 Hemingway was in an automobile accident with John Dos Passos in Montana and had his arm very badly broken. In *Green Hills of Africa* (1935) Hemingway was thinking of this pain when he wrote that the most "horror" he could remember going through he experienced

> one time in a hospital with my right arm broken off short between the elbow and the shoulder . . . the points of the bone having cut up the flesh of the biceps until it finally rotted, swelled, burst, and sloughed off in pus. Alone with the pain in the night of the fifth week of not sleeping . . .

This story, "The Gambler, the Nun and the Radio," transfers the injury to the leg, and tells again of that horror, and of life in the hospital. It introduces a gambler—honorable, according to the standards of his trade, and courageous— and a nun. Frazer, who is a writer, is having the bad time described just above but, the author reminded us, this was not the first time for him: "His nerves went bad at the end of five weeks. . . . Mr. Frazer had been through this all before. The only thing which was new to him was the radio. . . . He was learning to listen to it without thinking." Clearly, this is our old friend Nick, and Montana (the location of the radio stations he hears signing off at night suggests this, as the songs he hears suggest 1930; Hemingway's own recuperation took place in a Billings hospital).

Part of the story (the radio part) has to do with the hero's insomnia, his bad nerves ("when the nurse goes out I cry an hour, two hours. It rests me . . .") and with his attempts to avoid thinking, which, as always, makes things worse. Alcohol ("the giant killer") and the radio are what keep him going; he plays the radio all night so quietly no one else can hear it. Lying there and concentrating on the sounds becomes another rite with which to keep off the "evil spirits"—the equivalent of fishing on the Big Two-Hearted, in actuality or retrospect. The sickness leads him as before to an extreme bitterness, and it is in this story that rock bottom in Hemingway's pessimism is reached in the familiar passage: "Religion is the opium of the people . . . and music . . . and sexual intercourse . . . and bread is the opium of the people." *

This is one way to live in the world, but it is not a very good way. The nun, Sister Cecilia, represents an

---

* The nadir of that pessimism ("Our nada who art in nada, nada be thy be name . . .") is also reached in "A Clean, Well-Lighted Place," which involves neither hero nor code, but which surely belongs, despite some confusion at points as to who is speaking, among the great stories of the language.

alternative: she believes she knows what the world is all about and she lives in it by her faith. Though quite charming, this faith seems also naïve to Frazer; it is Cayetano, the petty gambler, who has the code to live by. The Hemingway hero, although he greatly admires this code, is not able to live by it. He is too tortured, too thoughtful, too perplexed, for that; he cries at night—a grown man. This is incredibly "messy" of him, and messiness is above all things forbidden. The hero tries, but he cannot make it, and that is why the stories which most clearly present the code have a separate character to enact it. It is Cayetano (who is in much more pain—as the hero points out—than Mr. Frazer) who does not show a single sign of his suffering.

This Cayetano, a Mexican cardplayer, is brought into the hospital nearly dead, with two bullets in his stomach. A detective accompanies him and tries to get the dying man to name the one who shot him. The detective tries to convince the cardsharp: "It's all right to tell who shot you. . . . You don't have to act like a moving picture." This is just the point; he does. Frazer, acting as interpreter, obliges the detective by trying too: "One can, with honor, denounce one's assailant," he says. But he doesn't really believe it and is proud when Cayetano "won't talk." The Mexican suffers on alone at the hospital; his only visitors come to see him involuntarily, and are really partisan to the man who shot him. He suffers without a word of complaint and finally Frazer talks to him again, and learns he has been shot by a man who lost money to him in a crooked card game: the gambler will cheat at cards as Jack will throw a fight, but he will not take revenge on the man who nearly killed him for cheating, or even complain of it —as Jack would not back out of his agreement—and he insists, when he is praised for his courage, "it was nothing." Clearly the hero believes it was a good deal.

These distinctions between the hero and his tutor— the man whom the hero emulates, who has the code he would like to operate by, too—clarify and enrich a couple of Hemingway's later, best, and best-known stories, "The Short Happy Life of Francis Macomber," and "The Snows of Kilimanjaro." These long pieces are both clearly ritualistic—one a ceremonial triumph over fear, the other a rite in which a part of the self is destroyed. They present certain difficulties, however, because of new approaches the author took to his material and his protagonists.

Hemingway distinguished between "true" and "made up" stories. Both of these, though they use a great deal of autobiography, are of the latter type. These are personal stories, but they are not literal ones: in Africa in the Thirties Hemingway did not die of an infection, nor was he chased by a lion and murdered by his wife. The protagonists are also "made up" in that in each of the stories the writer adopted a mask that is for once grotesque, incongruous and truly a distortion. Both Macomber and Harry (in "Kilimanjaro") exaggerate some of the hero's weaknesses, failings, shortcomings. Harry is a failure as a man and as a writer; Macomber is a coward. It is very much as if Hemingway was getting rid of things again, but here he took a new and hypercritical attitude toward his protagonists. These men are not wholly unfamiliar as leading players in Hemingway, but they are outside the pattern he built in that they are seen through a glass very darkly or, to put it more cogently, they are seen *in* a glass —as in a Coney Island funhouse—which mirrors into magnified prominence the growing paunch, the receding hairline, the sagging muscles.

"The Short Happy Life" is, among other things, a detailed description of the process of learning the code and its value. Macomber, a frightened man, is seen in the story learning the code from Wilson, his professional hunting guide. He is presented as being very ignorant at first, but he painfully learns and he becomes a man in the process. Before that happens, however, it is apparent that Hemingway was using this plot of instruction in courage and honor to comment, as he had not done to this extent before, on many other things. The story is, for example, an analysis of the relationship between the sexes in America, and the relationship is in the nature of declared warfare.

D. H. Lawrence, in an essay on *The Scarlet Letter,* launches an assault on the American male who, he says, has lost his "ithyphallic authority" over the American woman, who therefore dominates and then destroys what is left. "The Short Happy Life" develops and intensifies Lawrence's notion with enormous skill. Francis Macomber, when under the tutelage of the hunter Wilson, learns courage and honor and to embrace the code; he attains his manhood, which is not the same thing as losing his virginity or reaching his twenty-first birthday, as the characters point out. When he attains this manhood he regains the ithyphallic authority he had lost and his wife, now panicky herself in her new role, must destroy him literally. Before he became a man she had committed adultery almost in his presence, knowing him helpless to stop her. When he becomes a man, and she can no longer rule him in the Lawrencian sense, she sends a bullet to the base of his skull.

Obviously Macomber is something different from a grown Nick Adams. What he represents instead is an extreme projection of the hero's problem of fear, and the story about him delineates an imagined solution to that problem. Unlike Macomber, Hemingway had never "just shown himself, very publicly, to be a coward." When he wrote the story he had just very publicly and maliciously been *called* one by Gertrude Stein in her *Autobiography of Alice B. Toklas* (1933); he retaliated in *Green Hills of*

Africa by calling her a "bitch." But the facts of the matter seem to indicate that she had no more reason for calling him "yellow" than that she knew it was an insult which would hurt, for reasons to be examined later.*

However, Macomber is not so extreme a projection that all contact with the hero and with Hemingway is lost. He was given Hemingway's age, his physical fitness and athleticism, and his expertness with big game and fish. Hemingway's own guide, "Pop," in *Green Hills of Africa,* looks very like Wilson, hunting guide of the story. In addition, the extraordinary "immediateness" with which the sensations of fear are felt by Macomber suggests the extent to which the author could feel for him. And fear, after all, was the hero's central problem.

In the course of this story Macomber completely disgraces himself in the presence of his wife and his hunting guide before he learns the code and wins their respect. He has already committed the unpardonable sin when the story opens: he ran away from a charging lion, and, as Wilson says, this is just not done—"no white ever bolts." Not only that, but he goes right on committing errors: he asks Wilson not to talk about his cowardice to other people, which for the professional hunter and possessor of the code's book of etiquette is "supposed to be bad form," and after Wilson insults him he spinelessly apologizes. In addition he cannot control his wife, who hounds him without mercy. It had all happened when it came time to track a lion, which he had wounded badly, into the long grass where it lay in wait for those who had shot it. But he had completely failed. First he wanted to send the inadequately armed African "boys" in after the animal; when Wilson refuses to be party to this type of slaughter he

* This famous quarrel is said to have been patched up in Paris in 1945 but if so, and if Miss Stein could read *A Moveable Feast,* things would assuredly unpatch.

suggests they leave the beast hidden in the grass. He could not have stumbled on a more wretched violation: someone else might meet him unawares and be killed; even if this doesn't happen it is certain that the lion is in considerable pain and it is their responsibility to do for him what cannot be done for human beings. And then when they finally search out the lion Macomber bolts, running wildly away in panic. When the three hunters are reassembled in their car after Wilson has killed the charging, wounded animal, Margot Macomber celebrates the complete loss of her husband's authority by leaning in front of him and kissing Wilson on the mouth. That night Macomber wakes to discover that she is not in her cot in the tent with him. "He lay awake with that knowledge for two hours." This activity does not go against Wilson's code, it is explained; as a matter of fact he "carried a double size cot on safari to accommodate any windfalls he might receive." The standards of the people who hired him were his standards: "They were his standards in all except the shooting."

It is these shooting standards which Macomber eventually learns and which, although they bring his death, make him for a short happy lifetime a man. Quite suddenly when shooting a buffalo he loses his fear. The lessons Wilson has been teaching him are now his own. A wounded buffalo gets away, as the lion did, and he can hardly wait to go in after the beast. In 1942 Hemingway, writing from his own experience an introduction to a collection of war stories, had this to say: "Cowardice ... is almost always simply a lack of ability to suspend the functioning of the imagination." In "the Macomber affair" he explains it the same way:

> It had taken a strange chance of hunting, a sudden precipitation into action without opportunity for worrying beforehand, to bring this about with Macomber. . . .

Fear was "gone like an operation. Something else grew in its place. . . . Made him into a man."

Putting the bad things into words may rid one of them, but it is necessary for the earlier-initiated Wilson to make clear to the hero that the same principle applies to so good a thing as the transformation into manhood, which he has just undergone: "You're not supposed to mention it. . . . Doesn't do to talk too much about all this. Talk the whole thing away." Wilson, warming now to Macomber, also confides to him the "thing he had lived by"— a quotation from Shakespeare. The extent to which Hemingway was able to project himself even into this maladroit and cowardly Macomber is further brought out by these lines from Shakespeare. Hemingway revealed this, perhaps without realizing it, in 1942 in the introduction just cited, when he told how in the war, in 1917, *he* learned courage from a British officer (Wilson is very British) who gave him, Hemingway, the identical message Wilson here gives Macomber:

> "By my troth, I care not; a man can die but
> once; we owe God a death and let it go which way
> it will he that dies this year is quit for the next."

The climax of the story has come, and Macomber's wife, recognizing the hero's new life as a man, cannot tolerate a long denouement. When her husband goes in after the wounded buffalo she—ostensibly and "intentionally" aiming for the beast in order to save Francis—kills him. Aiming at the buffalo, as Hemingway specified, she shot her husband "by mistake on purpose," as wise children put it—or, for adults, in a monumental "Freudian slip." When Wilson accuses her of murder she does not deny it; he prepares to exonerate her with explanatory photographs, and the story ends. Wilson is like the prizefighter Jack and the gambler Cayetano: he kills—as a profession—animals who have insufficient chance of protecting themselves; he consorts with rich decadents and adopts their moral standards; he lives a lonely, compromised life. But out of this he builds what he lives by; he has his courage and his honor: he would not "squeal" on his employer; he will not leave the animals he has pitilessly shot to suffer. He bristles with "won't do," "isn't done," "bad form," and "not supposed to." Macomber—not the hero, but like the heroes in this—admires all this code and tries to attain it. He makes the grade, but it costs him his life.

As the Macomber story dramatizes the casting off of fear, so "The Snows of Kilimanjaro" is a fictionalized purge, in this case of a whole bundle of guilty feelings. In this story Hemingway sourly depicted himself (there is no question of his identity here) as an abject failure, dying from an infected scratch five thousand miles from home. The story, interesting in many ways, is probably less tight and dramatic than the Macomber one, but it attempts different and more difficult things. There is a conscious and explicit use of symbolism—which is most unusual with Hemingway—and there is plenty of ammunition for the critics who have attacked the author for his preoccupation with death. That preoccupation is at least ostensibly what the story is about.

There is no question that the protagonist Harry is the Hemingway hero. Harry is a writer as was Nick in "Fathers and Sons"; he has thought a great deal about death, as Hemingway had done; he thinks of his part in the war against the Austrians, whom Nick fought; he later went skiing with them, as Nick did; he tries to keep himself from thinking, as Nick tried; he had "sold vitality, in one form or another, all his life," which is a way of putting what Hemingway did; Africa was "where he had been happiest," which the author said of himself in the *Green Hills;* and no one who had read that book, in which the second Mrs.

Hemingway figures, could fail to suspect in Harry's wife a less flattering portrait of the same woman. Here, too, is again the man who had "seen the things that he could never think of and later still he had seen much worse." Harry is very autobiographically drawn: he thinks of that room in Paris (in which Verlaine once lived) where "he had written the start of all he was to do." He also identifies himself, to knowing readers of F. Scott Fitzgerald at least, by remembering "poor Julian" and his romantic awe of the rich. Julian had "started a story once that began, 'The very rich are different from you and me.' And someone had said to Julian, 'Yes, they have more money.' " The story was Fitzgerald's "Rich Boy," and it was Hemingway who made the joke.

There cannot be many writers who stuck so rigorously to writing of themselves, and—in a way—*for* themselves, asking at the same time that an audience take an interest in what they were doing, and at the same time succeeding with a very large part of the reading public, as Hemingway did. "The Snows of Kilimanjaro" is widely read, widely anthologized, widely interpreted, and Hollywood paid an all-time high for it. But despite the fact that several versions of what the story is "about" are meaningful, this is also a special and private thing: a statement by Hemingway of his aesthetic aims and beliefs, and an analysis of his past failures as a writer of prose fiction, as of 1936, a year that was crucial for him. It can be read quite legitimately as a more objective and generalized piece of prose—as, for instance, a story of a writer dying on a safari in Africa, reviewing his past and previewing his future. But for its author it was an exercise in personal and aesthetic hygiene.

In his curious, stubborn way, Hemingway was a writer absolutely and wholeheartedly dedicated to his craft, and—as is the way of serious artists—he dreamed of immortality for some of what he had done; he thought, that is, of writing prose that would be so pure that it could never spoil, that would be permanent. In 1935, in *Green Hills of Africa,* a nonfiction work which supplies considerable background for "Kilimanjaro," he spoke of "how far prose can be carried if anyone is serious enough and has luck." As for luck, no man knows, but about his prose Hemingway was serious enough—grimly, humorlessly serious—and in a book on writing and bullfighting he had announced that he himself was trying very hard to write prose "which would be as valid in a year or in ten years or, with luck and if you stated it purely enough, always."

But as ample evidence testifies, 1936 found Hemingway disgusted with himself. This story itself is eloquent. He had been chasing about Europe and Africa with the very rich (though they "were dull and they drank too much, or they played too much backgammon"), and drinking all the time himself ("so much that he blunted the edge of his perceptions"). Seven fallow years had elapsed since he had written a first-rate book, *A Farewell to Arms* ("and you made an attitude that you cared nothing for the work you used to do, now that you could no longer do it"). Two marriages, both discussed in the story, had ended badly; he felt he had been disgracing himself in *Esquire:* "He had destroyed his talent by not using it, by betrayals of himself and what he believed in, by drinking so much . . . by laziness, by sloth, and by snobbery, by pride and by prejudice. . . . It was a talent all right but instead of using it, he had traded on it." To make matters worse, "for years" death had "obsessed him": now in horror he sees the possibility that it could all end like this—on an idle safari, haggling with a woman. And very little stated purely enough to last always.

It is apparent that in 1936 Hemingway made a mighty resolve that he would not, like poor Julian, really be "wrecked," that he would achieve permanence despite everything he had done wrong. First it was necessary to inventory everything in the place, and to heave out everything that could not be used—to destroy it, indeed, to spit it away—before such a radical development as occurs in a book of the next year, *To Have and Have Not,* could be possible. "The Snows of Kilimanjaro" does precisely these things, in addition to describing the goal which is the reason for the stocktaking, and presenting the purge itself, and even to prophesying what the final outcome will be.

"The Snows" opens with an introductory paragraph whose symbols state the better part of the story's meaning:

> Kilimanjaro is a snow covered mountain 19,710 feet high, and is said to be the highest mountain in Africa. Its western summit is called the Masai "Ngàje Ngài," the House of God. Close to the western summit there is the dried and frozen carcass of a leopard. No one has explained what the leopard was seeking at that altitude.

This passage can seem enigmatic enough, and has been widely struggled with, but in this context at least one meaning emerges. It is Hemingway himself who "explains" what the leopard sought at that altitude: the House of God, immortality. The leopard did not quite make the summit, and in his mysterious attempt to reach it perished, but his carcass is dried and frozen: he died in the attempt to save his soul, as all who try it must, but frozen at that temperature and height the leopard is permanent. He can never spoil, and he presents a perfect contrast to Harry with a gangrened leg, who is very mortal, rotting fast away in the heat of the lowlands.

But Harry is a writer, and if a thing is said perfectly, if it is perfectly immaculate, if it is said "purely enough," it cannot spoil, it is frozen, and its author is immortal.

At the end of the story Harry "dreams" of a plane which comes to rescue the writer, and after taking off with the pilot he sees, there, "unbelievably white in the sun . . . the square top of Kilimanjaro. And then he knew that there was where he was going." It was at this precise moment that Hemingway reorganized his forces and left the hero as a failure for what he hoped would be greater things. Leaving it back under the mosquito bar with the woman who had come in some way to stand for all the things which had corrupted it, he here sloughed off his contaminated skin—"somehow he had gotten his leg out and it hung down alongside the cot. The dressings had all come down and she could not look at it."

3 | DEATH AND TRANSFIGURATION

*The world breaks everyone and afterward
many are strong at the broken places.*

A FAREWELL TO ARMS

It was in Hemingway's novels that his
hero became strong at the places where he
had broken. When last we saw him, even
untwisted by guilt, he was rather badly
broken. He was Frazer, holding tight to his
sanity in a Montana hospital; he was
"I" barely maintaining mental equilibrium
through the scrupulous fishing of an imagined river, and was Nick fishing one in
reality but for the same reason. He was the
hero of Hemingway's short stories—sensitive, masculine, impressionable, honest, and
out-of-doors—a boy then a man who had
come up against violence and evil and been
wounded by them. The manhood he had
attained was thus complicated and insecure,
but he was learning a code with which he
might maneuver, though crippled, and he
was practicing the rites which might exorcise
the terrors born of the events that crippled

79

him. In the course of his wounding the world had broken along with the other things his relation to society and its ways. He had served time for it and democracy and the rest quite young, as Hemingway once remarked of himself, declining any further enlistment.

But Hemingway had of course written a lot of things besides short fiction, and although the stories provide a background without which a real understanding of the rest of his work is impossible, it is for the rest—especially for the novels—that he is best known. This work, basically, does one or more of three things, two of which have already been discussed in connection with the stories. That is, the rest of his prose re-presents this wounded hero and the process of his injuring, disillusionment and break with respectability; secondly it re-presents also the hero's emulation of the man with the code, and his efforts to attain to it; lastly it offers a kind of solution to his problems—in the metamorphosis of *To Have and Have Not,* the third important novel. The next book, *For Whom the Bell Tolls,* does all these things. The three concerns, the wound and the break, the code, and a working adjustment of them, are the subjects of almost all Hemingway's significant work lying outside the short story genre. This comes to eleven book-length novels and a short one, a burlesque, a book on big game hunting, one on Spanish bullfighting, another of reminiscence, and a play. We should now be in a position to revisit them with profit.

Chronologically, the burlesque—a "satirical novel" —came first. This was an anomalous book for Hemingway, *The Torrents of Spring,* which appeared in 1926, a year after *In Our Time.* F. Scott Fitzgerald put him up to this ridiculing of Sherwood Anderson, or so the story goes, as a device with which Hemingway could break his contract with Liveright, who had published the earlier book. The idea was that Liveright, also the publisher of Anderson, would reject the satire on one of his star performers; this would nullify the contract, and then Hemingway would join his friend Fitzgerald at Scribner's to deal henceforth with Maxwell Perkins. In any case, that is what happened, though Hemingway certainly had more in mind than the single purpose. He knocked out *The Torrents* in haste, Liveright rejected it, Scribner's published it, and thus Scribner's got the next book, *The Sun Also Rises,* which in time became a best seller.

The Torrents of Spring (Hemingway apparently liked Turgenev's titles) was *not* a best seller, and recent critics have seemed to feel that a relative neglect of the book constitutes no great injustice. Balancing this judgment are the many extravagant reviews it originally received.* It is possible to take the compromise stand that if one goes to the trouble of reading Anderson's *Dark Laughter* (1925) first, and then goes through Hemingway's parody it is indeed moderately funny. But it is doubtful that this procedure is worth the effort. For one thing, Hemingway could be a lot funnier; for another, Anderson was an extremely fat target and in *Dark Laughter* was at times his own burlesque, as in a profundity like "if life were not so complex it would be more simple," or "if there is anything you do not understand in human life consult the works of Dr. Freud." If Hemingway had waited a while the job might have done itself.

Part One of the satire pointed its way with its title: "Red and Black Laughter." As Anderson had ended his book with the rich, deep laughter of Negroes (which was intended to suggest, in its primitive wisdom, a disparage-

* Several critics found it almost unbearably funny, and Allen Tate soberly judged it the most economically realized humor of disproportion he had encountered in American prose.

ment of the contrasted, frustrated whites) so several of Hemingway's chapters end with the sound of Indian war whoops. Another device is equally damaging: as nearly always in Anderson, so in Hemingway the characters are forever stopping to "wonder"—to ponder one of life's deep mysteries, usually suggested by some other book and always banal. Hemingway goes like this:

> Could it be that what this writing fellow Hutchinson had said, "If winter comes can spring be far behind?" would be true again this year? Yogi Johnson wondered.

Part Three of the book is called ". . . the Making and Marring of Americans," and would seem at first glance to announce that Miss Stein was going to be disposed of too, but Hemingway really waited for a later book to do that, and this one goes on declaring its author's independence of his old friend Anderson, and of the whole Anderson brand of sentimental primitivism.

The Sun Also Rises, which appeared later in 1926, reintroduces us to the hero. In Hemingway's novels this man is a slightly less personal hero than Nick was, and his adventures are to be less closely identified with Hemingway's, for more events are changed, or even "made up." But he still projects qualities of the man who created him, many of his experiences are still literal or transformed autobiography, and his wound is still the crucial fact about him. Even when as Robert Jordan of *For Whom the Bell Tolls* he is somewhat disguised, we have little or no trouble in recognizing him.

Recognition is immediate and unmistakable in *The Sun Also Rises.* Here the wound, again with its literal and symbolic meanings, is transferred from the spine to the genitals: Jake Barnes was "emasculated," to speak very loosely, in the war. But he is the same man, a grown Nick

Adams, and again the actual injury functions as concrete evidence that the hero is a casualty. He is a writer living in Paris in the Twenties as, for example, Harry was; like Nick he was transplanted from midwestern America to the Austro-Italian front; when things are at their worst for him, like Fraser he cries in the night. When he refuses the services of a prostitute, and she asks, "What's the matter? You sick?" he is not thinking of his loss alone when he answers, "Yes." He is the insomniac as before, and for the same reasons: "I blew out the lamp. Perhaps I would be able to sleep. My head started to work. The old grievance." And later he remembers that time, which we witnessed, when "for six months I never slept with the light off." He is the man who is troubled in the night, who leaves Brett alone in his sitting room and lies face down on the bed, having "a bad time."

In addition, Jake like Nick is the protagonist who has broken with society and with middle-class ways; again he has made the break in connection with his wounding. He has very little use for most people. At times he has little use even for his friends; at times he has little use for himself. He exists on a fringe of the society he has renounced; as a newspaper reporter he works just enough to make enough money to eat and drink well on, and spends the rest of his time in cafés, or fishing, or watching bullfights. Though it is not highly developed yet, he and those few he respects have a code, too. Jake complains very little, although he suffers a good deal; there are certain things that are "done" and many that are "not done." Lady Brett Ashley also knows the code, and distinguishes people according to it; a person is "one of us," as she puts it, or is not—and most are not. The whole trouble with Robert Cohn, the boxing, maladroit Jew of the novel, is that he is not. He points up the code most clearly by so lacking it: he will not go away when Brett is done with him; he is "messy" in every way. After he has severely beaten up Romero, the small young bullfighter, and Romero will not give in, Cohn cries, wretchedly proclaims his love for Brett in public, and tries to shake Romero's hand. He gets that hand in the face, an act which is approved as appropriate comment on his behavior.

Cohn does not like Romero because Brett does. She finally goes off with the bullfighter, and it is when she leaves him too that she makes a particularly clear statement of what she and the other "right" people have salvaged from the wreck of their compromised lives. She has decided that she is ruining Romero's career, and besides she is too old for him. She walks out, and says to Jake:

> "It makes one feel rather good deciding not to be a bitch. . . . It's sort of what we have instead of God."

In early editions, *The Sun Also Rises* had on its title page, before the passage on futility in *Ecclesiastes* from which the title is taken, Gertrude Stein's famous "You are all a lost generation." The novel provides an explanation for this observation, in addition to illustrating it in action. As in the story called "In Another Country," the picture of the hero wounded and embittered by his experience of violence is broadened to include other people. Brett Ashley, for example, and her fiancé Mike Campbell are both casualties from ordeals similar to those which damaged Jake. Brett has behind her the very unpleasant death of her first fiancé; Mike's whole character was shattered by the war. *A Farewell to Arms* can be read as background to the earlier novel: some of Brett's past is filled in by Catherine Barkley, whose fiancé had been blown to bits in the war, and most of Jake's by Frederic Henry.

The fact that characters in *The Sun Also Rises* are recognizable people, taken from "real life," does not contradict the fact that they are in this pattern. Various personages known to Paris of the Twenties have thought that they recognized without difficulty the originals—Donald Ogden Stewart, Harold Stearns, Harold Loeb, Lady Duff-Twysden, Ford Madox Ford, and Pat Guthrie—and even Jake had his counterpart in actuality. But Hemingway, like most authors, changed the characters to suit his purposes, and it is clear that whatever his origins, Jake, for instance, owes most to the man who created him, and is the hero.

He is the hero emasculated, however, and this must primarily account for the fact that he does not always seem entirely real. As he feels befits his status, he is largely a passive arranger of things for others, who only wants to "play it along and just not make trouble for people." But as narrator, at least, he is convincing, and if there is something blurred about him it helps to bring the participants into a focus that is all the sharper. Hemingway had always been good with secondary characters, finding them in a bright flash that reveals all we need know. Here, as he somehow managed to make similar people easily distinguishable, the revelations are brilliant. One remembers Brett and Cohn longest, for they get the fullest development, but Count Mippipopolous is wonderful, and wonderful too—save for their anti-Semitism, largely missing from an edition which advertised that "Not one word has been changed or omitted"—are Mike and Bill.

Chiefly it is Hemingway's ear, a trap that caught every mannerism of speech, that is responsible for the fact that these characters come so alive and distinct. That famous ear also caught a great many "swells" and "grands" that have dated—for slang is one thing almost certain to go bad with the passage of time—and some of the dialogue of camaraderie ("Old Bill!" "You bum!") is also embarrassing. But taken as a whole the talk is superb and, as a whole, so is the rest of the writing in the book. Hemingway's wide-awake senses fully evoke an American's Paris, a vacationer's Spain. Jake moves through these places with the awareness of a professional soldier reconnoitering new terrain. The action is always foremost, but it is supported by real country and real city. The conversational style, which gives us the illusion that Jake is just telling us the story of what he has been doing lately, gracefully hides the fact that the pace is carefully calculated and swift, the sentences and scenes hard and clean. This is true of the over-all structure, too: the book is informal and relaxed only on the surface, and beneath it lies a scrupulous and satisfying orchestration. It is not until nearly the end, for example, when Cohn becomes the center of what there is of action, that opening with him seems anything but a simply random way of getting started. This discussion of Cohn has eased us into Jake's life in Paris, and especially his situation with Brett. Suddenly the lines are all drawn. An interlude of trout fishing moves us smoothly into Spain and the bullfights. At Pamplona the tension which all try to ignore builds up, slowly, and breaks finally as the events come to their climax simultaneously with the fiesta's. Then, in an intensely muted coda, a solitary Jake, rehabilitating himself, washes away his hangovers in the ocean. Soon it is all gone, he is returned to Brett as before, and we discover that we have come full circle, like all the rivers, the winds, and the sun, to the place where we began.

This is motion which goes no place. Constant activity has brought us along with such pleasant, gentle insistence that not until the end do we realize that we have not been taken in, exactly, but taken nowhere; and that, finally, is the point.* This is structure as meaning, organization as content. And, as the enormous effect the book had on its generation proved, such a meaning or content was important to 1926. The book touched with delicate accuracy on something big, on things other people were feeling, but too dimly for articulation. Hemingway had deeply felt and understood what was in the wind. Like Brett, who was the kind of woman who sets styles, the book itself was profoundly creative, and had the kind of power that is prototypal.

Despite quite a lot of fun *The Sun Also Rises* is still Hemingway's *Waste Land,* and Jake is Hemingway's Fisher King. This may be just coincidence, though the novelist had read the poem, but once again here is the

* It happens that this is not precisely the point Hemingway intended to make. He once said that he regarded his first epigraph, "you are all a lost generation," as a piece of "splendid bombast." (Later he devoted one of the sketches, "Une Génération Perdue," of his *Moveable Feast* to an effective attack on the phrase.) It was his idea that the second epigraph taken from *Ecclesiastes* would "correct" the famous remark attributed to Miss Stein. As far as he was concerned, he wrote his editor Maxwell Perkins, the point of his novel is, as the Biblical lines say in part, that "the earth abideth forever."

Some support for this position can be found in the novel itself. Not quite all the people in it are "lost"—surely Romero is not—and the beauty of the eternal earth is now and then richly evoked. But most of the characters do seem a great deal of the time if not lost then terribly unsure of their bearings, and few readers have felt the force of Hemingway's intention. The strongest feeling in the book is that for the people in it (and one gets the distinct impression that other people do not matter very much) life is futile, and their motions like the motion of the sun of the title (as it appears to our eyes): endless, circular, and unavailing. Further, for all who remember what the Preacher said in this well-known Biblical passage, the echo of "Vanity of vanities; all is vanity" is rather loud. Thus what Hemingway proposed to do and what he did again seem two things, but it is doubtful that this hurts the book.

protagonist gone impotent, and his land gone sterile. Eliot's London is Hemingway's Paris, where spiritual life in general, and Jake's sexual life in particular, are alike impoverished. Prayer breaks down and fails, a knowledge of traditional distinctions between good and evil is largely lost, copulation is morally neutral and, cut off from the past chiefly by the spiritual disaster of the war, life has become mostly meaningless. "What shall we do?" is the same constant question, to which the answer must be, again, "Nothing." To hide it, instead of playing chess one drinks, mechanically and always. Love is a possibility only for the two who cannot love; once again homosexuality intensifies this atmosphere of sterility; once more the Fisher King is also a man who fishes. And again the author plays with quotations from the great of the past, as when in reply to Jake's remark that he is a taxidermist Bill objects, "That was in another country. And besides all the animals were dead."

To be sure, the liquor is good, and so are the food and the conversation. But in one way Hemingway's book is even more desperate than Eliot's. The lesson of an "asceticism" to control the aimless expression of lust would be to Jake Barnes only one more bad joke, and the fragments he has shored against his ruins are few, and quite inadequate. In the poem a message of salvation comes out of the life-giving rain which falls on western civilization. In Hemingway's waste land there is fun but no hope. No rain falls on Europe this time, and when it does fall in *A Farewell to Arms* it brings not life but death.

A Farewell to Arms (1929), which borrows its title from a poem of that name by George Peele,* reverts to

---

* As in the case of many of Hemingway's titles the allusion to the poem is slightly ironic, for Peele mourned the fact that he could no longer fight.

the war and supplies background for *The Sun Also Rises.* For the germs of both of its plots, a war plot and a love plot, it reaches back to *In Our Time.* An outline of the human arms in the novel is to be found among these early stories in a piece called "A Very Short Story." This sketch, less than two pages long, dealt quickly, as the novel does extensively, with the drinking and love-making in an Italian hospital of an American soldier, wounded in the leg, and a nurse, and had told of their love and their wish to get married. But where the book ends powerfully with the death in childbirth of the woman, the story dribbled off in irony. The lovers parted, the soldier leaving for home to get a job so that he could send for his sweetheart. Before long, however, the nurse wrote that she had a new lover who was going to marry her, though he never did; and then, shortly after receiving the letter, the soldier "contracted gonorrhea from a sales girl in a loop department store while riding in a taxicab through Lincoln Park." *

The war plot of *A Farewell to Arms,* on the other hand, is a greatly expanded version of that Chapter VI sketch in which Nick was wounded and made his separate peace—with Rinaldi, who also appears in the longer work. This wound, which got Nick in the spine, and "I" in the knee, and emasculated Jake, has returned to the knee, which is where Hemingway was most badly hit. Then the

---

* Except for the venereal element (which according to a paperback biographer was thus contracted by a *friend* of the author), it appears that this sketch tells how it actually was, the novel-to-be how it might have been. In life Catherine Barkley, the heroine of the novel, was Agnes H. von Kurowski, the Bellevue-trained daughter of a German-American father; Hemingway intended to bring her home from Italy and marry her. (Leicester's biography prints an excellent photograph of her; Marcelline's biography prints a picture Ernest sent home from Italy of a "nice-looking bearded older man . . . Count Greppie"—possibly the model for Count Greffi in the novel.)

same story is rehearsed again in lengthened form. (Recuperated enough to return to action after another convalescence in Milan, Lt. Frederic Henry becomes bitter about the society responsible for the war and, caught up in the Italian retreat from Caporetto, he breaks utterly with the army in which he is an officer. And this is again the old protagonist, who cannot sleep at night for thinking—who must not use his head to think with, and will absolutely have to stop it. He is also the man who, when he does sleep, has nightmares, and wakes from them in sweat and fright, and goes back to sleep in an effort to stay outside his dreams.)

Unlike Jake Barnes, however, Frederic Henry participates fully in the book's action, and as a person is wholly real. But he is also a little more than that, for just as the response of Americans of the period to the aimless and disillusioned hedonism of Jake and his friends indicated that some subtle chord in them had been struck, so something in the evolution of Frederic Henry from complicity in the war to bitterness and escape has made him seem, though always himself, a little larger than that, too. Complicity, bitterness, escape—a whole country could read its experience, Wilson to Harding, in his, and it began to become clear that in Hemingway as elsewhere "hero" meant not simply "protagonist" but a man who stands for many men. Thus it is that when historians of various kinds epitomize the temper of the American Twenties and a reason for it the adventures of that lieutenant come almost invariably to mind. And also, since these things could hardly be said better, his words:

> I was always embarrassed by the words sacred, glorious, and sacrifice and the expression in vain. We had heard them, sometimes standing in the rain almost out of earshot, so that only the shouted words came through . . . now for a long time, and

> I had seen nothing sacred, and the things that were glorious had no glory and the sacrifices were like the stockyards at Chicago if nothing was done with the meat except to bury it. . . . Abstract words such as glory, honor, courage, or hallow were obscene. . . .

It is on the implications of these sentiments, and in order to escape a certain death which he has not deserved, that Henry finally acts. He jumps in a river and deserts: the hell with it. It was an unforgettable plunge.

Memorable too, in her devotion and her ordeal— though much less memorable, and much less real—is Henry's English mistress. Idealized past the fondest belief of most people, and even the more realistic wishes of some, compliant, and bearing unmistakable indications of the troubles to come when she will appear as mistress of heroes to come, Catherine Barkley has at least some character in her own right, and is both the first true "Hemingway heroine," and the most convincing one. Completely real, once again and at once, are the minor characters— especially Rinaldi, the ebullient Italian doctor, and the priest, and Count Greffi, the ancient billiard player, and the enlisted ambulance drivers.

Chiefly, again, it is their speech which brings these people to life and keeps them living. The rest of the book, however, is less conversational in tone than before, and in other ways the writing is changed a little. The sentences are now longer, even lyrical, on occasion, and, once in a while, experimental, as Hemingway, not content to rest in the style that had made him already famous, tries for new effects, and does not always succeed. Taken as a whole, however, his prose has never been finer or more finished than in this novel. Never have those awesome, noncommittal understatements, which say more than could ever be written out, been more impressive. The book has passages which rate with the hardest, cleanest and most moving in contemporary literature.

The novel has one stylistic innovation that is important to it. This is the use of an object, rain, in a way that cannot be called symbolic so much as portentous. Hemingway had used water as a metaphoric purge of past experience before, and so Henry's emergence from the river into a new life, as from a total immersion, was not new. What is new in *A Farewell to Arms* is the consistent use of rain as a signal of disaster. Henry, in his practical realism, professes a disbelief in signs, and tells himself that Catherine's vision of herself dead in the rain is meaningless. But she dies in it and actually, glancing back at the end, one sees that a short, introductory scene at the very start of the book had presented an ominous conjunction of images—rain, pregnancy and death—which set the mood for all that was to follow, prefigured it and bound all the ends of the novel into a perfect and permanent knot.

This is really the old "pathetic fallacy" put to new use, and—since there is no need to take it scientifically or philosophically, but simply as a subtle and unobtrusive device for unity—quite an acceptable one, too. Good and bad weather go along with good and bad moods and events. It is not just that, like everyone, the characters respond emotionally to conditions of atmosphere, light and so on, but that there is a correspondence between these things and their fate. They win when it's sunny, and lose in the rain.

Thus, then, the weather, which as both omen and descriptive background (made once again to count for something) is a matter of style, cannot be extricated from the book's plot, or structure. This is of course built on the two themes involved in the ambiguity of "arms," which are developed and intensified together, with alternating emphasis, until at the extremity of one the hero escapes society, and the heroine everything.)Despite the frequency with which they appear in the same books, the themes of love and war are really an unlikely pair, if not indeed—to judge from the frequency with which writers fail to wed them—quite incompatible. But in Hemingway's novel their courses run straight and exactly, though subtly, parallel, and he has managed to fuse them.) In his affair with the war Henry goes from desultory participation to serious action and a wound, and then through his recuperation in Milan to a retreat which leads to his desertion. His relationship with Catherine Barkley undergoes six precisely corresponding stages—from a trifling sexual affair to actual love and her conception, and then through her confinement in the Alps to a trip to the hospital which leads to her death. By the end of Hemingway's novel, when the last farewell is taken, the two stories are as one, in the point that is made very clear, lest there be any sentimental doubt about it, that life, both social and personal, is a struggle in which the Loser Takes Nothing, either.

This ideology, which is the novel's, has two related aspects which are implicit in the united elements of the plot. In the end, a man is trapped. He is trapped biologically—in this case by the "natural" process that costs him his future wife in the harrowing scenes at the hospital, and is trapped by society—at the end of a retreat, where you take off or get shot. Either way it can only end badly, and there are no other ways. How you will get it, though, depends on the kind of person you are:)

> If people bring so much courage to this world the world has to kill them to break them, so of course it kills them. The world breaks everyone and afterward many are strong at the broken places. But those that will not break it kills. It kills the very good and the very gentle and the very brave impar-

tially. If you are none of these you can be sure that it will kill you too but there will be no special hurry.

It does not really matter very much that there is something a little romantic about this passage, perhaps the finest in all of Hemingway, or that the novel is a romantic one as a whole. It must be just about the most romantic piece of realistic fiction, or the most realistic romance, in our literature. Henry's love affair, which blossoms glamorously from the mud of the war, is but the most striking of several factors which go together to make his war a remarkably pleasant one, as wars go, and much more attractive than wars actually are. The lieutenant has a somewhat special time of it, with orderlies and porters and little or no trouble with superiors, and good wine and good food and a lot of free time in which to enjoy them. But it is not important that these aspects of his army experience are highly untypical. Nor does it matter on the other hand that women usually survive childbirth, and many men are discharged from armies in good shape, and then life goes on much as before. What matters instead is that this time Hemingway has made his story, and the attitudes it enacts, persuasive and compelling within the covers of his book. And after we have closed the covers there is no inclination to complain that this was, after all, no literal transcription of reality which exaggerated neither the bitter nor the sweet. It was rather an intensification of life. Willingly or not, disbelief is suspended before a vision that overrides objections, withers preconceptions and even memory and imposes itself in their place.

This novel has the last word, always. Catherine Barkley, as it happened, was very good, very gentle, very brave. Unlike the hero, who broke and survived to become eventually quite strong, she would not break and so she was killed. It was very likely in rebuttal to the people who rejected the pessimism of this denouement that Hemingway pointed out three years later, in *Death in the Afternoon*, that love stories do not end happily in life, either:

> There is no lonelier man in death, except the suicide, than that man who has lived many years with a good wife and then outlived her. If two people love each other there can be no happy end to it.

Death in the Afternoon (1932)—like *Green Hills of Africa* (1935)—is a book of nonfiction in which the hero is to be found pretty much at the end of his rope. It is a book on bullfighting, and represents Hemingway in complete escape from the society he renounced in his first war novel. It is not simply a coincidence that it also finds him in the depth of his pessimism, which is here, however, a depth lighted by a certain humor. It is in conversations with the "Old Lady," who appears from time to time to keep the reader awake, the Author says, that this disenchantment is best illustrated. Hemingway is talking to the Old Lady about venereal disease:

> Ah, madame, you will find no man who is a man who will not bear some marks of past misfortune . . . but a man throws off many things and I know a champion at golf who never putted so well as with the gonorrhea.
> *Old lady:* Have you no remedy then?
> Madame, there is no remedy for anything in life.

If this is true then of course it follows that the remedy is death. That is what the book is about: the death of bulls, bullfighters and horses: death in the afternoon. Death had become Hemingway's principal subject, for a while at least; his preoccupation with the idea is never more evident than here. Bullfighting is "about death," too, and all of the author's tortured theories of art and tragedy and bulls—though not entirely silly—do very little to hide the fact that it is his fascination with highly stylized dying which primarily accounts for his presence in the grandstand.

Not that there are no other things in the book. The Spanish critics, who ought to know about these things, said that it was the best book on bullfighting ever. If one is not particularly interested in this aspect, there are many other attractions. The dialogues with the Old Lady (they have not much to do with bullfighting) are extraordinarily funny and cover a wide range of topics. There is also a good deal of excellent advice on how to write prose fiction; and, if it should ever again be possible to tour a "normal" Spain as a vacationist, the book would serve as a helpful, if hefty, cross between Baedeker and Duncan Hines. If one is interested in none of these things, there are still the photographs, a rather self-indulgent and pedantic glossary, and the case histories of certain *aficionados*.

But the aspect of the book which most obviously integrates it with the rest of its author's work is the code which Hemingway admired in the bullfighters. These men are previews of the guide Wilson, who taught Macomber. As Wilson with his animals and customers, so the bullfighter with his. In each case a man finds himself in a compromising position. Each makes his living by killing animals for pleasure and pay, and—therefore?—each has the strictest rules by which the activity may be pursued. There cannot be many zones of human endeavor in which more things can be classified as "done" or "not done" than in bullfighting. And governing this etiquette, which prescribes one's behavior to the last curve of the last finger, are the all-important qualities of honor and *cojones* (for which the English "courage" is a euphemism). Here is "grace under pressure" epitomized. The bullfighter is the man with the code, whom the hero studies, admires and emulates. More than this, Hemingway seemed to see bullfighting as a ritual which acts out his conception of men as the creatures who pit themselves against violent death, and to see the bullfighter as high priest of the ceremonial. With a behavior that gracefully formalizes the code, he administers the death men seek to avoid. The view itself was not uninteresting, and most readers were at least willing to give it a try. The chief trouble was with the rather hysterical or blood-drunken manner in which it was presented.

The grinding need for self-justification and the nervous, eloquently belligerent attitudes struck in this book are even more striking in *Green Hills of Africa* (1935). This is an account of a big game expedition, in which the author repeats that he is doing what he likes most, is enjoying himself and is happy—nine time in the first seventy-two pages!—until the reader unavoidably infers that something is most certainly wrong. To be sure, "it was my own damned life and I would lead it where and how I pleased," but if readers came to feel the truant was really wondering what was happening back at school, and if perhaps he ought to be there, that is their own business, too.

Be that as it may, Hemingway liked Africa. As for his own country, "a country that is finished":

> Our people went to America because that was the place to go then. It had been a good country and we had made a bloody mess of it. . . . Now I would go somewhere else.

The extent to which the big game hunter had lost touch with the finished land in the year 1935 is harshly indicated by passages in which he discusses, somewhat jocosely, "What's going on in America?" ("Some sort of Y.M.C.A. show," is one answer.) But *Green Hills of Africa* includes more than social criticism. Inferior to

Death in the Afternoon, the book does contain "something for everyone." There is the hunting itself, some autobiography, and some literary discussion. Although he becomes involved in a few long and weirdly contorted sentences (which mark another change from the famous shorter ones) the book is well written on the whole and is moderately entertaining. It has a wonderfully keen awareness of people (even of the natives, from a *bwana* point of view) and of the country, and is excellent on the hunting. But about the only over-all interest in the thing centers around the problem of whether or not Hemingway would finally shoot a kudu, and this is a matter some people find it very hard to care about. One's total impression is of a man who had so completely cut himself off from the roots that nourish, since that separate peace, that he had developed a vitamin deficiency. The more nervous and uncomfortable he became the more he asserted his happiness; something had to give and it did.

There is a great difference between the man who was chasing animals in Africa, with servants, Scotch and sodas and all the rest of it on a twenty-five thousand dollar safari-honeymoon, and the one who drew the protagonist of *To Have and Have Not* (1937). This Have Not finds it impossible to make an honest living for himself, and will not dig sewers for a government which pays him less for digging than it takes to feed his wife and children. Harry Morgan, named perhaps for another hard-drinking buccaneer who worked some of the same territory and also evacuated people for high prices (and based on an actual rumrunner named Josey Russell), becomes an outlaw as a result. What had happened was a revolution in Hemingway of equal importance to the one Nick underwent when he renounced the society which was responsible for the pious slaughter of the First World War. By 1937 Ernest Hemingway had re-embraced the society he had quit some twenty years before, and was back in another "war for democracy."

It was not easy to plot the course of this rough circle, for although it is not exactly unique in the history of the developments of contemporary writers Hemingway came home from lands farther off than most, and he had been away longer. By 1936 his friend John Dos Passos (who had been an "expatriate" and had written an anti-war novel and a book on Spain in his earlier days) had published all three volumes of *U.S.A.* We do know, however, what *To Have and Have Not* means in the context of its author's development, and we know a little about how the meaning was arrived at.

The novel is a book with a "message," and that message is stated by the author in one sentence. It is a sentence which "had taken him a long time to get out," and which "had taken him all of his life to learn." It is a deathbed conversion; the words are Harry's last on earth: "No matter how a man alone ain't got no bloody f---ing chance." The conflicts and anguish involved in turning from an America where everyone was "quitting work to go on relief," to one where some kind of cooperative society seemed clearly the implicit answer, can only be guessed at, though it is pretty certain that the purge of "Kilimanjaro" was a part of the transformation. So, without doubt, was the slaughter of hundreds of U.S. Army veterans left by their government to perish in a Florida hurricane in 1935, which Hemingway reported with savage indignation for the communist *New Masses*. What we also know is that the novel was started as early as 1933. When, early in 1937, Hemingway went to Spain to report Loyalist news of the Spanish Civil War, a first draft of the book (which was much longer than the one we have) was completed. It ended in utter discouragement. When the author returned to this country later that year he was ardently pro-Loyalist; he destroyed a good deal of the novel and changed the ending. Doubtless Morgan's speech, Hemingway's Manifesto, was written at that time, too, and the fact that this concluding message does not grow very inevitably out of the action is further ground for such a guess. Hemingway broke the back of his book, and must very nearly have broken his own.

To Have and Have Not is an anomaly in the development of Hemingway's prose, for it is one of his very few full-length works in which the hero does not appear. Although Morgan has a very few points of resemblance to the hero, and is usually mistaken for him, he is really not our man. He has neither the background, the troubles nor the personality. But all the same, we have seen the like of him before: he is the man who teaches the hero. He is the prizefighter, the bullfighter, the gambler, the hunting guide, who appears always to illustrate something important that the hero must know, and knows in his next appearance. But this time it is not so much the necessity for having the code that he primarily illustrates, although he has it and the book is packed with praise for his *cojones*. This time it is that human beings cannot strike out alone with impunity; they must cooperate.

The novel is a very uneven one and it is more significant for the way it marks this revolution in the course of the author's thinking than for anything else. There are some excellent scenes, like the one of a brawl in a barroom, but there are some poor ones, too. For the first time the uncomfortable feeling that one has in the presence of the poseur is really marked. When Hemingway writes, for example, "I felt bad about hitting him. You know how you feel when you hit a drunk..." it is quite proper to reply, "No. How does it feel to hit a drunk? Tell us how it feels to hit a drunk."

The contrast between the Haves and the Have Nots

in the novel, which is really structure and support for the whole book and message, is unconvincing. The basis of the superiority of the Nots lies chiefly in the Morgans' bedroom talent, and while there can be no objection to the notion that Harry and his wife perform more admirably than, say, the solitary rich girl who masturbates, it must at the same time be conceded that a large part of the Morgans' superiority is directly attributable to the somewhat chance fact that he has only a stub for one arm.

On the other hand, however, there is a certain catharsis, doubtless written before the conversion in Spain, for the accumulative disgust which the various scenes among the Haves build up. This is the savage rhetoric with which Richard Gordon's wife (he is a successful novelist in the book) denounces her husband; it must be a peak in something or other:

> Love was the greatest thing, wasn't it? . . . Slop.
> Love is just another dirty lie. Love is ergoapiol pills
> to make me come around. . . . Love is quinine. . . .
> Love is that dirty aborting horror that you took me
> to. Love is my insides all messed up. It's half cath-
> eters and half whirling douches. I know about love.
> Love always hangs up behind the bathroom door.
> It smells like lysol. . . . Love is all the dirty little
> tricks you taught me that you probably got out of
> some book. All right. I'm through with you and
> I'm through with love. Your kind of picknose love.
> You writer.

Just how all these things lead to Harry's final pronouncement is Hemingway's business, not ours, and it is not skillfully transacted. Nor are the Johnny-come-lately explanations of how the Haves got their money very impressive. Actually, if the author could have assembled his thousands of readers in one place and said, "Look, I was wrong. From now on things will be different," he would have accomplished the biggest part of what his novel accomplished.

That we are not making too much of the simple statement that a man has no chance alone is proved by the book that came from Hemingway one year later. *The Fifth Column* (1938), a play full of wonderful talk but Rover boy action, finds our old friend the hero—this time called Philip—a counterespionage agent of the Stalinist underground in Madrid. A kind of Scarlet Pimpernel in the clothes of a twentieth-century American reporter, Philip appears to be a charming but dissolute wastrel, a newsman who never files any stories. But actually, and unknown to his mistress Dorothy (with whom he is more or less in love), he is up to his neck in the Loyalist, communist fight.

Although he has become somewhat jocular (perhaps as a result of relief from guilt feelings got rid of in the last novel, and with the tone of the hysterical humor of soldiers facing death) Philip is the hero as before. He has the old troubles still; he has "the horrorous"—a "sort of super horrors"—in the night. He is able to joke about them because he has known them for so long: "I never tell anybody when I get the horrors. . . . I've had them so long I'd miss them if they went away." Dorothy wants him to tell her about these horrors, but the hero says, "No. Everybody gets their own, and you don't want to pass them around." Actually, everyone doesn't—Dorothy doesn't, for example—but she accepts the excuse. "If you want me to go to sleep," he tells her on returning tired from a raid at five o'clock in the morning, "just hit me on the head with a hammer."

There is still the superstition and still the knowledge-ability. There are good signs and bad signs—little irrelevant things which portend success or failure for a venture. Hot water in the hotel, for instance, is a good sign which the hero takes seriously. At the same time, his knowledge of his way around has deepened and even become subtle. He is able to decide that a guard who claims to have fallen asleep is telling the truth by examining what the man says he dreamt, and finding it rings true. He knows about dreams, and what sort of thing the man would have made up if he had been lying.

In the play the wounds of the hero's personality are reopened by the work his job in Madrid entails. He is required, for example, to be present at the torturing of two captured fascist leaders, which turns out to be a lot like things he does not need to be reminded of. But of course Dorothy knows nothing of all this and she says, "You're a perfectly vicious commodity. Never home. Out all night. Dirty, muddy, disorderly." However, along with the horse-play and the cops-and-robbers action, Hemingway was trying to show that he meant business in *The Fifth Column*. The hero has finally to get rid of his mistress, whom he had intended to marry. She is rich, she is unconscious of the class meaning of the war, and she takes time from his work. He has no right to keep her any more: "We're in for fifty years of undeclared wars and I've signed up for the duration." At one point he says of the Lincoln Battalion: "It's such a good battalion and it's done such things that it would break your damn heart if I tried to tell you about it." The hero, it scarcely needs pointing out, has come a long way from the lieutenant who some ten years before had said that words like sacred, glorious and sacrifice were obscene.

But it is hardly any distance at all from "a man alone ain't got no . . . chance" to "No man is an *Iland,* intire of it selfe. . . ." These words from Donne which supply a title for Hemingway's next book, *For Whom the Bell Tolls* (1940), signified at the start that Hemingway and the hero, now named Robert Jordan, had not gone back on anything. However, Jordan has by now thought more about politics than Philip had, and he has come to a kind of position. The American college instructor, in Spain as a Loyalist guerrilla, is—he makes clear—not a communist. Maria asks him:

> "Are you a communist?"
> "No I am an anti-fascist."
> "For a long time?"
> "Since I have understood fascism."

But his position is always a fluctuating one, and when Pilar asks if he has her great religious faith in the Republic he answers, " 'Yes . . .' hoping it was true." When he himself inquires into his politics he is at times able to reply that he has none:

> What about a planned society and the rest of it? That was for the others to do. . . . He fought now in this war because it had started in a country that he loved and he believed in the Republic. . . . Here in Spain the communists offered the best discipline. . . . He accepted their discipline for the duration of the war because, in the conduct of the war, they were the only party whose program and whose discipline he could respect.
> What were his politics then? He had none now, he told himself.

At other times he is "realistic," "cynical," or "superficial" —according to one's own politics—about the possibilities of socialism. Mark Twain once said—using a saw that must have been already dull—"I know too much about human nature" to believe in a cooperative society. Jordan has a very similar comment: "If you had three together, two would unite against one, and then the two would start to betray each other." It is easy to see why American communists were confused about the novel, which was thoroughly denounced in the *Masses* and in the *Daily Worker,* and prominently displayed in Party bookshops in New York. However, despite Jordan's doubts, and the confusion in the Party line, the final impression of the book is one of at least tentative affirmation—affirmation of a just cause, and of the goodness of life:

> If we win here we will win everywhere. The world
> is a fine place and worth the fighting for and I
> hate very much to leave it.

That last sentence is a good one, and most people have accepted it. But other important passages in the novel, like the following one, have caused trouble:

> You felt, in spite of all bureaucracy and inefficiency
> and party strife something that was like the feeling
> you expected to have and did not have when you
> made your first communion. It was a feeling of
> consecration to a duty toward all of the oppressed
> of the world. . . . You felt an absolute brotherhood
> with the others who were engaged in it.

Many skeptics have found all this hard to believe in Hemingway, or hard to believe as anything more than a passing fancy. And it must be admitted that they have a point. It is not at all that his novel has oversimplified the issues, or overlooked objections, which are the pitfalls of propagandistic fiction. To Jordan there is nothing black and white about his enemies and his friends; as in life, there are shades of gray. The most barbaric atrocity in the novel is perpetrated by his friends, the Republicans—an important irony which looms so large that it alone would protect the book against the charge that it had falsified the complexity of the problems by stacking the moral cards. But it is not alone. Indeed the things Jordan learns in this war are, he realizes, "not so simple" in general. Through hard, old

Pilar he has become aware of odd and mystifying things about sex and fate; from others he has learned, the hard way, the difficulty of subscribing to any cause, which will invariably pervert in practice its original aims.

The trouble is, instead, that readers have regretfully found that the bitterness and cynicism of *A Farewell to Arms* ring somehow truer than Jordan's expressions of faith and belief, which he *hopes* are true. The man seems to be forcing himself, to be forcing something that does not come naturally and is thus not wholly his own. And he must apologize for it: his belief is "true no matter how trite it sounded," he tells himself, and this is surely an obscure kind of admission that even he senses that something is wrong. Hemingway seems involved here in a difficulty he had referred to years before, the difficulty of "knowing what you really felt, rather than what you were supposed to feel, and had been taught to feel." This difficulty is an appalling one, actually, and it is Hemingway's inability to surmount it completely, and thus convince his readers of the full and untentative sincerity of the hero's ideals, that primarily keeps this novel from greatness.

But it is a very good novel which displays the gifts that Hemingway at his best always had. Not even *The Sun Also Rises* evokes more richly the life of the senses, or is thicker with an awareness of them, or gives a closer feeling of the presence of a solid physical world in which the action takes place. And this action is plotted as surely and skillfully as ever, the minor events growing directly out of deeply understood characters, and the final tragedy wholly prepared for. The secondary characters are as real as ever. Pilar and Pablo, a supporting heroine and an off-and-on villain, respectively, are most fully developed, but equally impressive are the other Spaniards—Anselmo, Augustín, Primitivo, and a wonderful, worthless gypsy. Their conversation, written down in translated Spanish as the ear of an American would hear it (a device practiced occasionally with French in *The Sun Also Rises* and with Italian in *A Farewell to Arms*) is a triumph. The speech gives the full taste of the original, is both enormously expressive and extraordinarily precise, and is all the while entertaining. The substitution of the word "obscenity" for the incessant Spanish obscenities is not a completely successful circumvention, but on the whole the dialogue is witty—or even, at times, hilarious—and would alone make the book a joy to read.

In other ways this novel is different from, say, *A Farewell to Arms*. The prose, for instance, is more graceful, and less tense; there is almost no use of understatement, now deprecated by Jordan as an "English pose," the obverse of the Latin's "bravado." The chief differences, however, between this book and the rest of Hemingway's novels result from the fact that here the author has shortened the time span of the action to a few packed days while at the same time greatly lengthening the treatment of them. The book cannot have, then, the quick clean brilliance of some of his other work. And though one is unwilling to say that in going slower than before Hemingway has also gone deeper, it can be said that he does give a solider and much broader view of things, and that his characterizations are on the whole less spectacular but more substantial—all as befits the more leisurely pace. This is the most underrated of his books.

It must be admitted, however, that the important statement that Jordan does not wish to die is a simplification of a complicated matter. In *For Whom the Bell Tolls* there is a subterranean struggle between his wish to live and the old obsession with death. The opening sentence of the novel finds the hero stretched prone on the pine-needled floor of the forest; as he awaits the bullet which will end his life in the closing sentence of the book, he is in the same position. In between, as others have pointed out, there has been for him only this long tendency toward the grave. This attraction toward death not only brackets the novel, as if to say that the whole book is to be read in the light of the inclination toward returning to earth which Jordan's posture indicates. The entire novel is impregnated with the atmosphere of the violent extinction of life. Corpse is piled on corpse, and the tendency toward death is steered on its long way by the novelist, who offers up one body after another to mark the route.

At the same time, Robert Jordan shows the same appetite for living which as hero he has always had. The exigencies of a rugged, outdoor existence greatly increase the old sensual pleasures—food, drink and sex—which have always been important. First, though, among the reasons for living is of course Maria, companion of Jordan's sleeping bag, and girl of his dreams.

In a foreword to *Green Hills of Africa* Hemingway had written: "Any one not finding sufficient love interest is at liberty . . . to insert whatever love interest he or she may have at the time." One might guess, then, that what the author had done in this novel of the Spanish war was to insert his own contemporaneous love interest—presumably his third wife, to whom the novel was dedicated, and whom in appearance Maria somewhat resembled. Even if it is not to be taken literally, however, his inscription, "To Ingrid Bergman, who is the Maria of this book," in a gift copy for the actress who later played the role in the movies, confuses the issue. But whatever her origins, such considerations point to the trouble: Maria is far too good to be true. It must be that Hemingway was aware of this, for he had Jordan himself state the objection: "Maybe it is like the dreams you have when someone you have seen in the cinema comes to your bed at night and is so kind and lovely." In real life, he thinks, "Such things don't happen." There exactly is the difficulty, and these devices —designed to anticipate and forestall us—are unavailing.

The hero's whole attitude toward women is curious. It is frequently either warlike or sentimental. He started out rejecting his mother in defense of his father, and since then the partners Hemingway drew for him are either vicious, destructive wives like Macomber's, or daydreams like Catherine, Maria, and Renata, the most recent version of the ideal. More than Catherine, though rather less than Renata, Maria is just too ethereal for the world she is in—is submissive and devoted beyond credibility and to the extinction of her own character. She does not like to drink (that's for Men); she exists for her lover alone and has no other interest or function in all life or the world but to serve him. Although she is for a while a very lovely vision, as we get to know her she becomes more and more a vision until ultimately she ceases to be a person at all.

This idyll, Jordan's love affair with Maria, is compounded of romanticism like that in *A Farewell to Arms*. For the couple, "it is possible to live as full a life in seventy hours as in seventy years," for instance. Related to this view of things is more of the melodrama to be found in *The Fifth Column*. At one point in the novel, referring to his job as saboteur, Jordan tells Maria darkly, "I cannot have a woman doing what I do." But he has one, and they are "as good as married," as they agree.

Connected with the romantic element in the book is a theme of superstition which, as always, exists side by side with realistic attitudes and a considerable amount of handy knowledge. Right at the start Jordan is able to get the confidence and admiration of his fellow guerrillas by showing that he knows a great deal about their horses, simply by glancing at them. He knows everything that must be done and exactly how to go about it—is indeed a little too knowing, sure, and capable for complete credibility. At the same time he is always seeing good and bad "signs." Often these are empirical, often they are not; there is no attempt to discriminate. In addition, although he wants to reject the notion, Jordan is bothered throughout the long story by something Pilar, the wise old gypsy, saw in his hand when he first met her. While they were discussing "luck" she asked to see his palm. Jordan offered it; she took one look and dropped it. He wants to know what it is that she saw: "I don't believe in it. You won't scare me." But Pilar won't tell.

To be sure, Robert Jordan doesn't believe in it, but just the same he is always wondering about it and asking her what it was. He fights against the idea that it has any meaning; when she asks if he believes a man can tell what is going to befall him he replies:

> "No. That is ignorance and superstitution."
> "Go on," Pilar said. "Let us hear the viewpoint of the professor." She spoke as though she were talking to a precocious child.

This is the situation of *A Farewell to Arms* again. Just as Catherine saw herself dead in the rain, and Lt. Henry deprecated the vision, which turned out to be a true one, so now Pilar (who had presumably seen a short and abruptly terminated "life line") foresees that the hero's life is soon to be terminated. He is bothered by this suspicion, though he will not admit it, and it turns out true again.

But Jordan is the hero become at last relatively strong at the broken places. He bears the scars of all his wounds, but over the long years of his history he has learned a good deal about how not to reopen them. The scars are still very evident in the novel. Jordan begins to worry and becomes nervous and then stops, because it interferes with his job. He is continually telling himself to "stop thinking," because he "would not think himself into any defeatism"—because thinking brings up old troubles, new blood from old hurts. Thought is a kind of dis-ease with the hero, and it must be cured lest it become an impediment to carrying out the actions which were implicit in Harry Morgan's dying words. "Turn off the thinking," Jordan tells himself. "You're a bridge-blower now." Remembering the old days of "Big Two-Hearted River" and "A Way You'll Never Be" the hero is very careful, because sometimes you think and "you can't stop and your brain gets to racing like a flywheel with the weight gone. You better just not think."

The hero remembers well enough the days when he nearly fell off the edge of his sanity, but after all it is a lot to ask the reader to remember back fifteen years to *In Our Time*—if he ever read it, and is able to make the connection. Partly for this reason, it seems likely, Hemingway goes back in *For Whom the Bell Tolls* to fill in some of that past once more. As we have seen, the war experiences of the hero have been, since Nick became a war casualty, the most obvious and immediate sources of his difficulties. But Jordan is the first hero who is too young to have been in that war: if Hemingway is to account for those ever-visible scars he has got to fill in again the strokes that made the original injuries, so that he can show them, and how they are being overcome.

A world war has specific dates; to have been in it Jordan would have to be in his forties when he appeared in Spain, and that is too old for the picture Hemingway wanted to give. The kind of thing that happened to Nick up in Michigan, however, cannot be precisely assigned to certain years. Thus in this novel Hemingway reached all the way back into Nick Adams' childhood and came up with a new "short story" which is as representative of the early Nick stories as any of *In Our Time*.

Jordan tells the incident to Maria and Pilar: aged

seven, he went with his mother on a trip to Ohio, where he was to be in a wedding ceremony. As he looks out a hotel window onto the strange town he is visiting he sees a Negro being hung to a lamppost to be burned alive. The Negro has been tied to the place where the lamp itself should be, and is being hauled up into the air by means of the mechanism which hoists the arc light when something breaks and the man falls to the ground. He is being pulled up again when Robert's mother sees what the boy is watching and hauls him from the window.

That is all there is to the story. It is, just like the early Nick stories, "pointless," unless one sees what the point is. Just as "Indian Camp" was not about Indians, nor "The Killers" about gangsters, but were about Nick, so this story is not about a Negro but about young Robert. Hemingway was going to rehearse this process only once, in *For Whom the Bell Tolls,* and so he had to make his meaning unmistakably clear, for if the point of this Negro-burning incident is missed there will not be much in the book to account for the discomfort the hero must overcome if he is to perform his task and blow his bridge. And so Hemingway finally lifted the curtain on the process he had been working for so many years and once and for all gave away the whole show: after hearing Jordan's little story, Maria, quicker to get the point than any reader, says, "You were too young at seven. You were too young for such things." And then just as Maria has analyzed the whole difficulty so Pilar gives a solution: "Don't speak of such things. It is unhealthy."

The hero finds this good advice. He must go over such events in order to master them, but he does not speak of them often. When he is talking with Pablo of his predecessor at this demolition assignment (the man was captured and committed suicide to avoid being tortured) Pablo wants to know the details of the story. Jordan lies that he does not know them. They are too like the things he will not think about. He attempts not to speak of such things; it is unhealthy.

However when—toward the end of the book—he begins to face the likelihood of his own destruction he begins to think, quite unavoidably, of the death of his father. This is what bothered the hero a good deal back when he was Nick in the story "Fathers and Sons." Then he did not like to think of that death, and could not yet write about it and get rid of it. By 1940 he could do it, and it is done here. He tells Pilar a little about it: his father committed suicide. Pilar, as a guerrilla and a peasant who can understand this phenomenon only within the limits of her own experience, asks, "To avoid being tortured?" Jordan answers with a metaphor: "Yes. To avoid being tortured," and changes the subject. His father shot himself with a pistol, Robert reminisces later. This bothers him intensely, of course: it is in violent contradiction of the code he has been learning; it is "not done." "I understand it," he tells himself, "but I do not approve it." And thus we now know yet another of the things that crippled the hero even after he was grown. (By now, indeed, we should know a little more. We should know, or very strongly suspect, that Dr. Hemingway must have committed suicide too, as he did.)

The function of alcohol in the life of the hero is never more clear than in this novel: that Negro, falling from the lamppost, that pistol shot which destroyed Jordan's father, that Indian with his head cut nearly off, that Bugs who nursed an ex-prizefighter—all these things, and many others, are "giants," and alcohol is the "giant-killer" for Robert Jordan. He has a flask, small but infinitely precious, which he keeps always with him; it contains absinthe. Pablo asks what this greenish, numbing liquor is, and Jordan answers, "A medicine. . . . It cures everything." Pablo tries the drink and finds it too bitter to swallow. He says, "It is better to be sick than have that medicine." When one remembers that Pablo himself is an alcoholic, and a miserable and very sick man, then the fact that Robert Jordan does not agree that it is better to be sick is somewhat impressive.

Thus there is no doubt of it: Jordan is the hero as before. But the complicated man of insomnia and nightmare, damaged by what he has seen and been through, has come to a climactic triumph over his disabilities. The end of *For Whom the Bell Tolls* does not find him like Jake sitting hopeless in Paris waiting for rain; nor like Frederic Henry, walking in it away from the only thing that had meaning for him. It ends with Jordan lying on the forest floor awaiting his death, to be sure. But it is a death dedicated to life that he awaits; this time the hero has won. He was won over his incapacitating nightmares; he has held off the giants, grasped the code, worked his way out of his long bitterness and blown the bridge, which was his job to do.

Probably no one supposed that Jordan's was the last death the hero would die, and in various ways Hemingway's next book announced itself as a novel about dying before it appeared in 1950. First there were the reports of the writer's serious illness in Italy, and the fears that caused him to lay aside a long novel he was reported to have been working on for years in favor of a short one on a topic that seemed of more immediate importance to him. Then there was the announcement of the title itself, *Across the River and Into the Trees*. The meaning of the phrase was clear, at least to those familiar with the story of the death of Stonewall Jackson, for near the wood-fringed Rappahannock the wounded general is said to have become delirious, and then to have struggled from a coma to speak his last words, which are a highly expressive and rather Jungian metaphor for dying.

Then when the book appeared there was the opening paragraph, which seemed to presage the ending with suggestions of Dante's *Inferno* and a mood of Stygian strangeness, as a man makes a difficult crossing of a canal in Italy with the help of a surly and Charon-like poler. And the suspicion that this overtone was quite intentional is hardly weakened when later in the novel a girl says to the man, "You sound like Dante," and he replies, "I am Mister Dante . . . for the moment." ("And for a while he was and he drew all the circles.") Indeed the first chapter of the book perfectly introduces the theme, as the duck shooter dispenses substitute deaths in a highly ritualized preparation for his own which, like those of the birds, must be perfectly accomplished, and ultimately is.

The man is Richard Cantwell, a badly marked-up colonel in postwar Italy. He goes briefly to Venice for the duck shoot and to see Renata, a "nearly nineteen" year old countess who loves him, and with whom he is in love. As he returns to duty after the visit his heart, the most defective part of his war-ravaged body, finally gives out. After reciting his version of the words of General Jackson, his source, to T/5 Jackson, his driver, Cantwell dies, as all had known he soon must do.

In very many ways, this is the mixture as before. As Robert Jordan is about as far as the hero ever gets from being Hemingway himself, so Richard Cantwell is about as close to him. The author protested vigorously against people who suspected this identification, and if one went too far with it his complaint was legitimate. Hemingway was not a professional at arms, but a learned amateur (though this colonel is an officer of an oddly literary sort). The author did not die in Italy, and Cantwell did not display all sides of his character. But not in a long time, and never at such length, had Hemingway presented himself, "strictly controlled and unthinking," in so thin a disguise. When the novel was published, ex-General Cantwell, who has "been beat up so much he's slug-nutty," had Hemingway's age to the year. He had grown into his middle period from the hero we once knew particularly as Lt. Henry, for it was Frederic Henry, "a lieutenant then, and in a foreign army," who fought and was wounded—like Cantwell and Hemingway—at Fossalta. The eccentric, battered soldier with high blood pressure, who chases the mannitol-hexanitrate tablets with alcohol and stays, in Venice, at the Gritti, was very nearly Hemingway.

Here too is the heroine as before, staying young as the hero ages, but as lovely, compliant, devoted and recognizable as ever. "I would not want you to be in any way other than you are," the colonel said. And since he created her himself, it is not surprising that she is indeed not otherwise than he wished.* Here also is the traditional writing-off of the heroine's foil, the ex-wife: she was conceited, ambitious and sterile. ("But that was in another country, and besides the wench is dead," said the colonel.)

Then there is the code, which is represented by the "Order of Brusadelli," a formal organization of five men who have been through the fire that necessitates a code,

* The critic long ago was told, however (by a novelist and friend of Hemingway's), something about an original for Renata; since the facts had not appeared in print they did not appear here. But in the fall of 1965 the lady, who was Renata's age at the time of the writing of the book, identified herself—as Adriana Biagini, now thirty-five, and married to a German in Milan. She said the author had asked that his novel not be published in Italy until after his death (it did not appear there until 1965), and said also that in 1950 she had gone to live with the Hemingways in Cuba. (He called her "daughter," which is how the colonel addressed his teenage mistress, the countess.) There does not seem to be any particular reason for doubting her; the essentially autobiographical nature of Hemingway's fiction is once again confirmed.

and have adopted one. There are the superstition and the know-how, all the usual equipment, and the characteristic mixture of love and death that Hemingway is known by. The situation in the novel ("a girl nineteen years old in love with a man over fifty years old that you knew was going to die") is perilous, to be sure. But that fact does not fully explain why, with the methods and materials which have been in other Hemingway novels so satisfying, this is one of his weakest books. The failure is the sum of many errors—the tone of emotion recollected in rage, the savage and quite irrelevant attacks on another American novelist, the wholly embarrassing conversations with a portrait of Renata, and with the girl herself, for instances.

More basic difficulties are the result of two delusions under which the book was written, and by which it is conditioned. One of these was more or less conscious, and the other not so. The unintentional delusion under which Hemingway labored throughout the novel is that he was being interviewed. T/5 Jackson, Renata and others act as straight men, setting up implausible questions so that Cantwell can pontificate. When obliging reporters were not about, Hemingway interviewed himself. Thus we get estimates of prominent writers, generals, admirals, and presidential candidates—and of Red Smith, a sports columnist who writes a little like Hemingway. (The colonel likes *him*.) Also the Russian situation, the Tito situation, and "inside" bits about various battles of the Second World War. Most of this is not very interesting to read: "Nobody would give you a penny for your thoughts, he thought. Not this morning."

The other delusion was more or less conscious, for in the book Hemingway realized, in fiction, a wish—quite patently envisaged a dream of how he himself would like to die. He supplied for his hero an ideal girl, and ideal meals with perfect wines in his favorite city, and—the crucial piece of preparation—"the best run duck shoot I have ever shot at." Then when it is over Cantwell gets the signal from his heart, gets to speak his appropriate last words and to write his will, and expires. The whole book is written in the tone of an answer to a question sometimes asked by the very hungry or bored: "What would you order if you were in the best restaurant in the world, and could have anything you wanted on the menu, all free?" Little things go wrong with Cantwell's leave to make the dream seem possible, but save for the necessary exception that he must after all die, everything is just as perfect as it can be and still seem real to him. This method produced a novel which for its author, he indicated, was almost intolerably poignant, but which readers sympathetic to Hemingway found painful for other reasons.

There are other reasons for the failure of the book, too. Since there never was less distance between Hemingway and his hero, the writer was almost completely uncritical of him. The discipline which once kept Hemingway from the self-indulgence of chronicling his every opinion, taste and whim broke down utterly. Cantwell is much less upset than he was as Nick in "A Way You'll Never Be," but his driver's petulant claim—"the old son of a bitch really *is* crazy"—though false, makes more sense than it ought to. Correspondingly, the heroine was never less real, being more than ever the girl who exists so for her lover that she ceases to exist for herself. Anyone who considers the hero's very real preoccupation with death, and the heroine's very unreal personality—not to mention the demolished fellow novelist and the purged ex-wife—can find with unhappy ease more meanings than one in this author's version of the usual introductory Note: "There are no living people . . . presented in this book."

As the characters deteriorate in *Across the River,* the

code itself becomes for the most part a joke. "El Ordine de Brusadelli" was named after a man who had "accused his young wife . . . of having deprived him of his judgment through her extraordinary sexual demands." Other protective gestures, once meaningful and even moving, now become empty mannerisms which are either comic or pathetic, depending on one's sympathies. Much that is important to the author has become unimportant or even ludicrous to the reader. Cantwell "reaching accurately and well for the champagne bucket," Renata who "chewed well and solidly on her steak," and Cantwell selecting always the table in the far corner with his back to the wall and his flanks covered—these make up a parody of the grace of execution and the need for defense which once made Hemingway distinctive. The writer was imitating himself, and the result is a more telling travesty than anyone else composed. Aside from the kind of medical information forced on the hero by his health in order that he can successfully fake his way through a physical examination, the know-how has become show-off, and is chiefly taken up with embarrassing displays of gastronomical wisdom. Some of the background in the novel is excellent. The Venice winds, waters and lights are marvelously captured. But as the marks on the colonel's shoulders which show where the general's stars had been are faint, so too the marks of Hemingway's earlier stature as a novelist.

However, this was a writer who had been broken and then promoted before. Immediately after *The Torrents of Spring* came *The Sun Also Rises;* after *To Have and Have Not, For Whom the Bell Tolls.* More pertinent is the recollection that the defects of *Green Hills of Africa* were overcome in "Macomber" and "Kilimanjaro"—chiefly with a more critical attitude toward more objectively seen material. The hope that this could be done again, and that the bitterness which impregnated *Across the River* could be purged, was to be fulfilled in *The Old Man and the Sea.*

However, while the earlier book of Hemingway's is among his weakest, it is also very nearly his most revealing, for it offers a gesture which in a flash brilliantly epitomizes him, once and for all. This gesture occurs in a scene in which Cantwell journeys to the place by the river Piave where he (and Hemingway, and Adams and Henry) "had been hit, out on the river bank." "This country meant very much to him, more than he could, or would ever tell anyone," Hemingway says. Actually, however, he had found a most remarkable way to express what that region meant, and here Cantwell takes instruments, and surveys in the exact spot on the ground where he had been struck. Then in an act of piercing and transcendent identification:

> the Colonel, no one being in sight, squatted low, and looking across the river . . . relieved himself in the exact place where he had determined, by triangulation, that he had been badly wounded thirty years before.

At this point as never elsewhere, Hemingway confronted and acknowledged the climax of his life, after a pilgrimage which binds this book to his first one with an iron band. In his effort to come the full circle before he is done, the hero does not end his journey at the place where first he lived, but at the place where he first died. Then in the most personal and fundamental way possible to man he performs this primitive ceremonial, which is revelation as nothing else could ever be of his mingled disgust and reverence for that event of his life by which the whole may be known, and by which it was unalterably determined. As Poe was drawn helplessly to the site of his pain, the tomb of his decaying beloved, and as Hawthorne was long unable to escape Salem, the scene of the inherited and acquired sins he held in horror, so Hemingway must someday have made this trip to Fossalta, and found this place by the bank of the river. Now it is done, and the hero can die. No doubt he would die again, before Hemingway was finally finished with him. But never again could he perform so dazzling and apocalyptic an act. For here Hemingway tightly unified and glaringly spotlighted the core of all he had done; and Cantwell in his eloquent rite squats low over the place of his first death, while his eyes look out at the last one, across the river and into the trees.*

It was difficult to know what sort of thing, in a writer's career, could follow such a climax. The best guess that could be made was simply that since it would be impossible to go farther in the direction the writer had been taking, the direction would have to be different. So vague a prediction as that stood an excellent chance of proving true. And true it proved, for Hemingway's next book was *The Old Man and the Sea,* the story of Santiago, an old Cuban who reads happily of baseball, and dreams of lions he saw on dazzling African beaches in his youth. But Santiago is also a fisherman, and he has been eighty-four days without a fish. Manolin, the boy who used to fish with him, has been sent by his parents to a luckier boat, and on the morning of the eighty-fifth day the old man

* *Across the River* appeared exactly one hundred years after publication of *The Scarlet Letter* (1850), in which Hawthorne had written: "There is a fatality, a feeling so irresistible and inevitable that it has the force of doom, which almost invariably compels human beings to linger around and haunt, ghostlike, the spot where some great and marked event has given the color to their lifetime; and still the more irresistibly, the darker the tinge that saddens it."
From Hawthorne himself, and Poe, from Hester Prynne and Ahab right down to Salinger's "Zooey," who is unwilling to leave New York ("I've been *run over* here—twice, and on the same damn *street*")—no one has demonstrated the notion with the force and clarity of Hemingway's hero. Hawthorne's is the classic American statement of the principle and, marking its centennial, Hemingway is its apotheosis.

ventures far out to sea alone. On the deepest of his baits, trolled at various precise levels, he hooks his fortune, a giant marlin. His line is heavy and strong, and since he cannot budge the fish an inch he holds the line against his back until it is so taut that beads of water jump from it. Then it begins to make a "slow hissing sound in the water," and the boat begins to "move slowly off toward the North-West."

For the rest of that day, then, and that night, and all the next day and that night, the fish—the greatest Santiago has ever even heard of—tows the skiff. The old man lives on plain water and raw fish, he goes almost without sleep, his hands are cut open by his line. But he has a vast, quiet courage and great, unself-conscious skill; he knows the "tricks," his modest term for his craft, and he holds on. He thinks of many things—of Joe DiMaggio ("Do you believe the great DiMaggio would stay with a fish as long as I will stay with this one?") and also of the worthiness of his adversary, and if perhaps to kill him is a "sin" ("I have no understanding of it and I am not sure that I believe in it"). But much of the time he is too busy to think, as when the line finally rises, slowly and steadily, and there is a bulge in the sea ahead of him, and the fish, eighteen feet long, comes out "unendingly," bright in the sunlight, the water pouring from its sides. Much later he succeeds in bringing the great thing alongside, in harpooning it, and in lashing it to the skiff. By this time his hands are cut badly, he is nearly blind from exhaustion, and he is too tired to think of anything.

It is not long, then, before the sharks come to take his prize away from him. He kills the first one, which plows off like a speedboat, three-quarters out of the water, jaws clicking and tail thrashing the water white. But he loses his harpoon in it, and when more sharks arrive his knife-blade snaps in the brain of one of them, and now he can only club them. In the end he has nothing but the splintered butt of his tiller to fight with, and his marlin, "a fish to keep a man all winter," is nothing but a skeleton. He tows that home, makes his way to bed, and falls asleep, to fish again another day.

This book has many roots in the rest of Hemingway's work. Much of it goes back to an essay, "On the Blue Water (A Gulf Stream Letter)," which the author published in *Esquire,* in April of 1936. In this piece he tried to explain what there is about deep-sea fishing in the Stream that makes it exciting—the mysteries of that largely unexplored place, the indescribable strangeness, wildness, speed, power and beauty of the enormous marlin which inhabit it, and the struggle while their strength is bound to a man's, his thick line "taut as a banjo string and little drops coming from it." He also included a paragraph of more specific interest:

> Another time an old man fishing alone in a skiff out of Cabañas hooked a great marlin that, on the heavy sashcord handline, pulled the skiff far out to sea. Two days later the old man was picked up by fishermen sixty miles to the eastward, the head and forward part of the marlin lashed alongside. What was left of this fish, less than half, weighed eight hundred pounds. The old man had stayed with him a day, a night, a day and another night while the fish swam deep and pulled the boat. When he had come up the old man had pulled the boat up on him and harpooned him. Lashed alongside the sharks had hit him and the old man had fought them out alone in the Gulf Stream in a skiff, clubbing them, stabbing at them, lunging at them with an oar until he was exhausted and the sharks had eaten all that they could hold. He was crying in the boat when the fishermen picked him up, half crazy from his loss, and the sharks were still circling the boat.

Here, of course, is the germ of the novel.* And the old man himself, Santiago, is also an outgrowth of past performances. Just as Col. Cantwell presented the Hemingway hero aged for the first time beyond his young manhood, so Santiago is the first of the code heroes to have grown old. Particularly he is related to men like Jack, the prizefighter, and Manuel Garcia, "The Undefeated" bullfighter, who lose in one way but win in

* On October 21, 1965, one Anselmo Hernandez, a gnarled, weathered old man allegedly 92 years old, made it to Key West, Florida, in the midst of thousands of anonymous refugees from the Castro regime. He became conspicuous, however, by announcing that he had "inspired" Hemingway's Nobel Prize-winning *The Old Man and the Sea:* "I knew Hemingway for thirty years. . . . He said he would write a novel about me and he did." This claim, widely printed in the press with a current photograph of the old fisherman, was immediately dismissed by Mrs. Hemingway, who commented that a dozen Cuban fishermen made the same boast—further that although her husband had known Hernandez well the book was not based on any one person. Her statement was accepted as authoritative. But on seeing the photograph of Anselmo Hernandez, and seeming to recall both the image and the name in connection with the novel, the present writer dug up another picture (published by *Vogue* in June of 1953), and disputed Mrs. Hemingway on two counts. This earlier photograph was taken by Leland Heyward, producer of the film based on the book, and it shows a threesome seated in a bar "on location,"—purportedly the author of the story, Ernest Hemingway, together with the actor who was to play the old man, Spencer Tracy, and with the old man himself, who was identified only as "Anselmo." The Anselmo Hernandez whose picture was in the newspapers of October 22, 1965, is older and thinner and unmistakably the Anselmo of the 1953 photograph. Surely the character of Hemingway's old man is no transcript of any Anselmo's; it is chiefly the character of the author-fisherman himself. But if the experience of the old man in the book is not based on exactly what happened to an actual, single fisherman then Hemingway in 1936 gratuitously invented what he pretended in *Esquire* to report. And if Hernandez is not the same old man then Hemingway was party to a second deception when he sat for Heyward's photograph. Neither deceit is probable: Hemingway had a fondness for facts as well as fictions.

another. Like Manuel, Santiago is a fighter whose best days are behind him, who is too old for what his profession demands of him and, worse, is wholly down on his luck. But he still dares, and sticks to the rules, and will not quit when he is licked. He is undefeated, he endures, and his loss therefore, in the manner of it, is itself a victory.

"A man can be destroyed but not defeated," is how Hemingway put it this time. And so the theme—"What a man can do and what a man endures" ("plenty," as Santiago admits of his suffering)—is also familiar. So are other things—Hemingway's concern with fishing as a deeply meaningful occupation, for instance, and his awareness of death, expertly delivered and received, as the source of much of life's intensity. In a way we have even known the boy before, for in providing that sentimental adulation which in his need for love and pity the other hero once required, Manolin has taken over some of the functions hitherto performed by the heroine.

There is little that is new, either, in the technique. The action is swift, tight, exact; the construction is perfect, and the story is exciting. There is the same old zest for the right details. And there is the extraordinary vividness of the background—the sea, which is very personal to Santiago, whose knowledge of it, and feeling for it, bring it brilliantly and lovingly close. Again there is the foreign speech translated—realistic, fresh and poetic all at once. In short, *The Old Man and the Sea,* in manner and meaning, is unmistakable Hemingway. But where characteristic methods and attitudes have on rare occasion failed him in the past, or have been only partly successful, this short novel is beyond any question a triumph.

This is the first time, in all of Hemingway's work, that the code hero and the Hemingway hero have not been wholly distinct. Wilson the guide, Cayetano the gambler, Morgan the smuggler—all embodied ideals of behavior the Hemingway hero could not sustain. They balanced his deficiencies; they corrected his stance. Of course Santiago is not Hemingway, and is not the Hemingway hero; he is the code hero, based on the experience of an unfictional Cuban fisherman. But now the relation of the author and the code hero is very close. Though Hemingway was thought with the phrase to be acknowledging his eccentricity, whereas Santiago makes it clear that he means he is formidable, both figures were given to remarking "I am a strange old man." And both men were preoccupied with their "luck"—a kind of magic which people have in them, or do not. Indeed it is the only flaw in the book, beyond our involuntary recollections of the heroine, that there are times when the old fisherman sounds a little like Col. Cantwell: "Do not think about sin," Santiago tells himself with uncharacteristic sarcasm. "There are people who are paid to do it."

What this means, among other things, is that Hemingway was narrowing the gap that had always existed between him and his code heroes. Actually he narrowed it to the point where it is possible to show that on one level *The Old Man and the Sea* was wholly personal: as he seemed obscurely to acknowledge his demotion in *Across the River* by removing the stars from Cantwell's shoulders, so here Hemingway seemed, but more obviously, to promote himself back. Harry, dying in "The Snows of Kilimanjaro," was himself a writer, and the Hemingway hero, but not even that story contained a more transparent or confident discussion by the author of those constantly absorbing problems of his professional past, present and future. *The Old Man and the Sea* is, from one angle, an account of Hemingway's personal struggle, grim, resolute and eternal, to write his best. With his seriousness, his precision and his perfectionism, Hemingway saw his craft exactly as Santiago sees his. The fishing and the fishermen turn out to be metaphors so apt that they need almost no translation: Santiago is a master who sets his lines with more care than his colleagues, but he has no luck any more. It would be better to be lucky, he thinks, but he will be skillfully exact instead; then when the luck comes he will be ready for it. Once he was very strong. "The Champion" they called him, and he had beaten many rivals in fair fights. The boy agrees: "There are many good fishermen and some great ones. But there is only you." Still there are many who do not know this, and the whole reputation is gravely imperilled by a streak of bad luck. And so the ex-champion musters his confidence: "I may not be as strong as I think. . . . But I know many tricks and I have resolution."

Santiago needs these things, for he is still out for the really big fish. He has assured the boy he is a strange old man; "Now is when I must prove it." (The times that he has proved it before "meant nothing. Now he was proving it again.") And he does prove it. The sharks may eat his fish, and spoil everything, as they always try to do. But even a young fisherman in the prime of his strength would have done well to land this marlin, and so at the end Santiago is secure in bed, dreaming happily of the lions. (As for these lions, they play like cats on beaches "so white they hurt your eyes"—as white, we might think, as the "unbelievably white" top of Kilimanjaro that Harry dreamed of, the magical goal of the artist, where the leopard froze. And so we could say here, as Hemingway said of Harry, that Santiago is happy in the end because he knows that "there was where he was going.")

But this time it is the public and not the private parable—the generalized meanings which underlie and impregnate the action—that matters most. On this level there is no allegory in the book and, strictly speaking, no symbols. The marlin Santiago catches, the sharks that eat it away and the lions he dreams of are not so much symbolic of other things as broadly suggestive of them. To pin them down by naming equivalents they do not have would be to limit and decrease, vulgarly and gratuitously, the power of what Hemingway had written. On the public level the lions, for instance, are only so vague as the "poetry" in Santiago, and perhaps the sign of his nostalgia for his youth. The marlin is not even anything so general as "nature"—which would justify the most obvious trap, a man-vs.-nature allegory—for as brothers in this world and life, inextricably joined by the necessity of killing and being killed, Santiago and the fish are tightly bound up in the same thing. If we ask ourselves what *The Old Man and the Sea* is "about" on a public and figurative level, we can only answer "life," which is the finest and most ambitious thing for a parable to be about. Hemingway has written about life: a struggle against the impossible odds of unconquerable natural forces in which—given such a fact as that of death—a man can only lose, but which he can dominate in such a way that his loss has dignity, itself the victory.

The stories of all the best parables are sufficient to themselves, and many will prefer to leave the meanings of this one unverbalized. Such a reading, however, would comprehend less than Hemingway clearly intended. By stripping his book—as only this novelist can—of all but the essentials, and Santiago himself of all but the last things he needs for his survival (the old man owns almost nothing, and hardly even eats), and by the simplicity of the characterization and the style, Hemingway has gently but powerfully urged a metaphor which stands for what life can be. And it is an epic metaphor, a contest where even the problem of moral right and wrong seems paltry if not irrelevant—as in ancient epics, exactly—before the great thing that is this struggle.

If all this sounds a little "classical," it is because this tale of courage, endurance, pride, humility and death is remarkably so. It is classical not only technically, in its narrow confines, its reduction to fundamentals, the purity of its design, and even in the fatal flaw of pride (for Santiago exceeded his limits and went out too far). It is also classical in spirit, in its mature acceptance, and even praise, of things as they are. It is much in the spirit of the Greek tragedies in which men fight against great odds and win moral victories, losing only such tangible rewards—however desirable the prizes and heartbreaking the losses—as will dissipate anyway. It is especially like Greek tragedy in that as the hero fails and falls, one gets an unforgettable glimpse of what stature a man may have.

The story has affiliations, too, with Christian lore. These are not so much this time in its spirit, despite the virtues of pity, humility and charity with which it is invested. They are in its several allusions to Christian symbolism, particularly of the crucifixion. This orientation was not entirely new to Hemingway. Nearly forty years ago he published a little play, "Today Is Friday," in which a Roman soldier who was present at Calvary kept saying of Jesus: "He was pretty good in there today." In *Across the River and Into the Trees* the Colonel, whose heart goes out to anyone who has been hit hard, "as every man will be if he stays," has a twice-wounded and misshapen hand, which he is very conscious of. Renata, running her fingers lightly over the scars, tells him she has strangely dreamed it is "the hand of Our Lord." Now it is Santiago's hands, and the noise that comes from him when he sees the sharks ("a noise such as a man might make, involuntarily, feeling the nail go through his hands and into the wood"), which first relate his ordeal to an ancient one. Then when at the end he carries his mast uphill to his cabin, and falls, exhausted, but finally makes it, and collapses on his cot, "face down . . . with his arms out straight and the palms of his hands up," the allusion is unmistakable.

All this does not indicate that Hemingway was embracing, or even necessarily approaching, the Christian faith. Such passages as the one on the possible nonexistence of sin explicitly disavow it, as does the running insistence on the story as a wholly natural parable, confined to the realms of this world and what we know by experience. Instead Hemingway is implying another metaphor, and seems to say here, as in *Across the River:* the world not only breaks, it crucifies, everyone, and afterwards many are scarred in the hands. But now he has gone further, to add that when it comes, and they nail you up, the important thing is to be pretty good in there like Santiago.

One of the virtues of this short novel is that its meanings emerge from the action with all the self-contained power of the marlin breaking the surface of the ocean. Hemingway did not drag up anything, and one of the means whereby he kept the parable from obtruding is the baseball—that force in Santiago's life which, beside the lions, is all the life he has beyond his calling. Baseball stars are the heroes of this simple man; their exploits are the incidents, and their pennant races the plots, of his mythology. Baseball works a charm on the pages of this book. The talk about it is vastly real, it gives a little play to the line when unrelieved tension would be dangerous, and the sober conversations about it, which Santiago conducts with himself and with the boy, are delicious in their own right:

> "The Yankees cannot lose."
> "But I fear the Indians of Cleveland."
> "Have faith in the Yankees my son. Think of the great DiMaggio."
> "I fear both the Tigers of Detroit and the Indians of Cleveland."
> "Be careful or you will fear even the Reds of Cincinnati and the White Sox of Chicago."

Nowhere in the book is there the slightest touch of condescension in the humor of this childlike preoccupation. Hemingway gave it without irony, without patronizing his characters, without unkindness. This is because he profoundly respected his characters, and wrote his book with a tenderness that was new to him and to his work. And that is an important perception, because it leads to the heart of the book's power.

"I love more than any son of the great bitch alive," said the Colonel in *Across the River,* and although he said it "not aloud" it sounded foolish anyway. But it sounds a little less silly now: *The Old Man and the Sea* is a powerful book, and a large part of its power is the power of love.

Santiago's respect for his foe, the marlin, which is love, actually, as for a brother, is surpassed by Hemingway's respect for both that fish and Santiago himself, and for the whole of life which this battle epitomizes, and the world that contains it. An extraordinary thing had happened, for somehow or other a reverence for life's struggle, which this contest dramatizes, and for mankind, for which Santiago stands as a possibility, had descended on Hemingway like the gift of grace on the religious. This veneration for humanity, for what can be done and endured, and this grasp of man's kinship with the other creatures of the world, and with the world itself, is itself a victory of substantial proportions. It is the knowledge that a simple man is capable of such decency, dignity, and even heroism, and that his struggle can be seen in heroic terms, that largely distinguishes this book. For the knowledge that a man can be great, and his life great, might be in itself an approach to greatness. To have had the skill, then, to convince others that this is a valid vision is Hemingway's achievement.

This is to say, among other less abstract things, that Hemingway had reached the point where he was able to affirm without forcing, or even apparent effort, certain things about brotherhood, man, and life which he had tried and crucially failed to affirm in *For Whom the Bell Tolls.* Indeed, since Santiago is a man alone and without the boy—for, after all, a man faces certain final things alone—and since the old man catches his fish, Hemingway had sharply qualified the pronouncement of *To Have and Have Not,* which was even more forced. *The Old Man and the Sea* is pregnant with implications about the contestants and the contest, but this time there is no need to say anything about them outright. It seems you never have to say it if you really mean it.

It is the heartening vision of this story, then, and the deep sense one has of a writer who is at long last completely at home in this life and world, which chiefly account for the power of the book. The rest of its force is the result of its remarkable surface virtues. And it may be that the action—so taut that beads of water seem to jump off the lines, all in a world miraculously alive and lasting—will seem one day the greatest thing after all. Hemingway's hope for his short novel, that "all the things that are in it do not show, but only are with you after you have read it," is mostly fulfilled; and, in the end, vicarious experience is the finest gift literature has to offer. It is the genius of Hemingway that our response is intense, rich, and deep. Without that, the vision and the meanings would count for nothing.

"It's as though I had gotten finally what I had been working for all my life," Hemingway also said, and there are many ways in which it would seem that he had. One of the more subtle ways lies in the fact of Santiago's survival: all the rest of the characters Hemingway projected himself deeply into have, if they struggled and attained the code, died in the process; at the end of this story Santiago is confident, happy, and ready for more. In addition, though *The Old Man and the Sea* is not necessarily Hemingway's greatest book, it is the one in which he said the finest single thing he ever had to say as well as he could ever hope to say it.

And so the question occurred to the faithless: then what was left for this one to do? To ask such a question was to reckon without the personal triumph Santiago represented and to forget what the old man said when the boy asked if he was strong enough then for a truly big fish: "I think so. And there are many tricks." Besides, this was indeed a strange old man.

4 | THE MAN
AND THE LEGEND

*Since he was a young boy he has cared
greatly for fishing and shooting. If he had
not spent so much time at them . . . he
might have written much more. On the
other hand he might have shot himself.*

HEMINGWAY

Henry Thoreau once concerned himself
briefly with the problem of whether or not
a boy should be taught to shoot. He decided
that "We cannot but pity the boy who has
never fired a gun; he is no more humane,
while his education has been sadly neglected." But he went on to limit his approval
sharply by saying that he gave it while
trusting that the youngsters who were bent
on the pursuit "would soon outgrow it."

It would be good if we could go on to
ask this man what we are to think of an
adult—and, what is more, an adult who
was very likely the finest writer of American
prose to come along since Thoreau himself
—who never did outgrow it. It is not easy
to know why a man must kill animals in

order to keep from killing himself, but Hemingway was never easy to understand. In his boyhood a runaway, in his early manhood a shattered personality who put some of the pieces together and became famous, in his thirties an *Esquire* sportsman who abruptly took off for a war against fascism, and later a man gathering a reputation for being quite an eccentric, Hemingway never seemed simple. But a lot of his behavior can be illuminated by a short account of his life.

The story started in an intensely middle-class suburb of Chicago called Oak Park, Illinois, where Ernest Miller Hemingway was born on July 21, 1899. He was the second child in a family of six children; there were four sisters and a younger brother. His father, Clarence Edmonds Hemingway, a large, bearded doctor of medicine, was famous for his eyesight and his devotion to hunting and fishing. His mother was Grace Hall Hemingway, a religious and musical woman, who sang at The First Congregational Church and named all her daughters after saints. The conflicting interests of the parents evidently came into the open over the question of what the first son was to be like. The big stucco house had a music room with a stage in it. The boy's mother gave him a cello, and for many years made him practice it. But before Ernest was three his father had given him a fishing rod, and by the time he was ten he had a shotgun.

As a short story called "The Doctor and the Doctor's Wife" was to record, the "masculine" interests won out over the "feminine" ones. Hemingway became fonder of the woods than the suburbs, never became a cellist or a chorister. But this, though an important victory, was not a simple one, for the doctor, in giving way to the workman in that story, was something less than completely admirable in the eyes of his son. And as the later "Fathers and Sons" confesses in the name of Nick again, Ernest was not entirely pleased with the parent who had died so suddenly. In *For Whom the Bell Tolls* Jordan seems to be summarizing Hemingway's own dissatisfaction when he recalls the doctor's suicide and says, "I'll never forget how sick it made me the first time I knew he was a . . . coward." Nevertheless, the early story must state the matter of the writer's ultimate judgment on his heredity pretty well. He still favored his father, and Jordan goes on to think: "if he wasn't a coward he would have stood up to that woman and not let her bully him. I wonder what I would have been like if he had married a different woman?"

The parts of the childhood which stuck were the summertimes up in Michigan. The Hemingways had a house on Walloon Lake, in a region which was populated chiefly by the Ojibway Indians. Here the boy, like Nick, did his real growing up, and learned to hunt, fish, drink, and know girls. Here too he went on professional errands with the doctor. Oak Park seems to have offered a lot less, though the boy as an adolescent participated in its life in a fairly customary way. At fourteen he wanted boxing lessons, and went in to a Chicago gymnasium to take them. He got his nose broken by a professional on the first day, as a result of his zeal; he completed the course, however.

At Oak Park High he was especially active, and already interested in writing. He was an editor of the school weekly, for which he wrote a news and gossip column. He wrote also for the quarterly and composed the class prophecy.* He played in the school orchestra for a while, belonged to the debating club and the rifle club, played right guard on the football team, made the swimming team and managed track. "None are to be found more

* Predating the Kansas City *Star* days, there is just a touch of the "later Hemingway" in some of the high-school writing, as in this conversation taken from the class prophecy: "A loud noise and commotion started outside, and I hastened to the door. 'Let me come in and see him. I know him. He'll be glad to see me. Let me in.' "

clever than Ernie," the yearbook for the class of 1917 says. But his friends also said that he was a lonely boy. And that he was discontented with his life at this time in this environment is pretty well proven by the fact that he tried to escape it, and ran away from home on two separate occasions.*

The United States went to war in the April that preceded his graduation, and the boy, who had firmly decided against college, saw his chance and tried to enlist. He was repeatedly rejected for a bad eye, however, and since the odd jobs he had performed as a runaway—day laborer, farm hand, dish washer, sparring partner—promised no future, he now left Oak Park for good and made his way to Kansas City. Here he lied about his age ** and landed a job as a reporter for the *Star*. But by spring of the next year he found he could get into the war after all as an ambulance driver for the Red Cross, and he went. He served on the Italian front in this capacity, and here he went through some of the bitterest fighting of the war. He was badly wounded in the leg at Fossalta di Piave, was hospitalized at Milan, and decorated by the Italians with their most coveted medal, the Medaglia d'Argento al Valore Militare, equivalent to the French Médaille Militaire, and with three Croci al Merito di Guerra.

After the war, Hemingway returned to this country to recuperate. He was having a good deal of trouble sleeping, and having been blown up at night he could not for a long time sleep in the dark at all. He was soon able to hold down a job, however, and in 1920 he got one editing the house organ of the Cooperative Society of America. He

* Leicester Hemingway in his book about his brother strenuously objects to this allegation, "freely reported by biographers": "Ernest always sent postcards"!

** This accounts for the fact that his birth date is still often erroneously given as 1898: he added a year to his age on this occasion and only took it back in middle age.

lived in an apartment on Chicago's North Side, and here
it was that he met Sherwood Anderson, and other writers
and painters of the "Chicago Group." Here too he fell
in love with Hadley Richardson, a girl from St. Louis he
had known, years back, in Michigan. He married her in
September, 1921, and after a honeymoon in the Michigan
woods went with her to Toronto. By fall he was a by-lined
reporter, and by winter a European correspondent for the
Star of that city. He reported the Greco-Turkish War for
the paper, and went to Paris with a note from Anderson
presenting him to Gertrude Stein. By now he was writing
stories and a novel on the side, but en route to Lausanne,
where Hemingway was covering a peace conference, a
suitcase containing practically all the manuscript he had
written was stolen from Hadley, who was bringing it to
her husband "as a surprise," so that he could work on it
in off-hours if he liked.

This was a good time for a new start. Reporting now
for the Hearst papers in Paris, and trying to write seriously
at the same time, was not working out. And there was
very little money. Then, too, Hadley was "enceinte," in the
phrase of the time; according to Miss Stein the young
writer was a little bitter about this. Finally the decision
was made: the couple would go back to America, have
the baby, work hard and save money, and then return
within a year, at which time Ernest would give up newspaper work and take his chances as a writer of fiction.
Unlike most plans of the type, this one was carried out.
Within the year they were back; the Misses Stein and
Toklas had acted as godmothers at the christening of a
son, John; and Hemingway had quit his job.

It was in these days that he took his stand and established his seriousness in a way which his friend Gertrude
found humorless, and perhaps a little silly. At first it was
hard to sell a story—editors refused to concede that they

were "stories"—but before long three or four got placed in German and French magazines. Then the *Atlantic Monthly* took "Fifty Grand," and soon the writer was deluged with offers, all of which he turned down. A Hearst editor made one which would have supported him in great comfort for many years but Hemingway, who feared he might write less well if he knew what he wrote was already sold, refused it. By this time Hadley had gone, and he was living in a single room with only a bed and a table as furnishing. He was allowing himself five sous a day for a lunch consisting of a few fried potatoes, and he was often hungry.

Hemingway has said that integrity in a writer is like virginity in a woman—once lost it is never recovered. He must also have had considerable hope for his ultimate success, and it was not long now in coming. Both *In Our Time* and *The Torrents of Spring* were miserable failures from the financial standpoint, but *The Sun Also Rises* had a more substantial sale. With it Hemingway, still well under thirty, found himself a famous man, with the literate young going about everywhere in what they took to be his manner—speaking his dialogue, adopting his attitudes, and drinking with new purpose and assurance. After this time he sold well no matter what. Throughout the Thirties and Forties he managed to live handsomely, and for the most part on what he made by writing. Later his income from Hollywood alone would have made him at least temporarily rich. Despite the fact that thousands of magazine readers issued ominous rumors about *Across the River* before it appeared as a book, and despite predominantly bad reviews, the novel took a firm place at the top of the best-seller lists immediately after it was published. Its author was soon to turn down as insufficient an offer of a quarter of a million dollars for the motion-picture rights.

From standpoints other than financial, Hemingway's

story was of mixed success and failure. By 1927 his marriage to Hadley was obviously wrecked, and they were divorced. Hemingway never took his divorces easily, as the misery smuggled away in a story called "Homage to Switzerland" testifies. But later that year he married another St. Louis girl, a wealthy fashion writer for the Paris office of *Vogue,* the late Pauline Pfeiffer. They returned to this country, and here *A Farewell to Arms* was written, and published in 1929. Another son, Patrick, was born that year, and in 1932 a third son, Gregory. By now Hemingway was "settled" in Florida, and embarked on a decade which in many ways was the least distinguished of his mid-career. From 1928 to 1938 he lived mostly at Key West, more in the public eye than ever before or since, and in a light that flattered less than a more subdued one might have done. These are the years of *Death in the Afternoon,* and *Green Hills of Africa,* and of the establishment of a reputation as a sportsman. He became a champion fisherman, with several exploits of strength and skill attaching to his name, including the capture of a 468 pound marlin which he landed without a harness. A species of rosefish (*Neomarinthe hemingwayi*) was named in his honor. He earned a small fame as a duck shot and slayer of big game, and as a boxer. He once went four rounds in an exhibition with the heavyweight champion of Great Britain. He had a handsome cruiser, the *Pilar,* built to his specifications as a fishing boat, and fished from it in various tournaments which he won. Much of this activity was reported by him in *Esquire,* to the accompaniment of some swashbuckling photographs.

However, it is possible to be unnecessarily severe—as some, including Hemingway, have been—about the Key West period of his life, and particularly about his connection with *Esquire.* For one thing, during this time that magazine was also offering its public in the barbers' chairs of America: Thomas Mann, Theodore Dreiser, Aldous Huxley, Ezra Pound, Clarence Darrow and Havelock Ellis, not to mention Anderson, Stein, Fitzgerald and Dos Passos, and these authors are not generally known for their frivolity. For another, a good deal of what he published there—aside from a couple of his best stories—was unpretentious and workmanlike journalism, and a little of it was very good indeed. He wrote several pieces which showed a clearer (though, at this time, isolationist) view of the impending world war than most people could boast, and two of his articles on writing contained some excellent material. One of these gave quite a bit of extremely practical advice on how to write, and the other was a very effective defense against the complaint (current in the Thirties) that his own work was not political.*

But in 1935 Hemingway's isolationism and apoliticality were not to last for long. The Spanish Civil War broke out the next year, and more than anything else it seems to have brought him wholly back to the world. Spain he had for a long time loved, and now he borrowed

---

* Read *War and Peace,* Hemingway said in *Esquire* (December, 1934), and see how you will have to skip the "Big Political Thought passages" that Tolstoi "undoubtedly thought were the best things in the book when he wrote it . . . and see how true and lasting and important the people and the action are. . . . That is the hardest thing of all to do." He went on to say that it is also a lonely thing: not a critic will "wish you luck or hope you will keep on writing unless you have political affiliations":

> You are just as well off without these reviews. Finally, in some place, some other time, when you can't work and feel like hell you will pick up the book and look in it and start to read and go on and in a little while say to your wife, "Why this stuff is bloody marvelous." . . . If the book is good . . . you can let the boys yip and the noise will have that pleasant sound coyotes make on a very cold night when they are out in the snow and you are in your own cabin that you have built or paid for with your work.

heavily and personally purchased some ambulances which he gave to the Loyalists. To pay off his debt he made several trips to Spain as correspondent for the North American Newspaper Alliance, and managed to aid the cause again by working on a movie called "The Spanish Earth," and by giving, in June of 1937 before the Second National Congress of American Writers, his only, however eloquent, public speech—on the problem of Spain and the necessity of defeating fascism. He published word of his conversion in *To Have and Have Not,* and a play on the war, *The Fifth Column,* and then in 1940 brought out his longest work on war, democracy and Spain, *For Whom the Bell Tolls.* A few days after this was published, Pauline Pfeiffer divorced him for desertion, and a few days after that he married still another St. Louis girl, the novelist Martha Gellhorn. She had once come to Key West as a reporter to interview him for *Collier's,* and they had met again in Spain. They were married in Cheyenne, and went off together to China as war correspondents; later they settled near Havana.

This marriage did not last either, however, and the last Mrs. Hemingway was born Mary Welsh, a girl from Minnesota whom Hemingway met in London in 1944 when she was working there for *Time.* He was in England as a correspondent accredited to a tactical command under Air Marshal Coningham, and had gone on several missions with the RAF. His World War II adventures, however, had started some time before this. In 1942 he had volunteered himself and his boat for various projects to the Navy, and for two years he cruised off the coast of Cuba with a scheme for the destruction of U-boats. The *Pilar* now had a crew, radio equipment, and some high-powered munitions. The idea was to get hailed by a submarine, and then when alongside to blow it up. The mission had been authorized and outfitted by Spruille Braden, then our ambassador to Cuba, and although Hemingway's somewhat suicidal plan never had a chance to prove or disprove itself, he did help to locate submarines which the Navy subsequently is presumed to have sunk, and he was recommended by Braden for a decoration.

When the invasion of southern France was undertaken in 1944, Hemingway managed to get attached to the Third Army as a *Collier's* correspondent. He didn't much like the role of nonparticipant, however, and did very little work at it. Moreover, he had small use for General Patton, and as a result stayed pretty much away from the army to which he had been accredited. After the breakthrough in Normandy at St.-Lô, he attached himself instead to an infantry division of his liking, the Fourth of the First Army. With this outfit Hemingway saw a great deal of action. His adventures were climaxed at Hürtgen Forest, where the regiment he was operating with sustained such appalling casualties that it lost, in eighteen days, over 80 per cent of its officers and men. Hemingway was in the slaughter from start to finish, and it was his disgust over a "stupid frontal attack," tactically unfeasible but ordered from above and carried out, which chiefly animated the bitterness of Richard Cantwell. He was with the Fourth Division also at Schnee Eifel and in Luxembourg.

There was plenty of color in his wartime adventures, which were less distinguished for good reporting than for other activities. At one point in a battle, according to the two-star commandant of the Fourth Division, Hemingway was sixty miles in front of anything else in the First Army. With the Germans on both flanks and before him, he was sending back intelligence, and asking for tank support in order to hold out. On another occasion, at Rambouillet to the southwest of Paris, he took charge of a group of French irregulars, set up headquarters in a hotel, and conducted full-scale operations. He guarded the roads, dispatched patrols to attract the fire which would reveal the German positions, and sent out civilians on bicycles who returned with similar information. When Leclerc arrived in the town to begin his official march on the French capital, Hemingway presented the general's chief of staff with the sketches and the other particulars he had assembled. In the opinion of an OSS colonel, it was this material that made the Frenchman's famous undertaking a success. Hemingway, however, made his own entrance and his own liberating gestures. At the head of his personal army, now motorized and over two hundred strong, he followed Leclerc until the attack bogged down momentarily at a spot where Hemingway had anticipated it would, and then took off on his own route. When Leclerc's army was at the south bank of the Seine, Hemingway's was in a skirmish at the Arc de Triomphe.

This episode brought down a formal investigation which lasted nearly eight weeks. Under "suspicion" of having violated that section of the Geneva Convention which prohibits the carrying of arms by correspondents, he was very nearly court-martialed. But the result of the investigation might have been anticipated: a good deal of testimony to the effect that others had seen no weapons on him eventually freed him, and brought a medal instead.

After the war, his activities were for a time less flamboyant. Living for the most part in Cuba when not traveling abroad, he said he was writing, off and on, a very long book which would be divisible into four separate books—and *The Old Man and the Sea* was presumably one of them.* Aside from the war, the thing that most interrupted the task was a serious infection which resulted from a trivial hunting accident abroad, late in the Forties.

* He described this "long work" variously and often, but it seems not to have existed on paper.

This was disturbingly like "The Snows of Kilimanjaro," and Hemingway, apparently fearing to die without having written the story of his dying in full, and without having acknowledged in full the significance of his experience at Fossalta, put aside all other matters to write and publish *Across the River*. Sixteen million units of penicillin saved him from having to cross it himself, and he was shortly back at work.

Hemingway long wrote wherever he was. Unable to sleep in the light in maturity, like Santiago, as he once could not in the dark, like Nick, he woke automatically with the sun, and worked till lunch time, when he counted up his meager wordage for the day, had a drink, read the papers, and went swimming, fishing, or hunting, depending on the country. His nose was as sensitive to smells as his eyes to light; and he could identify various animals at a distance by their characteristic odors. He drank but did not smoke. He had high blood pressure for which he took pills. He loved France, Italy, Africa and Spain, and Wyoming, Montana and Idaho; he despised New York City.

When he was not abroad Hemingway lived for a long time at Finca Vigia ("Lookout Farm")—longer than he was to live anywhere after he left Oak Park as a very young man. This large limestone villa, with a white tower he had built onto the house for a workroom, is on a hilltop at San Francisco de Paula, nine miles outside Havana, and fifteen minutes from the Gulf Stream, where he berthed his fishing boat, *Pilar*. There with him were an extraordinarily attractive and competent wife, Mary— as well as some dogs and cows, a legion of cats and pigeons, and one noisy undomesticated owl. The "farm" encompassed thirteen acres of banana trees, shrubs, and informal gardens; also a tennis court and a swimming pool. There was a staff of servants, including a handy-man

chauffeur and an engineer for *Pilar*—and also a small collection of choice paintings, among them a Braque, a
Miró, a Klee, and two works of Juan Gris. The walls of
a living room sixty feet in length were heavy with African
trophies; there was no cello, no stage, plenty of (recorded)
music but no music room.*

Such a biographical sketch performs some service,
however small, in recording as it does a colorful life and
giving background to a career which by many counts must
be rated a success. But what it demonstrates as well as
anything is how little we need a full-scale biography in
order to make at least some sense of a writer who was almost from the beginning at work on the psychological
core of his own. Of course Hemingway left out a lot, but
a good many of the main outlines and really significant
events of his life he recorded in the guise of fiction. It is
always risky to take any kind of fiction as a presentation
of fact, but it is less of a risk here than it would be
in most places. *Green Hills of Africa,* an autobiographical
book, seems no more factual and a lot less revealing than
Across the River and Into the Trees, for instance.

In one way or another Hemingway told almost
everything one would wish to know about him. His
parents were in essence Nick's and Jordan's, as was his
boyhood. His first war was Nick's, and Lt. Henry's and
Col. Cantwell's. The effects of that experience were given
in the image of Nick again, and of Jake Barnes. Two
works of nonfiction, plus Mr. Frazer in Montana, brought
the story into the bitter Thirties. Then there is the purge
of "Kilimanjaro," the conversion announced by Morgan,

---

* When Hemingway went, as he did frequently, to Havana
it was usually to drink in "Papa's Corner" of the inelegant
Floridita. It has, he once said, "a wonderful john." ("Makes
you want to shout: Water closets of the world unite; you have
nothing to lose but your chains.")

and the fights against fascism of Philip and Robert. Subtract the silver eagles, and Col. Cantwell presents a picture of the writer at fifty which matches the pictures we had of himself. Hemingway's dependence on the therapeutic value of what he wrote practically guaranteed that we know or will know at least most of the really significant things about himself that he knew. Added to these things are whatever insights we can make for ourselves. In a world where all understanding is relative and very partial, we frequently settle for much less.

At the same time, it would be naïve to accept in a crude and literal way Hemingway's picture of his hero as a picture of Hemingway as a man. Artists create and rearrange, they do not copy, and there are many differences between the telling of the story and the living of it. These differences have partly resulted from a rather natural tendency to romanticize the facts somewhat, particularly as regards the isolation of the hero, although the facts themselves would seem romantic enough. In addition to this, it is difficult to measure the vague and controversial distance that separated the man from the public picture we have of him.

The Heroic Hemingway and the Public Hemingway somehow conspired to produce a Mythical or Legendary Hemingway. This was an imaginary person who departed from the actual person at some point that is very difficult to determine. He was partly the product of a branch of myth known as hero worship, which tries to make a man familiar to us by elaborating actual details of his life and career while at the same time exaggerating unusual or colorful traits in order to make the man seem very special, and a little more than human. This figure was also the product of Hemingway himself, who seemed at times to be both creating and imitating his hero. When this romanticized and rather Byronic legend began to catch on, there were plenty of other people who were willing to contribute to it.

Thus we have the man who administered a very bad beating to a boxer who had fought a dirty fight, who spectacularly rescued John Dos Passos from an afternoon death on the horns of a bull, and so on. Very often, the stories turn out to have been true. Years ago, Hemingway did (with a water bottle) beat up a prizefighter who had nearly succeeded in killing a lighter boxer. When not drinking the writer was himself modest about his own exploits, of an extraliterary sort. But even when the stories about him were factual, they had an air of having been gone over by a press agent, as though everyone who came in contact with him must respond extravagantly. This Hemingway was the "gossip columnist's delight," whose activities were regularly reported in the newspapers and news magazines. Whenever he was in New York, the Broadway columns were given over in large part to accounts of what he said, did, looked like, and was drinking. His name was forever cropping up on such lists as enumerate the ten most "Fascinating Men I Ever Met," or "Distinguished Heads (or Stimulating Faces) I Ever Saw." One came across his picture—either bearded or bandaged—more often than one saw pictures of, say, Faulkner, Dos Passos and Steinbeck combined.

It is very hard to know the facts about a man whom journalists took over in this way, and his adoption by the photographers resulted in no great clarification. Pictures of Hemingway showed first a round-faced but stalwart youngster with bangs and a Dutch cut. Later they presented a thin, shy adolescent with a large frame not grown into, and then a very youthful soldier with sensitive, clean-shaven face. In the Twenties the face took on a dark, full mustache, and a pleasant yet grimacing grin. The legend was beginning to develop, now, and in the Thirties it was full-blown. There were pictures of a quite handsome figure squatting with gun beside the corpse or head of some large beast, or with rod beside some enormous, strung-up fish. In the Forties there were pictures of a man coarsely dressed in a not-quite-regulation field uniform, with pensive, tactical eyes, and a pair of binoculars hanging carelessly from a pair of massive shoulders. (It was at this point that Edmund Wilson noted an ominous resemblance to Clark Gable; and shortly thereafter Hollywood offered the novelist a part in a movie.) Later there were pictures of a tremendous beard, opening in broad smiles beneath steel-rimmed G.I. spectacles; these framed grinning eyes that looked up from a typewriter or a bomber. Well into the Fifties the photographs seemed to offer the head of some fuzzy, great-jowled lion, much given to riding in boats and swimming, and still rather handsome when occasionally shaved and down to fighting weight. Far from presenting the literal record of a life which might counteract the legend, until the last years the photogenic Hemingway vastly confused the record by glamorizing it further.

Once in a while the confusion broke noisily into the open. Several years ago, for instance, the author was sitting quietly in a night club when a broker named Chapman came up to him, sneered, "So you're Hemingway . . . tough guy, huh?" and pushed him in the face. Mr. Chapman was guilty of the simplified notion that the myth was all false and suffered severely for it. Max Eastman made the notorious charge that the chest hair was faked, too. After Gertrude Stein published to the world the opinion that the man was yellow people quite regularly took a swing at him. They all lived to regret it, as far as is known, but at least one of them had to repair for several days to a hospital, for like all legends this one had taken off from facts and was nourished by them. Hemingway was an expert shot and fisherman and in earlier years was a fine boxer and skier. He was an amateur at arms who has the respect of many professional soldiers. And yet on the other hand it is hard to believe literally, as we are asked to, all that we read—such as that *For Whom The Bell Tolls* was used by both the American and the Russian armies in World War II as a textbook of guerrilla fighting.

The factual record merges murkily with legend, and Hemingway's exploits in World War II instance nicely the difficulty of knowing what proportion of each went together to make up the blend. The plan for sinking submarines and very likely himself, for example, is the sort of spectacular stuff that legends are made on. Yet Spruille Braden went on record with the statement that in his opinion Hemingway would have been victorious in an actual encounter. The pictures of Hemingway ranging ahead of his division as it swept out of Normandy, and of him pinned down sixty miles in front of anything else in the First Army, are materials for the building of heroes. But it all appears to have been true, and the commanding general of the division told other correspondents: "I always keep a pin in the map for old Ernie Hemingway."

The French irregulars who put themselves under Hemingway's wing in this war had a hard time comprehending the fact that the reporter was not a general. It is easy to understand their confusion, for it was widespread, and like a general the correspondent had a lieutenant as an "aide" and "personal-relations officer," and was assigned a cook, a driver, a photographer and a special liquor ration. The outfit must have been in actuality colorful enough to give support to any legends that might spring from it. According to Robert Capa, who traveled for a time with this task force, Hemingway's unit was equipped with "every imaginable" German and American weapon. Hemingway himself was forever getting shot at, and so endeared himself to the command that its members copied even his ways of walking and talking, and issued short sentences in their own tongues. They carried more munitions and alcohol than a battalion might normally control. The pinnacle of their success was reached with the capture of Paris, when under Hemingway's personal direction the Ritz was exclusively liberated. Capa arrived a little late, and was greeted at the entrance to this excellent billet by a posted guard who told him, "Papa took good hotel. Plenty stuff in cellar. You go up quick."

Legends not only grow with ease from such adventures, but are already involved in them. One morning in the Hürtgen Forest a correspondent rode before daybreak with Hemingway to the command post. As he later recalled it: "Everybody knew his jeep. Out of the dark woods you could hear hundreds of voices saying, one after another, 'Good morning, Mr. Hemingway.' It was like a royal progress." This greeting manifested an unaccustomed degree of formality, however, for he was usually known as "Papa." Ignoring his own styling of "Ernie Hemorrhoid, the poor man's Pyle," he was said to be Papa to all the soldiers, and to most of his acquaintances afterward. According to the testimony of Malcolm Cowley, if you ordered a Daiquiri in Havana the waiter would brighten up and say "Como Papá?" If you said yes, then came a double Daiquiri, without sugar. The last accounts of him in Cuba told of a paternal grizzly bear who picked up all the checks and gave counsel on love, life and literature to all the young who wished it.

It must all have been at least stretched or simplified a little. And even what must have been true does not necessarily need to seem plausible. An artist named Groth suggested this very nicely when during the war he encountered Hemingway at the front, and deserted his sketchbook momentarily to relate in words what he saw and heard. "Who is Ernest Hemingway?" one American soldier asked. "A big shot," another replied in respectful tones and awed. "I don't know exactly what he does, but he's really a big shot." Groth at the time was staying with this very important person in a farmhouse designated at headquarters as "Task Force Hemingway." The house was right at the front, and the Germans frequently sent patrols into its yard. All of Groth's first night the novelist himself stood guard. After Hemingway had given elaborate orders for a cross-fire defense against a very possible attack, and had issued a startled visitor some hand grenades, Groth went up to bed. He had a little trouble going to sleep: there was "the Hemingway I had read so much about downstairs on guard with a tommy-gun and with grenades hanging from his belt." It was Groth's ingenuous yet excellent judgment that "All this was exciting and a little unbelievable."

There is something about Hemingway that excited strange loyalties, and even stranger antipathies. These in turn inspired some extravagant estimates of the man, particularly as a writer. Some people were stimulated by him on the one hand to an enthusiasm which passed all the bounds of sense. Novelists have been especially afflicted in this way. Arthur Koestler's claim that Hemingway is "the greatest living writer" might be questioned, for instance, by many who realize that Mann, Eliot, Shaw, Faulkner and Gide were all alive when the pronouncement was uttered. But John O'Hara made Koestler seem timid, and broke the record for all time by asserting that after due cognizance of the millions of writers who have lived since 1616, it was his belief that Hemingway was "the outstanding author since the death of Shakespeare." ("What makes Shakespeare better?" someone wanted to know.)

Such a reputation stood in unquestionable need of deflation. In the same piece where Mr. O'Hara went thus on record he also railed bitterly at a magazine which had published an "attack" on Hemingway which may have been calculated to fill that need somewhat. Chiefly, however, it provided more confusion.

"I can tell you," Hemingway's friend and editor, the late Maxwell Perkins, once wrote another acquaintance, "that Profiles in the *New Yorker* are something to dread." Perkins went so far as to consult a lawyer to see if there was not some way to prevent the drawing of his own by Malcolm Cowley, though it turned out to be flattering. Hemingway's was not so flattering, and it produced a certain amount of bafflement when it appeared, for it made its subject out to be as colorful in an eccentric way as he had ever been made to seem in a Byronic one. "I'm a strange old man," said Hemingway to his interviewer, while proceeding to document one interpretation of his contention with considerable force.

First there was the appearance, featuring above all a pair of steel-rimmed spectacles with a small wad of dirty paper under the nosepiece. (It "cuts him up brutally," Mrs. Hemingway explained. "When he really wants to get cleaned up he changes the paper.") Then there was the speech—for a while the kind of Indian talk that is achieved by dropping the articles from sentences, and restricting all verbs to the present plural, and then a dialect which consisted almost wholly of sports metaphors, selected from baseball and boxing and often inscrutable. There was the drinking, too. Hemingway turned down an offer of four thousand dollars to pose as Man of Distinction ("I wouldn't drink the stuff for four thousand dollars"), but the consumption of other wines and liquors was steady and heavy. Then there were the substitute claims for distinction of another kind, as the author emphatically backed Koestler and O'Hara in his own vernacular. Throughout the piece he moved his fiercely competitive, lumbering way, filling the air with right and left jabs (which were countered only by a dead-panned but gloating reporter), and when outdoors pointed an arm at pigeons in the air, "shooting" them, while complaining that the birds of New York do not fly properly.

There was not anything really ruinous about this picture, while there was a good deal about it that was ingratiating. Also, there was little in it which Hemingway himself did not effectively corroborate in subsequent, written interviews or in *Across the River and Into the Trees*. The curious speech was not an unprecedented mode of expression for him, according to recent reports; Cantwell started on the Valpolicella immediately on waking, and before daylight, simply as a starter; and Hemingway never made much of an effort to conform to New York standards of grooming. The piece was cold and cruel, and it was written in the tone of bland superiority which frequently characterizes the periodical in which it appeared. Chiefly what the sympathetic reader missed was any sense that this was a first-rate writer, or awareness that the personal reflections of this fact are more important than the eccentricities which help to make a "character." Too, the interviewer had less of the writer's company than she pretended. But despite all these things, the sketch did not distort its subject past recognition.

This was, though, a "strange old man" indeed, and if a picture of him provided us by the *New Yorker* was designed to cut him down to size somewhat then it was by no means a first attempt in this direction. Balancing the extravagant estimates, there have been for a long time the attacks of certain literary critics who sought to puncture what they took to be a vastly swollen reputation. Hemingway claimed not to read the critics, but his wariness suggested that he read them rather closely. If he did, he knew that some of them called him everything from fake to fascist fool, roundly insulted him on occasion and ridiculed him frequently.

More interesting than the attacks, however, were Hemingway's retaliations. He always had an advantage over his adversaries in that whereas he never conceded them a thing, they rather nervously rushed to concede him a great deal. Practically no critical enemy of Hemingway's but has guarded himself round, before launching his attack, with such admissions of talent as would satisfy most writers no matter what followed. Many of the critics Hemingway despised have agreed, for example, with his own judgment of himself, that he was the American champion. Most of those who disagreed would have given the crown to William Faulkner whom, Hemingway once said, he would have been proud simply to have managed. (Later he changed his mind.) But Hemingway was not satisfied, and he hit back in ways which did nothing to increase his stature, but which brought out another curious side to his nature.

Sometimes this warfare broke into the open when the writer was acting the role of literary critic himself. He wrote, for instance, a critical introduction to Elio Vittorini's *In Sicily,* and in doing so composed a document that reveals a lot more about the American than it did about the Italian. It was quite clear, first of all, that the basis of his admiration for the work was its resemblance to some of his own. Close in spirit to *A Farewell to Arms* and *For Whom the Bell Tolls, In Sicily* has an isolated young man in the rain who despairs of all values, but finally finds—in the solid pleasure of the senses and in the greatness of his Pilar-like mother—that life is worth the struggle, and even the armed struggle of war. "Every man is ill once, half-way through his life, and knows this stranger that is the sickness inside him," Vittorini remarks. But the most notable thing about Hemingway's introduction was that it consisted largely of an attack on the sterility of the "New York literary reviews," which bordered on the neurotic in its lack of true relevance to the matter at hand. Hemingway admired Vittorini because, among other reasons, he ran away from home when he was seventeen. One gets the notion that the trouble with the critics is that they never did, although there are no available figures on this point. Instead of running away, and learning their country, they feed on "schism and the dusty taste of disputed dialectics . . . their steady mulch the dehydrated cuds of fellow critics. . . ."

It is an inadequate critic, to be sure, who never feels about his trade as the poet Marianne Moore has felt about hers: "I, too, dislike it: there are things that are important beyond all this fiddle." But Hemingway's contempt approached hysteria, and he seized inappropriate opportunities to sound it. It would not be hard to cite a good number of critics whose knowledge of their country outdistanced Hemingway's. And it is interesting to notice that when Hemingway endeavored to write literary criticism himself, he took up a good deal of his space to chew on the work of those who were temporarily his fellows.

The critics who write for what are called the "little magazines" are very nearly the only serious critics we have, and it is interesting to consider Hemingway's objections to what he called "the Kierkegaard circuit." He had only one big objection, really. It was to anything which he did not regard as virile enough, and for some reason any kind of intellectualism seemed to indicate a lack of masculinity. In writing a blurb for Nelson Algren's *Man with the Golden Arm,* for instance, he managed to voice his confusion: "Truman Capote fans grab your hats, if you have any, and go. This is a man writing. . . ." * He once tried less delicately but by the same tactics to dispose of Proust, Racine, Radiguet, Cocteau and others. He had a certain point in this sort of thing. He had it for years, and he became shrill with it.

It is always odd when virility insists so stridently on itself. Many people have for some time figured, with Gertrude Stein, Max Eastman and others, that the much-vaunted masculinity was a simple pose. Miss Stein once remarked rather superciliously that Hemingway should write the "real" story of Hemingway, which would be a "yellow" tale, and not at all the tale of courage that he wrote. This would be an interesting suggestion except for the fact that it was based on a failure to see that Hemingway had already written the story Gertrude had in mind. The Nick Adams who drank ether to get through an attack, and confessed his terror to Capt. Paravicini, and fastened a chin strap across his mouth to keep his lips from getting out of control, is but one instance of Hemingway's long recital of his fears and of the means whereby he tried to overcome them. The whole notion—and it is still widely held—that Hemingway pretended to courage which he did not have is based on a false and superficial reading of his work. In the same way, the idea—also still around—that the masculinity Hemingway paraded was but the reverse side of a "real" effeminacy is glib and ignorant. It would be hard to deny, however, that Hemingway's literary tastes were often determined by his insistence that modern fiction to be acceptable must in many ways resemble his own. It would be as difficult to show that his

* Taking his own sweet time about it, Algren in 1965 repaid the compliment in kind, while at the same time bidding "Good riddance to all . . . praise-me-and-I'll-praise-you . . ." critics. His *Notes from a Sea Diary: Hemingway All the Way*, 1965, a critical disaster.

note of anti-intellectual virility was not sounded until it became monotonous. That the man adopted a mask is clear. Sometimes he was very careful to afford his careful readers the opportunity to peer behind it. But he did not always do this, and when he did not it was difficult to know what was there.

The mystery as to what was "there" would be largely cleared up if the people who knew Hemingway personally were agreed about him. But this is not the case. The man was assaulted at one time or another for practically everything, and not always by strangers. He had, however, a good many friends, and occasionally the attacks on him became insulting to the point where an ally was moved to come to the rescue with a defense. This happened when Sinclair Lewis abused his competitor so thoroughly that Elliot Paul wrote an indignant and persuasive dissent, putting it down for the record that Hemingway was shy, diffident, unsure of himself, eager for constructive criticism, loyal, gentle, considerate and generous. Paul also remarked that as an old reporter himself, Hemingway was generous to reporters, who frequently took advantage of him.

All this is true, and yet it is also true that the man clearly demonstrated that there was another side to his character. One would have thought that Paul's effective rejoinder, written chiefly to combat that insulting and patronizing article by Lewis (in which he called Hemingway both "puerile" and "senile") would have been sufficient. But Hemingway seems to have come back in his own way in *Across the River,* after thirteen years had elapsed, with a portrait of an American writer who has been widely taken to be Lewis. If it was indeed this man then Hemingway got the better of it, for though in the book version the magazine portrait was cleaned up a little, nothing in Lewis's attack struck so fiercely as the description of that face (Lewis had cancer of the skin; so did Hemingway): "a strange face like an over-enlarged, disappointed weasel or ferret . . . like Goebbels' face, if Herr Goebbels had ever been in a plane that burned . . . like a caricature of an American who has been run one half way through a meat chopper and then been boiled, slightly, in oil."

Hemingway had people swinging at his head so often at least partly because he stuck his neck out so much. He entertained at various times, for example, a preposterous opinion of his own aesthetic stature. Not even John O'Hara could really say much for *Across the River,* which Hemingway once insisted was his greatest. On occasion he was also a show-off and fatuous. Yet there was always the stubborn honesty and the sense of personal integrity. There was always a lot of derision for the Hemingway beard, which covered the skin infection, and of Hemingway's fishing, which apparently covered the fear of a mental contamination. It is surely better to shoot a kudu than to shoot yourself.

Another reason for the extremity of people's responses to Hemingway is the fact that several facets of his personality were set at an extreme slant. The man was, for example, fabulously ambitious and extraordinarily competitive. He saw himself in the ring not only with everyone who wrote but also with everyone who has ever written. Read everything, he once told a young writer, so you'll know what you have to beat; Hemingway once fully intended some day to beat them all. He was also inordinately vain. He struggled to hide this fact, but people who knew him well say that when he had been drinking hard the truth would come out, and he would begin to let you know that he had beaten more good writers than you would have thought possible.

On the other hand Hemingway was unusual in ways

that were thoroughly ingratiating. He could be wonderfully, even excessively, generous. His manner of operation here was wholly intuitive or instinctive. He liked or disliked a person on first sight, and that was just about it. Sometimes this was not particularly helpful, as when he decided on meeting Zelda Fitzgerald, years before her mental collapse, that she was "crazy." But if he liked a person he listened, he helped, and he also gave away a great deal of money. Another honorable aspect which has been hidden for the most part from the public view is of Hemingway the student. Since he had trouble sleeping, he drank and read instead; he must have very nearly carried out the advice he gave the young writer and read "everything." But he did not read so much as he studied. He learned very quickly, and he studied more than the art of writing. Almost in the spirit of a scholar hot in the pursuit of a Ph.D., and possibly as a defense against that unwarranted insecurity that haunts educated men who never went to college, Hemingway became very learned—but in his own unorthodox fields. He was not only a bit of a linguist, but also qualified with experts as an expert in such matters as navigation, military history and tactics. He was truly—even, for some, absurdly—erudite about large animals and fishes, as well as prizefighters and bullfighters. His knowledge of terrain—of where animals, weapons and tanks will go—is reported to have been incredible.*

* It may come as surprise to some who don't know it already that rolling rather freely about the world (gathering, one would expect, little moss) Hemingway at the end had a personal library several times the size of that gathered by William Faulkner, who seldom strayed from Oxford, Mississippi. In addition to all kinds of magazines, and American, London, and Paris newspapers, Finca Vigia was by 1954 "awash with books" (Robert Manning, *The Atlantic Monthly,* August, 1965). There were nearly 400 in Mrs. Hemingway's bedroom; more than 500, "mostly fiction, history, and music," in a sitting room; 300, "mostly French works of history and

Hemingway was also remarkable for his will power, and he owed to a rigorous and determined exercise of it the strength he made of his broken places. This has of course been most clear in the way he overcame the fright which seems once to have been nearly incapacitating. By continually walking into the face of danger he somehow managed to get the better of his fears. The idea, as with Macomber, that a sudden precipatation into action could cure a man wholly and for good seems mystical. But the fact is that in Spain and elsewhere in the late Thirties and Forties several experiences apparently did cure Hemingway: veterans, and among them professional soldiers, have testified that in the Second World War he seemed to them quite simply the bravest man they had ever seen.

Still a certain part of our picture of him must remain an unresolved paradox. Here was the writer who announced the death of all the gods save those of the senses and attended mass at a Roman Catholic church every Sunday, and who read regularly a periodical called the *Southern Jesuit.** He would confess readily that he read a

---

fiction, in an elegantly tiled . . . Venetian Room; and nearly 2000 in the high-shelved library, these carefully divided into history, military books, biography, geography, natural history, some fiction, and a large collection of maps." In the writer's own bedroom, in addition to piles and boxes of letters, two filing cabinets, and a great lion skin with letters stuck in its mouth ("That's the Urgent in-box," Hemingway explained), were 900 books, "mostly military manuals and textbooks, history and geography in Spanish, and sports volumes"; in a tower the writer had built to write in but did not use much, another 400 volumes; in a small guesthouse, 700. Hard to visualize, since there was already a serious shortage of space, by the time Hemingway left the villa for good in 1960 he had somehow acquired an additional 3,800 volumes.

---

* According to Leicester's book his brother, during all of his marriage to his second wife, Pauline Pfeiffer, was "as strong a Catholic as she was," but he broke from the Church when he broke with her.

good many sporting magazines as well, but he would not admit that he subscribed as he did to the *Partisan Review*. This was the man who wrote some of the most photogenic fiction of our time. But once when he was badly in need of money he refused forty-five hundred dollars a week for an "advisory" sojourn in Hollywood, and he flatly refused even to have a look at the movie version of *A Farewell to Arms* when a copy of the film was flown to him for a special, première showing. He prided himself on his practical knowledge and displayed the expertness with which he "knew his way around." But it is reported that he did not like to travel on a Friday and was thoroughly shaken by the sight of a black cat. He went about knocking on wood and was scared of snakes.

But it is not all paradox, and there are two explanations for several of Hemingway's peculiarities, and especially of his recent eccentricities, that make a certain degree of sense. These explanations are Hemingway's own, in a manner of speaking, for they are given by him to help account for Richard Cantwell's idiosyncrasies. In *Across the River* Hemingway first of all continued to chronicle a steady and heavy consumption of alcohol by his hero, who had been drinking hard for at least a quarter of a century, and it is no secret that this activity—like many another activity of the protagonist—had its autobiographical basis. Readers have often complained that no one could drink as constantly as Hemingway's characters do, but reliable reports would seem to indicate that the writer's own efforts in this direction persuasively invalidated the charge. The only restriction he apparently placed on himself was not to drink in the morning, which was when he worked, but it is further reported that in later years he frequently broke the rule.

Also in the same recent book, he had Cantwell's driver, T/5 Jackson, speculate: "He's been beat up so much he's slug-nutty." This may have seemed a very off-hand diagnosis, but the fact of the matter is that Hemingway's body must have retained the record of about as many blows as a man could take and live. Like Cantwell, he was scarred from top of head to sole of foot. As a boy he was forever getting hurt. The boxing lessons got him a broken nose. In his senior year at Oak Park High he was removed from both of the two big football games with injuries. It was apparently true from the start, as someone remarked to Gertrude Stein later, that "whenever he does anything sporting something breaks: his arm, his leg or his head." But although the history of his sporting injuries could be documented at some length, these were the very least of his woundings. There were, for example, three serious auto wrecks—the one with Dos Passos which nearly cost an arm, one in Cuba, and one in London that necessitated the taking of fifty-seven stitches in his head, stitches which he removed on the way to Fox Green Beach on D day. But most of his scars were picked up in warfare, and commemorate actual battles. In combat alone Hemingway was shot through both feet, both knees, both arms, both hands, and the scrotum, and was wounded in the head six times.

It is the head wounds which would most back the "theory" which he gave to Jackson to expound. Col. Cantwell answered his doctor's question as to the number of brain concussions he had sustained by saying ten, "give or take three." Hemingway had at least that many, and after this answer was given there were more—one "a Force 5 Beaufort concussion" from a blow, received on the *Pilar,* which also severed an artery and dug into the skull itself. His concussions go back to 1918, but in the short space of three years, 1943–1945, he had five serious ones. In addition, a car-mirror support once cracked the front of his skull, and he broke six ribs in 1946. His large body was criss-crossed with scars.

The big wound, however, was the one where the man

like the hero got "hit properly and for good," "out on the river bank." This is the injury Hemingway suffered on the night of July 8, 1918, at Fossalta di Piave. He had gone out in front of the trenches to a listening post on the bank of the river, and was hit by an Austrian trench-mortar shell called a *Minenwerfer,* or "ash can." "I died then," Hemingway said, speaking figuratively. The three Italian soldiers who were with him all died literally. All three of them had their legs blown off, and when the American recovered consciousness two of them were already dead, and the other was screaming. Hemingway could make himself walk, and he picked up the living but legless Italian and carried him back toward the trenches. On the way, however, an Austrian searchlight caught him in its beam and a heavy-caliber machine gun opened up on him, hitting him once in the foot and once in the knee. (I "leaned over and put my hand on my knee," Lt. Henry said. "My knee wasn't there. My hand went in and my knee was down on my shin.") When he got to the dressing station, the Italian was dead and Hemingway was himself for a while considered past help. When he was finally attended to, 227 fragments of steel were taken from his right leg alone.

A great deal about Hemingway was exciting and a little unbelievable. Several sides of his personality were curious, or overlaid with publicity or glamour, and hard to get at. But there is one thing that should be clear about him, and that is that more prominent in his life than anything else save the production of books has been the absorption of blows. It still seems obvious that for Hemingway and the hero alike the explosion at Fossalta was the crux of that life, and climax to a series of like events which had their start up in Michigan and were to be repeated and imitated in various forms over and over again. It remains likely that a great deal in Hemingway, such as his avowed preoccupation with death, traced directly to this source. "I had been shot and I had been crippled and gotten away," he later put it. But it is not clear exactly how he got away, or how far away he got. Actually it is not clear how any of these things work.

There is, though, one striking, comprehensive explanation for all of this. It was formulated as a theory by Sigmund Freud in his *Beyond the Pleasure Principle* (1922). Anyone with any of Hemingway's contempt for psychiatry would approach this theory with great caution. The author himself would go nowhere near it. When asked the name of his analyst once, as he told Earl Wilson, he accurately replied with a laugh: "Portable Corona No. 3." But it is pretty clear that his typewriter had chiefly to get rid of an experience of the First World War, and that in the period immediately following it Hemingway reorganized his personality, and developed himself as a writer. And so well does Freud's theory offer an interpretation of the man's difficulties at this absolutely crucial time that one would think, if he didn't know better, that the doctor had diagnosed the writer, and was in his book discussing Hemingway as a test case.

What Freud did was to suggest that there exists in psychic life a "repetition-compulsion," which goes "beyond the pleasure principle." Working with patients whom he thought to be suffering from "traumatic neuroses" which were the results of wounds or "shock" received in the First World War, he discovered that analysis of the dreams of these casualties contradicted one of his basic theories, that dreams are "wish-fulfillments." The dreams of the wounded, he wrote, obey rather the repetition compulsion, which "disregards in every way the pleasure principle."

Instead of reasoning that in some obscure fashion the neurotic masochistically finds what is for him really pleasure in this pain (a direction one might have expected), the doctor came up with his theory of the "death instinct," which explained for him the anomalous dreams of his patients. There is an instinct, he speculated, in living organic matter, "impelling it towards the restatement of an earlier condition. . . ." "Everything living dies from causes within itself, and returns to the inorganic. . . ." "The goal of all life is death." Then he took another step, and went on to account for the destructive drives in the human personality by tracing them back to this death instinct: in order not to destroy ourselves, we destroy other things. To keep from giving in to the death drive, we assist in other destructions.

Hemingway—who wrote, among other things, his nightmares—made both simple and justifiable the identification of "fiction" with "dreams" here. Once this is done the theory fits and we put it on: suffering from the wounds and shock crucially sustained in the First World War, Hemingway, in terms of Freud's analysis, was continually in his prose disregarding the pleasure principle, and returning compulsively to the scenes of his injuries. He had his preoccupation with death as a result of an overexposure to it. He saw too many helmets "full of brains," and he built his monument in recognition of the meaning of his own misfortune. Jordan, assuming the posture of burial, was with his preoccupation simply more sensitive than most of us to a force which impels us all backward to an earlier, inorganic state. And that is not all: before Hemingway, symbolically through his hero, submits to this drive he must occupy himself with vicarious dying—with witnessing and participating in many wars, many bullfights. Despite his contempt for psychoanalysis, he said it himself when he wrote that he spent a great deal of time killing animals and fish in order that he might not kill himself. He said it again in writing that "when a man is still in rebellion against death he has pleasure in taking to himself one of the god-like attributes; that of giving it."

There are of course bound to be risks in anything so pat; we rightly suspect the danger of a master key which unlocks all the doors in the corridor. The difficulty here, however, is not so much that this is too easy as that there is no evidence for the speculation that this tendency toward death is the expression of an instinct, as Freud himself admitted. His whole theory of "instinct" is disreputable in many quarters; modern anthropologists, particularly, have thrown a ghastly light on it. In addition, Freud argued from analogy, which is always a risky procedure. In the last analysis he could only say that the living exists *after* the nonliving, and *consequently* wants to return to the earlier form, at which point one gets a little dizzy.

However, there is no need for a theory of a death *instinct* in order to explain the phenomenon of a death *wish*. There is not even any need to look for such wishes only in neurotics, for certainly—consciously or otherwise —the most "normal" people imaginable can entertain them at times. The thought of death is one toward which we must sometimes be at least ambivalent, for just as death means the end of pleasure so it means, too, the end of pain; in this sense, if in no other, all of us with a part of our natures may occasionally wish to die. Death is the escape to end all escapes; when things are going badly it should not be hard to entertain thoughts of it, especially if one can dream up means to it which are attractive enough. In a traumatic neurosis (and the woundings of Hemingway and his hero certainly bear all the marks of what is called traumatic experience) perhaps the preoccupation with death becomes so insistent that wishes for death begin to look instinctual.

Freud's theory of the death instinct has been rather widely rejected, even by theoreticians who have come along in his name. But the theory of trauma has proved more acceptable, and in the "authoritative" *Psychoanalytic Theory of Neurosis* (1945) of the late Otto Fenichel a good deal is made of this illness. According to Fenichel, the term "trauma" is a relative one, and those who have a "high potential" for it are most likely to be afflicted. That Nick Adams, at least, had this potential seems patent, particularly in a story like "The Killers," in which the thought of violence that had not even taken place was enough to make him want to get clear of the town where it was impending. That what happened to Hemingway at Fossalta was sufficient to realize this potential seems even more obvious. The nightmares and insomnia which he suffered as a result of this experience are discussed by Fenichel as primary symptoms of this neurosis.

It is "unmastered amounts of excitation," the analyst tells us, which make for the sleepless nights and the dreams. In the daytime, "trauma creates fear of every kind of tension"—as is brilliantly demonstrated by Nick fishing the Big Two-Hearted on his return from the war. Nick felt sick and had to sit down after the excitement of a strike. "The thrill had been too much," and he did not dare to "rush his sensations any." This, Fenichel explains, is because even a little influx of excitement may have the effect of "flooding" the patient, as was clear in "A Way You'll Never Be," and also when Jordan feared the times "when you can't stop and your brain gets to racing like a flywheel with the weight gone."

It is the first characteristic of this neurosis that the trauma is constantly being repeated: "The patient cannot free himself from thinking about the occurrence over and over again." Both Hemingway and his hero testify to this, of course—whether asleep, in the nightmares which re-peated the wounding in Italy, for example, or awake, in writing of the incidents which hurt. The hero keeps saying he can "get rid of" the experiences which have damaged him by writing about them later. This is precisely the view of Fenichel, who argues that the function of these repetitions is that they "represent attempts to achieve a belated mastery, fractionally, of the unmastered amounts of excitation."

It is also a part of the theory of the traumatic neurosis that after the trauma itself has done its damage, the patient "then has to find new and better ways of adaptation. This . . . consists in nothing more than a complicated system of bindings and primitive discharges." This is a remarkably accurate description of the process the hero went through after he had been disabled in the war. For evidence of a complex system of bindings and primitive discharges it is unnecessary to go beyond the accounts of his ritualized fishing trips, and they were but the clearest instances of a process which was to color and control the rest of the hero's life. And these new ways of adaptation have certain consequences, for as a result of the necessary concentration on the crucial task of mastering the "excitation," many of the "higher functions" must go by the board. The personality is necessarily retrenched, and therefore to some degree impoverished, for the purpose of controlling the fear. For this phenomenon, Fenichel coins a startling word: "primitivation." The analyst shows no sign that he ever read the novelist, but with this term he sheds considerable light on the origin of Hemingway's "primitivism." It happens to be the only light, as we saw, by which some of Hemingway's stories—like the "Big Two-Hearted River," which contained a vivid description of how all this works—can be properly read.

And so it seems that a great deal in Hemingway—his preoccupations, limitations, attitudes, peculiarities—conformed to the hypotheses of psychoanalytic theory. Even his superstition can be seen as one of the "archaic features" which are common in obsessed or compulsive neurotics, no matter how well informed they may otherwise be. Even Cantwell's exorcistical gesture in building the monument to his great wound is not surprising if one accepts the claim that many neurotics overevaluate, in a magical way, the powers of the movements of the bowels.

When the doctors disagree, as they do, the layman— competent or otherwise—is forced to decisions. What he can say here is simply this: the diagnosis looks plausible, though it is of course an incomplete one. For examples, the guilt and anxiety which are products of any neurosis, and the Oedipean situation which is supposed to be primary and so often crucial, have not by any means been fully explored. The attempt has simply been to show how certain theories—of "trauma," of the "repetition compulsion" and of its function, of the "primitivation" of personality which is the price of readjustment, of vicarious dying and the implications of a preoccupation with the fact of violent death—throw a good deal of light on Hemingway and his work. They do not illuminate everything. The most complicated neurotic may follow quite a simple compulsive pattern of behavior, but that is by no means to say that the simple pattern is equivalent to the whole of his personality. It is doubtful that the simplest man alive could be totally explained by a single set of concepts, and the author was not that man. There were surely many other sides to Hemingway. But they were less obvious, more secretive and—one might guess—less important. Among the patterns that might go to explain Hemingway completely, moreover, it is the pattern of trauma that he told us about, which looks like the best key to his personality, and which affords the best single psychological insight into his work.

Perhaps it should be pointed out, too, that no reduction in the man's value or relevance is involved in any interpretation like this one. Hemingway's work is limited in many ways by his difficulties. A guide in narrow circumstances, for example, he is surely no broad guide to human relations. But the paramount fact is that in spite of and even out of his troubles and the limits they prescribe, Hemingway fashioned one of the most impressive literary careers of his time. It is not the trauma but the use to which he put it which counts; he harnessed it, and transformed it to art. With will power, hard work and a profound sense of his calling, he made the most of everything he had, and not only overcame his weakness, but made it strong.

His work has no single meaning, and it is the work that matters. Still the personality illuminates the work, and our curiosity about the writer himself is human enough. In the light of a Freudian explanation, moreover, our understanding of him as human or hero, man or legend, may be deepened and properly enriched. A picture which John Groth once meant to give of Hemingway's famous courage and indifference to danger is sufficient illustration of this, for in the context of pathology its meaning becomes ambiguous and complex. The picture itself becomes very nearly as memorable as a scene by the writer himself, and is every bit as terrifying: At a regimental command post, close to the German lines in the Second World War, Groth and Hemingway were eating dinner with some officers one night. Suddenly the German 88's began to break their way in. To a man, everyone everyone hit the floor in the accepted fashion, and groped for helmets. Or so Groth thought. But when the candles were lit, he was stunned with what he saw, for there was Hemingway still at the table—bareheaded, his back to the firing, still eating his dinner, alone.

5 | THE ORIGINS AND MEANING OF A STYLE

I was trying to learn to write, commencing with the simplest things.

DEATH IN THE AFTERNOON

"Hemingway should perhaps more than anyone else be allowed to escape the common literary fate of being derived from other people," Edmund Wilson once wrote. Gertrude Stein was not so sure: "He looks like a modern and he smells of the museums," she said. It doesn't look as if the truth of the matter is in either of these views. Hemingway derived from other people, all right. He owed a lot to other writers, and a large part of his debt can be assessed. On the other hand, he always made fresh and new and very much his own whatever he chose to borrow or rework or learn from. Whatever his faults, he very rarely smelled of others. He was not a reproduction; and if he had the look of a genuine original, who fashioned what is unquestionably the most famous and influential prose style of our time, it was because many ingredients had been thoroughly assimilated and revitalized by the force of an integrated and talented personality.

The problem of literary derivation is always difficult. Even if a writer should say that his books came to be what they are because he had read and been impressed by certain other books, or that he thinks what he thinks because of certain experiences he has had, we cannot be sure, and are suspicious about the finality of such statements. When on the other hand he submits no really clear claims about his origins, or makes contradictory ones, then the claims of anyone else become even more speculative than they might have been. And yet it is often possible, on the basis of certain facts, to speculate. Presumably no one who had read Hemingway's books would deny that the First World War had an effect on his ideas; and no one familiar with his prose style and the facts about Gertrude Stein would contend that she had no influence whatever on it. A writer is shaped, in one way or another and no matter how slightly, by everything that has ever happened to him; among the things that happen are the books he reads and the writers he has known.

Hemingway read a great many books, and he knew several writers when he was serving his apprenticeship in Paris. One of them was Samuel Putnam, who once heard him say, categorically: "that's how I learned to write, —by reading the Bible." He went on to specify: Old Testament, King James version. But this kind of remark is not really very helpful. For one thing, a man could say and believe this one day, and not the next; for another, it is common knowledge that people who claim descent from nobility mean mainly to speak well of themselves. It is not that there is a bar sinister in the heraldry of Hemingway's prose, but that his escutcheon should display the bearings of more antecedents than one, and not all of them so exalted.*

Another writer who knew Hemingway in Paris, in the months of 1922 when he was thoroughly learning his trade, named three more immediate teachers of the young stylist: Gertrude Stein, Sherwood Anderson, and Ezra Pound. In those days, said John Peale Bishop with insight, Hemingway wrote courageously, but out of pity; "having been hurt and badly hurt he could understand the pain of others." As far as prose was concerned, the novice saw only one man on the right track, and that was Anderson. However, he was also learning from Pound "the discipline of Flaubert" and the cutting out of adjectives, and from Stein the uses of repetition. Later famously he told Bishop: "Ezra was right half the time, and when he was wrong, he was so wrong you were never in any doubt about it. Gertrude was always right."

Very likely this was a good list that Bishop compiled, and as some of Hemingway's early stories show, it was possibly more or less of an oversight that the name of Scott Fitzgerald was left off it. And now, having suggested that the group numbers four influences, it is hard to decide to what extent they were really one, for these people knew and were reading each other, with the various forces mingling and interacting. In addition, once Hemingway got started he must have had some effect on the people who were affecting him; it is probably true, as he claimed, that Gertrude Stein learned to write conversation from him, and not the other way around. But such paths soon become

* It should be recorded, however, that at least according to his sister Marcelline, Hemingway as a boy was already a great reader and devoured everything from Horatio Alger to "every word of the King James version."

trackless, or so marked over that the most conscientious sleuth would give up the search.

*   *   *

The conventional but proper place to pick up a trail is at the point where it appears to begin. Ernest M. Hemingway is a name that was originally signed to some poetry. It is true that an insubstantial and unfunny piece of surrealistic whimsey called "A Divine Gesture," published in a "little magazine" called the *Double Dealer* in 1922, was prose. But this work was so unlike anything its author was to do again that it should be allowed to remain in oblivion, and the novelist's real debut was as a poet. There was first a quatrain called "Ultimately," which also appeared in the *Double Dealer* in 1922, and then in January of 1923 six short poems under the general heading of "Wanderings" came out in *Poetry*. "Ultimately" appeared below, in location and in quality, a poem by William Faulkner, which was the first time in print for the Southerner. The quatrain suggests that Hemingway had been reading the short poems of Stephen Crane pretty carefully:

> He tried to spit out the truth;
> Dry mouthed at first,
> He drooled and slobbered in the end;
> Truth dribbling his chin.

None of the "wanderings" led to much of anywhere, either. Most of them have to do in one way or another with war, and one of them begins in a patent imitation of Vachel Lindsay:

> Drummed their boots on the camion floor,
> Hob-nailed boots on the camion floor.
> Sergeants stiff,
> Corporals sore.
> Lieutenants thought of a Mestre whore ...

and does not mellow as it progresses. Three more poems of Hemingway's, which he once called "rather obscene," can be found by resolute scholars in the German magazine *Das Querschnitt* (for 1924 and 1925.) These are playful things, and rather funny; when they got back to Oak Park they caused quite a scandal. There was a last effort published in the opening number of Ezra Pound's *The Exile* (1927). The title, "Neothomist Poem," was garbled, the piece was signed E. W. Hemingway, and the complete work follows:

> The Lord is my shepherd, I shall not
> want him for long.

At this point in his career as a poet, Hemingway lapsed into a silence which was apparently going to last forever, but which later was shattered by an announcement made to a Broadway columnist. He had been filing poems in his pocket since 1921, the novelist said, and he had every intention of bringing out forty of them before long.* Like many of his published statements in the early Fifties, this was one which seemed calculated to delight his enemies and confound his friends—or at least those of them who remembered the early poems and the early prose.

The first prose of any importance that Hemingway published went into three good short stories that were added to his poetry and issued in a pamphlet, called *Three Stories and Ten Poems,* at Dijon in 1923. This was the author's "first book," and the gap that lies between the

---

* Unlike some of the fiction to which he occasionally referred, these poems do exist, and "Two Love Poems," rather unrewarding long ones in free verse written to Mary Hemingway in 1944, have been published (*Atlantic Monthly,* August, 1965). A small pirated gathering, *Collected Poems* (San Francisco, 1960), contains all the early published verses, including "The Age Demanded," which is worth reading only partly because it is a witty rejection of a part of Pound's well-known "Ode pour l'Election de Son Sepulchre."

prose in it and "A Divine Gesture" would be as baffling as it is profound if it were not for our knowledge of what happened to the things he must have written in between. Eighteen stories and the first draft of a novel would show the transition, but these were contained in the suitcase that was stolen from Hadley. The material that almost certainly traced the most imitative and faltering steps of a person learning a new skill is thus missing, and doubtless for good. But although the *Three Stories*—"Up in Michigan," "Out of Season," and "My Old Man"—are already accomplished performances, they still reveal quite a bit about their author's early debt to other writers. One of them is Hemingway's first really distinctive piece—his first attempt to write a story which is really the story he long continued to write.

The clearest direct obligation of the *Three Stories* is to Sherwood Anderson. "My Old Man," a good piece in its own right, is Hemingway's version of one of Anderson's best efforts, the widely reprinted "I Want to Know Why," which had appeared two years earlier. Both stories are about horse racing, and are told by boys in their own vernacular. In each case the boy has to confront mature problems while undergoing a painful disillusionment with an older man he had been strongly attached to. It doesn't look like coincidence.*

* "My Old Man" was written, Hemingway claimed, before he had read any Anderson. If this was the case the coincidence is astonishing. (Actually, from both literary and biographical points of view, incredible.) The story is, by the way, one of only two that escaped the theft of the suitcase at the Gare de Lyon: "Lincoln Steffins had sent it out to some editor who sent it back" (*A Moveable Feast*). Indeed it never was published at all until Edward O'Brien broke his rules and put it in his *Best Short Stories* of the year, otherwise culled from the magazines. ("I laughed and drank some more beer": O'Brien had in addition dedicated the volume to Hemingway, who was almost completely unknown, and "after all that he had spelled the name wrong.")

Nor does it seem likely that "Out of Season" would have been written quite the way it was without the example of F. Scott Fitzgerald's *The Beautiful and Damned,* which had been published in 1922. The debt is nowhere near as large as the debt of "My Old Man" to Anderson, it is less a matter of prose style, and the story is not as good. But, as sometimes in Fitzgerald, an attempt is made to convey the feeling of things falling apart in a way that seems to have intrigued the early Hemingway, and the discomforting atmosphere is persuasive. The story is concerned with everything going wrong with a marriage in a quiet and unexcited way: A young gentleman and his wife in the Tyrol want to go fishing. But it is illegal to fish there, the weather is raw and cold, they do not have the proper equipment, and the venture is finally abandoned. The piece moves in the mood of the aftermath of a quarrel the couple has had, and is quite like "The End of Something," that fishing story in which Nick Adams and Marjorie found themselves "quits." More prominent in Hemingway are the idealized relationships involving Renata, Maria or Catherine, and the more hostile ones with the Margots, but there are minor stories like this one—and "Cat in the Rain," "Hills like White Elephants," "A Canary for One" and "The Sea Change"—which present a discouraged picture of the rose with the bloom off, of couples under a spell of disenchantment, and they make one think of Fitzgerald, who had earlier portrayed such difficult subtitles, but less effectively.*

* A few of these stories are badly neglected, possibly because after all these years people still don't understand them very well. "The Sea Change," for example, is little known but brilliant. It concerns a man whose wife (mistress?) walks out on him, temporarily, for an affair with another woman. But failure to see that the title is submerged in Shakespeare's "Full Fathom Five" ("Nothing of him that doth fade, /But doth suffer a sea-change/ Into something rich and strange") gen-

"Up in Michigan" is the most interesting of the *Three Stories,* for it is the one that represents Hemingway's first attempt at what soon became his major theme. The locale of the story is the country around Horton's Bay, where the early Nick stories took place. By means of a title, Hemingway was soon to say what life is like in our time. Now he tries to say what life is like up in Michigan: Life, first in this place and then anywhere you go if you go there in our century, is violent, brutal, painful. Just as Nick was soon to be initiated into knowledge of these facts at a nearby Indian camp, so a girl named Liz is initiated into a ritual which teaches a similar lesson, but for girls, in this story. She is taken to a spot near a warehouse by a blacksmith who has had a good deal to drink, and is seduced, in pain and partly against her wishes. After the event the man falls off to sleep. Liz, who is cold, miserable, empty and alone, cannot wake him, so she walks off to her bed, crying. The dogged simplicity of the prose in this story suggests both Anderson and Stein, but it is too hardheaded for the former, and cut off by its subject matter from the latter. All Hemingway had to do, once he had written it, was to go on with a protagonist in whom he could see himself

---

erally results in a failure to see that, as with many of the Nick Adams stories, Hemingway is not presenting a situation so much as the subtle effects of a situation on a protagonist—which in this case very precisely fit the lines summoned up from *The Tempest.* With equal precision they fit as well the lines from Pope which the man in the story tries unsuccessfully to quote: "Vice is a monster of so frightful mien, /As to be hated needs but to be seen;/ Yet seen too oft, familiar with her face,/ We first endure, then pity, then embrace": exactly the process the man undergoes—a process not very easy to perceive if readers don't remember the lines better than he does. (None of this comes across as self-conscious, or the least bit pretentious; here, in his words, is the "ignorant bastard" who thought of "establishing a scholarship and sending myself to Harvard.")

directly, and he would have the adventures of Nick Adams.*

The qualities of these early stories which attracted most attention to Hemingway, and which seemed to mark his work as his own and no other's, were the rigorous objectivity with which they were told, their complete lack of "thinking," and the unbelievably sharp and simple prose. These qualities have never been more clearly marked than in a pamphlet called *in our time* which Hemingway published the year after the *Three Stories,* and later republished as the interchapter "sketches" in the book of stories called *In Our Time.* Since these sketches are very like self-set "exercises," brilliantly accomplished, it may very well be that they were written as early as anything that the mature Hemingway preserved. These sketches are arranged for the most part in the order in which their author experienced them, as the Nick stories in the book are in the order of his advancing age. They start with impressions of the war, proceed through Nick's wounding and several scenes of bullfighting, and end with a visit to the King of Greece, whom Hemingway had interviewed in connection with the Greco-Turkish War he was reporting.

The quality that most distinguished these sketches was

* "Up in Michigan" is the second of the two stories that were not stolen. "It had been in a drawer somewhere," Hemingway said, because Gertrude Stein had told him it was *"inaccrochable,"* an invented and rather difficult term no one seems to want to translate. Literally, "unhookable"—or, since *accrocher* can mean among other things "to pawn," "unhockable"? Probably not; perhaps she meant that because of the sex you couldn't hook it up with an editor; hence, in effect, "unprintable"—which, in 1925 when the first edition of *In Our Time* appeared, it was, as Hemingway failed to remark. Like *In Our Time,* incidentally, "Up in Michigan" is probably a sardonic allusion, in this case to a song of the period which extolled the bucolic virtues of life in the region: "How I'd like to be again /Way up in Michigan/ Down on the farm" (if for once memory serves).

a completely objective vividness, an unemotional approach which concentrated on presenting objects, allowing the responses of feeling and mind to take care of themselves. Hemingway saw this approach to his material as essentially a moral problem involving honesty. Writing in *Death in the Afternoon* of his apprentice days in Paris he put it this way:

> I was trying to write then and I found the greatest difficulty, aside from knowing what you really felt, rather than what you were supposed to feel, and had been taught to feel, was to put down what really happened in action: what the actual things were which produced the emotion that you experienced ... the real thing, the sequence of motion and fact which made the emotion.

In those days there was in Paris a "primitive" who had been for some time working with the simplest things and was willing to teach what she had learned. This of course was Gertrude Stein. Hemingway made his first pilgrimage to 27 rue de Fleurus two years before his *Three Stories*. The two writers talked a great deal. They walked and talked on many occasions, and she made the long trip across Paris to the Place du Tertre on the top of Montmartre and went over everything he had written. In return Hemingway, with Alice B. Toklas, copied out and later proofread fifty pages of *The Making of Americans,* and he got them published in Ford Maddox Ford's *transatlantic.* As Miss Stein has pointed out, it is not possible to be more directly exposed to a way of writing that has proved itself wildly infectious, and if Hemingway did not pick up something from this experience of Gertrude, who was "always right," then it must be that he had received inoculations from some source we shall never know anything about. Actually it is impossible to read very far in her book today without thinking of him.

Similarities between his prose and hers suggest indeed that he learned a lot. What she had tried to do in the days when Hemingway was a boy was remarkably like what the young man was going one day to try to do, too. Very early in the century she had been trying to get at the mental processes of a savage, and to approximate them in her prose. At that time there was a rage for primitive Negro sculpture, her friend Pablo Picasso was "going abstract," and all these forces were behind her "abstract" *Three Lives* (1909), which contained the famous primitivistic study of the Negro girl "Melanctha." This long story is told in a style that strikingly resembles the style Hemingway was to develop for his own uses. It is written in a simple, spare, concise and yet repetitive prose—clean, free of clichés or synonyms, and using the smallest and simplest of words. In addition, there is a passage of wild violence, a bloody razor-slashing of Melanctha's father, which is related with cold objectivity, with a total restraint of comment.

There was a lot here that Hemingway, finding his way, could use to advantage. The dogged simplicity of diction and sentence structure, although in one way "monotonous," was in reality completely appropriate to the meaning of much that he was going to try to say and show about a man under a tense, rigid control. Efforts to approximate the simple, primitive mind fit perfectly his hero's desire to escape his complex fears and be simple and whole as Melanctha—to feel, but "not to think . . . to remember and not too much remember. . . ." Hemingway's hero is no Steinian primitive, but he was trying very hard to be like one. The young Hemingway had a lot of use, too, for the devices of the unexcited violence in Miss Stein's fiction. Violence was his topic, and what he wanted to get rid of, and the essence of the ordeal his protagonist was going to undergo. How to treat violence effectively was written out plain in "Melanctha": describe "what the actual things were"—not the emotion but "the sequence of motion and fact which made the emotion." His aims were quite different from hers, but he could use for himself a good deal of what she had to teach, and it looks as if he did.

He may too have learned something of this sort from a less obvious source. A book of T. S. Eliot's called *The Sacred Wood* was in the hands of the advance guard in Paris in the early 1920's, and in these days Hemingway had apparently not yet developed his temporary distaste for the poet. Eliot had been worrying the problem of how to express emotion in poetry, and in his theory of the "objective correlative," included in this book in an essay on "Hamlet," he had come to the conclusion Hemingway was to announce in *Death in the Afternoon:*

> The only way of expressing emotion in the form of art is by finding . . . a set of objects, a situation, a chain of events which shall be the formula of that *particular* emotion; such that when the external facts . . . are given, the emotion is immediately evoked.

Hemingway claimed, in the same book on writing and bullfighting, that he learned to play with quotations from Eliot, and he may have learned more from the same source, for the poet is saying: "put down . . . the actual things . . . the sequence of motion and fact," and let the emotions take care of themselves.*

* In *Death in the Afternoon* Hemingway considered the death of a humanist: "I hope to see the finish of a few, and speculate how worms will try that long-preserved sterility; with their quaint pamphlets gone to bust and into footnotes all their lust." The Old Lady says, "That's a very nice line about lust," and the Author replies, "I know it. It came from Andrew Marvel. I learned how to do that by reading T. S.

Another widely read poet of the time, and another discovery of Pound's, was Robert Frost. Hemingway probably never studied him, or may have been totally unimpressed if he did. But the fact is that in poetry Frost was doing in the early 1920's for the speech and speech rhythms of New England precisely what Hemingway was soon to do in prose for a less regional way of talking: make a literary language of ordinary speech, in an effort to revitalize our writing. Such a force was "in the air," as they say, and many of Hemingway's effects—of irony and understatement, for example—are Frost's.

A more direct and specific set of instructions was offered a young writer by the Imagist poets. Hemingway would certainly have known about all this from Ezra Pound, who had once been head of the group, and the essence of the "Imagist Manifesto" was such that a prose writer could subscribe to it emphatically. The Imagists vowed to use the language of ordinary speech, and always the exact word; to present an image and to render particulars exactly, with no "vague generalities"; to be "hard and clear" and concentrated; and to demand a complete freedom of subject. In his prose, Hemingway stuck by these principles as fast as any of the poets who formulated them—faster.

Any list of writers who may have had a hand in the development of this one would be long if it intended to be

---

Eliot." Many a true word, they say, is spoken in jest, and Hemingway may have have learned from the same poet which poems to "do it" with. Eliot had already played with Marvel's "To His Coy Mistress" in his *Waste Land* (using lines which Frederic Henry later quoted to Catherine Barkley), and twice in that poem he had also used the song from *The Tempest* from which Hemingway borrowed his "Sea Change." The lines from Marlowe which gave Hemingway his much-worked phrase "in another country" had been quoted by Eliot in his "Portrait of a Lady."

complete. It seems very likely that the associated names of Joseph Conrad and Ford Maddox Ford should be on it, for instances. We know also that in what are called the formative years Hemingway read Stendhal, who presents pictures of the single man lost in the confusion of war or life that could not help providing examples for the isolated hero. There were, too, if we are to take him seriously, the painters in the Luxembourg Museum, which Hemingway often visited in the Paris days. He once remarked that he "learned how to make a landscape from Mr. Paul Cézanne," and then pointing to the background of a painting said, "We always have this in when we write." It may not be entirely clear how a writer learns to make landscapes from a painter. But it is not difficult to see that he might learn a few things about how to write natural description, and how to give fiction the sense of a physical background, in Turgenev. When Jake Barnes read *A Sportsman's Sketches* in Spain he probably watched with some care how the Russian dealt with hunting and fishing scenes, and was struck with the acute awareness one has of the out-of-doors in that book—the sense of what Hemingway has called "the places, and how the weather was," which he insisted all good fiction must contain. And it is doubtful that he missed the simplicity, the brevity and intensity which Turgenev's prose has even in translation.

But one quickly reaches the point of what are known as diminishing returns in looking for all the writers who may have a part in the making of a new one. In Hemingway's case, what is more, such a pursuit might preoccupy the zealous scholar to the point where he would miss something that is more interesting: for some time Hemingway has himself been dealing, in a rather obscure fashion, with the problem of his own aesthetic heredity. He has cast off several of the people who are said to have helped him, and he has claimed a new and perhaps more honorific set of forebears.

Of the four writers—Stein, Anderson, Pound and Fitzgerald—who generally are credited with shaping Hemingway, he has written off three. In "Kilimanjaro" that "American poet" in Paris "with a stupid look on his potato face" was probably not, as once believed, Ezra Pound, who was physiognomically a little lumpy, and known to have come from Idaho. Hemingway stayed on good terms with Ezra until the latter became a fascist; he never joined in the cry against him, and before his release from St. Elizabeth's Hospital in Washington the novelist had many times urged it. (He also favored giving the poet a Nobel Prize.) But the rest of these people have all at one time or another been firmly rejected. Back in 1933 Gertrude Stein accused Hemingway of having killed off a great many of his rivals (some of whom were also thought to be his mentors), and of having put them under the sod. Hemingway denied it. But it would have been difficult for him to deny it later. Perhaps she gave him an idea, though it was she who had taken the first swing. In any case, she got hers in *Green Hills of Africa:* "you never should have helped her," says Mrs. Hemingway, rather reversing the usual way of looking at it, and possibly with some justice. Fitzgerald got his in "Kilimanjaro" with the condescending passage on "poor Scott Fitzgerald" (as the original version read): "wrecked"—which rejects utterly one of his friend's major themes, the effects of wealth.* The most thorough early job, though, was of course done on Sherwood Anderson in *The Torrents of Spring,* where Hemingway, perhaps sensing in horror that readers might make unflattering comparisons between Anderson's "faux-naïveté" and his

---

* In both cases—Stein and Fitzgerald—the "attacks" were as nothing, of course, compared to what years later was going into *A Moveable Feast.*

own simplifications, sat down and in a burst of speed resolved to purge himself of the influence that man had once exerted over him, and to declare and publish to the world his independence of *that* contaminated source. Hemingway had also written off T. S. Eliot, who seems to have taught him a couple of tricks, by speaking wishfully (in an early tribute to Conrad) of "grinding Mr. Eliot into a fine dry powder," and of leaving "for London early tomorrow with a sausage grinder," although these are sentiments he long ago ceased to feel.

Of course these attacks did not necessarily indicate indebtedness on Hemingway's part; he hit out at many writers who could never possibly have helped him. Much of his disparagement had nothing to do with influences, and was motivated by jealousy of people he regarded as potential rivals—as Miss Stein claimed. He was in this rather like a champion fighter in defense of his title. He took on all comers—anyone who might make the weight and challenge his own supremacy. He fought rough, with only a passing glance at the strictures of the Marquis of Queensberry. If young, unseasoned fighters showed promise he would help them, as with O'Hara, Vittorini and many others. But if they looked like challengers he would knock them down.

Midway in this somewhat ungracious procedure of demoting his alleged influences and his rivals, Hemingway took time out, in a discussion of American literature, to elevate a few writers to take their places. In the *Green Hills* he had an Austrian interview him on the subject so that he might deliver a little lecture. There was not much, he conceded. Poe, though skillful, is "dead." Melville is marred by rhetoric.* Thoreau he "can't read." As for "Emerson,

* This decision must later have been revoked, as *Moby-Dick* (Melville at his most rhetorical) began to appear on lists, compiled by Hemingway, of indispensable books.

Hawthorne, Whittier, and Company," they were "English Colonials . . . who did not know that a new classic does not bear any resemblance to the classics that have preceded it."

If this last remark is not a succinct version of the burden of a good deal of Emerson, and particularly of his fundamental and famous "American Scholar," we have been misreading him all these years. And if Hemingway really saw a connection, beyond the geographical, between Emerson, Hawthorne and Whittier—and whoever goes in their Company—we have for some time underestimated his powers of intellectual synthesis. Even the Austrian might at this point have got the idea that this discourse was going to be unprofitable. But he does not seem to have, and the next section of the interview comes to life. It is here that Hemingway has claimed, for those who can read, what he would like to think of as his own true affiliations, and has taken on a new set of ancestors to replace the familiar ones he was in the process of disavowing. He praises three Americans: Henry James, Mark Twain, Stephen Crane.

The praise for James may not mean a great deal, to be sure. At the time when it was written Hemingway was developing a fondness for long and highly involved sentences, and these have been taken as evidence of "the Jamesian influence." But the complicated constructions Hemingway was occasionally attempting are often muddled, and look more like Faulkner's than James's. Hemingway's praise makes more sense if one takes it simply as an expression of admiration for the things he has applauded in Flaubert and Joyce as well: a sense of discipline, a command of form and structure, a devotion to the craft of prose fiction and a high seriousness in its practice.

The praise for Twain means a good deal more by way

of acknowledging influence and claiming affinity. What Hemingway said was that "All modern American literature comes from one book by Mark Twain called *Huckleberry Finn* . . . it's the best book we've had. All American writing comes from that." This rather loose overstatement is generally taken to mean that *Huckleberry Finn* is the source for the natural, colloquial, and nonliterary prose style in which much modern American literature, and particularly Hemingway's, is written. Whether the man knew it or not, his remark actually reveals so much more about himself that it should be examined at considerable length: he has provided so deep an insight into his origins that the topic will stand by itself. But for the moment it is enough to consider the remark in the way in which it is usually taken—as an acknowledgment that Twain's novel started a process of raising colloquial American speech to a full-grown literary language which more or less culminates, for our time, in Hemingway's own writing.

Stated this way the claim will stand up pretty well. It is not difficult to find any number of stylistic precedents for Hemingway in *Huckleberry Finn*. The opening paragraph of the novel, which has plausibly been called "the most important single event in American literature," establishes at once the "unliterary" tone. It also combines with this colloquialism a very artful use of repetition, which produces effects of rhythm and recurrence that are generally found in poetry, and are frequently found in Hemingway.

> You don't know about me without you have read a book by the name of *The Adventures of Tom Sawyer;* but that ain't no matter. That book was made by Mr. Mark Twain, and he told the truth, mainly. There was things which he stretched, but mainly he told the truth. That is nothing. I never seen anybody but lied one time or another, without it was Aunt Polly or the widow, or maybe

Mary. Aunt Polly—Tom's Aunt Polly, she is—
and Mary, and the Widow Douglas is all told about
in that book, which is mostly a true book, with
some stretchers, as I said before.

Throughout Twain's novel there is the same simplicity of
rhythm, vocabulary and sentence structure that we asso-
ciate with Hemingway. Hemingway's effects of crispness,
clarity and a wonderful freshness are there. Twain shows
the same gift for writing natural description, and giving the
sense of physical background, that Hemingway provides.
He has the same ability to make a minor character unforgettable in the briefest of spaces, and to get down the
precise manner of a person's speech, or dialect.

Gertrude Stein has usually received the credit for
teaching Hemingway the uses of repetition, though they
are written out plain in *Huckleberry Finn*. In the same
way she is said to be his instructor in the matter of how
to deal with violence in the most effective way—objectively, absolutely without comment. But *Huckleberry Finn*
is full of violence that is presented objectively, without
any comment whatsoever, and evidently on the same
theory that an episode of brutality, perfectly presented,
will speak for itself more eloquently than any author could
do. The episode, for example, in which a helpless drunk
named Boggs is shot and killed presents an exact precedent
for early scenes of Hemingway's like the one in which a
sick cabinet minister is shot and killed while sitting in a
puddle with his head on his knees. Both scenes produce
the same sickening effect; Twain's cries out for com-
passionate comment as loud as Hemingway's and gets as
little, which is to say none.

It is remarkable too that *Huckleberry Finn* is occasionally written in the stimulus-response, behavioristic
fashion that is so characteristic of Hemingway. Now and
then Twain does nothing to reorganize, reorder or analyze

his material, simply relating the events as they happen—
outwardly or in the mind of his protagonist—in the strict
order of their happening, as if he were drily making an
inventory. A passage like the one where Huck is escaping
from a cabin where he has been imprisoned by his father
("I Fool Pap and Get Away") is constructed in this
fashion. Twain lists each detail of Huck's escape, of his
preparation for a voyage, and of his feigning of his own
murder, in a strict one, two, three chronology of apparent
artlessness that is a prominent characteristic of such accounts as those of Nick's fishing trips.

It is a bit too much to say that "all American writing"
comes from Twain's book, but not too much to say that
Hemingway has accurately identified the progenitor of his
own prose. Still, there is a generation missing in this heredity; Clemens was born early enough to be Hemingway's
grandfather. And there is a quality of flat intensity in Hemingway that is usually absent in Twain. But we have a
writer who offers a general atmosphere of played-down
tension, and effectively links the two men—Stephen Crane.
Twain is one of the few novelists Crane is known to have
read while he was struggling to compose a style of his own,
and Hemingway correctly named him as the steppingstone
that makes the gap between himself and the author of
Huck's adventures negotiable.

The parallels which exist between Hemingway and
Crane as human beings are so numerous and exact that
they will go a long way toward explaining why the two
men so resemble each other as prose stylists, and even on
occasion as poets. Both Hemingway and Crane began very
young their careers as reporters, and quickly became
foreign correspondents. They traveled widely, and to the
same places: Key West, the American West and Cuba;
Europe, a Greco-Turkish War, and so on. Mainly, when
they were able, they journeyed to wars. Both had very

religious mothers, neither ever quite got over the death of his father, and both rebelled in various ways against their families. Each childhood was marred by the painful experience of violence; and it was eventually in warfare, sought out and embraced, that each man found a fascinating formalization of violence, and his essential metaphor for life. Both made an art of their preoccupations, and sought above all things the varied meanings of war. Chiefly they were compelled to learn what it had to teach them about themselves, and to test themselves against it, to make of danger a kind of mystic ceremony, or crucible. The results were identical. Each man found violence, pitted himself against it in terror, sought courage for its own sake, and was cited for its uneasy attainment. They worried at great length the problems of the relation of fear to bravery, and in the end they acted with a similarity that is startling. The pictures of Hemingway's behavior under fire in the Second World War are identical with those of Crane in Cuba, where the earlier reporter took suicidal risks in what appear to be truly desperate attempts to get hit.

Often dedicated in their attitudes and their work to the annihilation of romantic idealisms and lies, both men seemed themselves romantic individualists. Both stubbornly self-reliant, they disdained those who would not strike out for themselves, and as a result both held unpopular attitudes toward people who condoned or awaited a social reliance. Both opposed and insulted respectability, violated in dress, language, frankness and behavior the genteel traditions of their periods, and developed defiant affections for people in disrepute. Partly as a result, both men became the victims of gossip and found their characters the subjects of hot debate. They livened the literary scene with their color, and—handsome to women, a bit heroic—watched legends grow from their personalities and adventures. Crane had no devotion to bullfighting, but he was an amateur athlete of note; he also loved to shoot and was good at it. He ended his career in the midst of friends, fame, wealth, partial expatriation and small animals at Brede Place—an exact precedent for Finca Vigia. Crane's whole dark view of existence, of man damaged and alone in a hostile, violent world, of life as one long war which we seek out and challenge in fear and controlled panic—it is all an amazing forecast of Hemingway.

The work which Stephen Crane tore out of his sickness was rescued from the obscurity into which it had fallen after his death in 1900 at a moment which could not have been more perfectly timed for Hemingway than it was. Damaged himself, and in every imaginable way prepared to find in Crane what would have most meaning for him, Hemingway was in 1921 learning how to write the things Crane had written. This was the year in which Vincent Starrett selected among Crane's nearly forgotten stories and brought out a volume called *Men, Women and Boats.* A friend (at the time) of Hemingway's, Ford Madox Ford, called these the "best short stories in English," and the young writer could not possibly have missed them.

At any rate it does not look as though he missed them. In Crane he could find his own strict sense of personal integrity and honesty, exercised in a rigorous effort to look for himself directly and immediately at things, so that he might see them as if they had not been seen before. Here was a writer who must have worked on the theory that a complete honesty of vision would mean a new originality, so false are our clichés and our commonplace attitudes, and the notion was validated by the results on paper. Here, as he would hope for himself, the effort had resulted in a concentrated, exclusive and brilliant prose style, simple, bare and tense. Here were vivid, clear impressions and perceptions, fresh pictures of the sensuous surface of life, and a precision and originality in language. Here too a sense of tight design, a startling immediacy in description and even (in *The Red Badge of Courage*) a fascinated, glaring picture of a battle-field corpse, compulsive and intense. In Crane he could see also an attempt to make dialogue a true imitation of collo-quial American speech (though it often failed) and could always feel sharply the country in the background—"the places and how the weather was." Here there were even the laconic, understated endings to stories that people com-plained were "pointless."

In the *Green Hills* Hemingway chose two stories for special praise—"The Open Boat" and "The Blue Hotel." The first of these is often called Crane's masterpiece; at times it sounds enough like Hemingway to have been written by him. There are several such places, but take one in which Crane's ear did not fail him:

> ... the cook and the correspondent argued as to the difference between a life-saving station and a house of refuge. The cook had said: "There's a house of refuge just north of the Mosquito Inlet Light, and as soon as they see us they'll come off in their boat and pick us up."
>
> "As soon as who see us?" said the corre-spondent.
>
> "The crew," said the cook.
>
> "Houses of refuge don't have crews," said the correspondent. "As I understand them, they are only places where clothes and grub are stored for the benefit of shipwrecked people. They don't carry crews."
>
> "Oh, yes, they do," said the cook.
>
> "No, they don't," said the correspondent.
>
> "Well, we're not there yet, anyhow," said the oiler, in the stern.
>
> "Well," said the cook, "perhaps it's not a house of refuge that I'm thinking of as being near Mos-

quito Inlet Light; perhaps it's a life-saving station."

    "We're not there yet," said the oiler in the stern.

Here is all the flatness, and yet all the cadence, too, of Hemingway's famous conversation. Here is the realistic yet mannered effect, the same terse and unliterary tone, the same repetitions of words, phrases and statements, and the same muted tension.

    "The Blue Hotel" has as many resemblances, particularly to "The Killers," and has in addition a dead Swede propped up in front of a cash register—a device Hemingway used in "An Alpine Idyll" and reused in *The Fifth Column*. But it is a story that Hemingway failed to mention which most clearly establishes his great debt to Crane. This is "An Episode of War," and it is enlightening to compare it with a story of Hemingway's like "A Clean Well-Lighted Place," which has all the "monotony," the regularly rising and falling cadence, the depressed tone and the razor-edged impressions and perceptions for which Hemingway is famous.

    "A Clean Well-Lighted Place" is a fairly "typical" Hemingway story. An old man has tried to commit suicide, and has failed. He sits alone in a café, until late at night an unsympathetic waiter sends him along and closes the place. Another waiter is the central figure in the story, and he feels quite differently from his colleague about those who need a clean, well-lighted café to sit up late in. There is little else in life to help support it. "Hail nothing full of nothing, nothing is with thee," he thinks, echoing Mr. Frazer as he heads homeward in the realization that there is nothing else he can do but go to his room and to bed. The story ends with a characteristic understatement:

> Now, without thinking further, he would go home
> to his room. He would lie in the bed and finally,

with daylight, he would go to sleep. After all, he said to himself, it is probably only insomnia. Many must have it.

Crane's story is of a lieutenant who, while distributing a ration of coffee, is suddenly shot in the arm. The wound is not serious, but in the confusion of battle it is not properly cared for, and the arm is amputated. With the same flat, reserved, depressed understatement and absolute lack of comment for which Hemingway is well known, Crane ends "An Episode of War":

> And this is the story of how the lieutenant lost his arm. When he reached home, his sisters, his mother, his wife, sobbed for a long time at the sight of the flat sleeve. "Oh, well," he said, standing shame-faced amid these tears, "I don't suppose it matters so much as all that."

"After all, he said to himself, it is probably only insomnia. Many must have it."

Hemingway "had no basic relation to any prewar culture," wrote Alfred Kazin in his *On Native Ground*. But Hemingway himself knew better than this, and with the praise he bestowed in the *Green Hills* he has acknowledged his relations. If we read this praise as an admission of indebtedness, and read his attacks on other writers who are supposed to have influenced him as a refusal to admit anything, then a kind of sense can be made of this process of casting off immediate and familiar forebears, while taking on older ones. This is by no means to say that Hemingway learned nothing from his friends in Paris. It is to say instead that whatever he may have been taught there was an extension of what he could have learned at home. The route which goes from Twain to Crane to Hemingway has no uncharted areas which needed to be negotiated by a transatlantic crossing.

Just as Hemingway's general affinities can be discovered, so also may origins be found for a good many of the specific parts of his work. Two of his most famous stories, "Macomber" and "Kilimanjaro," are good examples of this. As the autobiographical *Green Hills of Africa* shows beyond any doubt, both stories are based in one way or another on their author's experience in that country. One would think that was all Hemingway would want or need to go on. But the fact is that just as the early "Out of Season" dates back to and reflects the breakup of Hemingway's first marriage, and owes something to the example of Fitzgerald, too, so these stories date back to the breakup of a second marriage, are built on their author's past in many ways, and at the same time take their structure from the work of other writers.

Early in the Second World War Hemingway collected and published the war stories that impressed him most, and he included the prototypes for both "Kilimanjaro" and "The Short Happy Life." The precedent for the unusual structure of the former ("technically Hemingway's most accomplished piece") is an experimental tale written in 1891 by Ambrose Bierce called "An Occurrence at Owl Creek Bridge." Both stories deal with a man at the point of death who imaginatively experiences his escape in such a realistic fashion that the reader is fooled into believing that it has been made, until at the end he discovers that the man has really died. Both stories open with the situation of impending death, then flash back to explain how the situation came about, and then flash "forward" with the imaginary escape, only to conclude with the objective information that the man has indeed died. Bierce's technique was praised by W. D. Howells, and Hemingway's by Malcolm Cowley; both stories are technically brilliant indeed. But Bierce's was first.

Even the basic symbols in "Kilimanjaro" may have been borrowed—the mountain itself from a letter of

Gustave Flaubert's, in which the Frenchman compares the perfection of art to *"une grande montagne à escalader,"* goes on to describe a mountain very like Kilimanjaro, and even speaks of perishing in the snows toward its summit. The leopard could be taken from the first canto of the *Inferno,* where it had to do with worldly pleasure which stood between Dante and his Holy Hill.

Stephen Crane admired "An Occurrence at Owl Creek Bridge," too. "Nothing better exists," he once remarked. In the same anthology, called *Men at War,* in which Hemingway reprinted Bierce's story, he gave over a good deal of space to Crane in order that he might print the whole of *The Red Badge of Courage.* Crane's soldier-protagonist is named Henry, and he resembles in several ways a lieutenant who went by that name. But Hemingway really waited for "The Short Happy Life of Francis Macomber" to use *The Red Badge.* It is the psychological plot that he reworked. Crane's study of cowardice and heroism focused on a youth who learned courage in the face of danger. He became "a man" in the process, Crane tells us, and began really to "live." He confronted the danger at first with a terrible fear. When it came he bolted, and fled in a wild panic. But the next time he was up against the enemy he was awakened from a kind of fighting trance to discover that his fear was gone, his manhood attained, his life begun. This is of course almost identical to the process which Macomber undergoes.

Even some of Hemingway's novels have fathers that a wise child could know. *To Have and Have Not,* for instance, is regarded as authentic, if inferior Hemingway —and so it is, in many aspects, but it seems indebted to other books anyway. The drunken conversation and brawling of some battered war veterans in a barroom is reminiscent of the famous Cyclops episode in Joyce's *Ulysses.* And it would be difficult to read Marie Morgan's soliloquy, with which the book ends, without thinking of the widely known ruminations of Molly Bloom which bring Joyce's novel to a close. But Hemingway's novel is concerned chiefly with the character and experiences of Harry Morgan, and it comes as something of a surprise to realize that this "typical Hemingway figure," as he has been called, is actually a rather stock figure in one branch of the traditional literature of American naturalism. The book is fully enrolled in the primitive school which was founded by Frank Norris and Jack London. Norris's *Moran of the Lady Letty* (1898) is a ludicrous performance, but it introduced to American literature a good deal that would stimulate others, if only to other inferior novels. The book is built around the Have and Have Not contrast (and the rich are effete, the poor robust); there is brutality for the subject race, the Chinese, and a lot of deep-sea fishing. Moran herself is the image of Marie—a great blonde, too big and strong to be pretty, but tremendously exciting as a "mate."

Jack London's *Sea Wolf* (1900) came without a blush straight from *Moran,* but introduced Hemingway's Harry Morgan in a character called Wolf Larson—a virile, brutal individualist whose survival-of-the-fittest ethics are, like Harry's, the interest of the plot. Like Norris's and like Hemingway's, the novel is a sea story charged with cruelty and violence, and the moral—though Larson himself dies *before* he learns it—is that it will not work: no matter how potent and pitiless, a man has no chance alone.

Morgan is the son of Larson, who is the son of Moran. And—to confuse the genealogy beyond hope of repair—Marie is the twin of Moran. Hemingway's book is in the main line of development of one of our minor literary traditions, in which naturalism goes primitive with a Nietzschean morality in Norris, and is tested and found wanting by London. Hemingway simply brought all of this into the line of his development, and redid it for himself with the settings, characters, meanings and wild brutalities of the prototypes. He also did it better. His novel is a weak one, for him, but nothing makes it look so good as to place it in the company of its progenitors.

So it is not true that Hemingway does not derive from other writers. But if he smells of museums, Gertrude Stein's nose has been one of the few to detect that odor, for even when he borrows most we connect his borrowings not with his sources but with him. *To Have and Have Not* does not, after all, seem to be derived, even if it is. Like most writers, Hemingway went to those who preceded him for what his experience made meaningful to him. With the force of his personality and the skill of his craft he made what he borrowed his own.

Once he had begun to make things his own it wasn't long before other writers were trying to make it all theirs. For well over a quarter of a century Hemingway's influence on prose fiction was so great that it was scarcely possible to measure it. For a while it looked as if practically no one had escaped it, at least in this country, and there are any number of modern American writers who could be called on to say that they all imitated him at one time or another. Nor have other countries failed to feel the stimulus of his style, attitudes and mannerisms. Malcolm Cowley has claimed that these things have extended even to the Russians. Mario Praz gives personal testimony of their prevalence in Italy, first on the novelist Vittorini, and then on just about everyone, so that you stumbled on him everywhere, it is said, not only in fiction but even in the correspondence of newspapermen. Very likely there is no country in which American books are read whose literature has been entirely unaffected by Hemingway's work. In his own country we are so conditioned to his influence that we stopped noticing it some time ago, and seldom stop to realize that the story we are reading might have been quite different, or not written at all, except for him. For quite a while, commencing in the late Twenties, it was standard operating procedure for young writers to start out with what they took to be their own version of Hemingway, and many of them never recovered. Some adaptations quickly reduced themselves to a cheap mixture of toughness and sex; a few directly profited. O'Hara appears to owe his subject matter to the example of Fitzgerald. But his style is modeled on Hemingway's, and after showing that he had mastered some of the Hemingway devices—particularly those for writing dialogue—he made a fetish of Hemingway's objectivity, and some (not all) of his most ambitious efforts distorted it into a rigorous and insistent pointlessness.

Hemingway's influence has extended particularly to fiction which is sometimes called "subliterary." The novels of Raymond Chandler, for example (the only "detective" Hemingway once said he read), are full of Hemingway. Unless it would be the author himself in *Across the River,* Chandler illustrates as well as anyone what can happen when the attitudes and mannerisms which have meaning in one writer are taken over by another, for whom they have rather different meanings, or none. Detective novels of the tough school, for instances, are compounds of vernacular dialogue, sex, and most particularly violence, which derive less from the work of Dashiell Hammett than from Hemingway. They travesty Hemingway by turning out mixtures of pain, gore, brutality, evil and all-around toughness which have no function except that they morbidly titillate. The brutality of gangster stories and murder mysteries, on the page or on film, owes a great deal to a man for whom violence was never pointless, who never offered it simply for the reason that millions of people get a kick out of it. Violence is the meaningful core of Hemingway, but in the thousands of minor novelists and story writers and script writers who have become infected with the virus, it is a disease which they profit from by passing it along to the public. Borrowing minor characters from his work—crooks and gangsters of many types, drunks, dope fiends, sexual cripples (these until recent years covert) and the like—and often basing their protagonist on a crude misunderstanding of Hemingway's, they write it tough and simple, bring in plenty of sex, alternate murders with beatings, call it realism and then, if it was not written for the movies in the first place, try to sell Hollywood the rights. Many of the people who turn out this fiction have probably quite forgotten their origins, and by now there may be quite a few who have never read Hemingway at all. There is no longer any need to read him. The tradition is established, and flourishes on its own. But a lot of its tricks were developed by Hemingway. They were not exactly "tricks," though, when they were originated, because they existed not so much for their own sake but as means of saying other things.

The rather thin shell of the "callous" Hemingway hero was painfully drawn over a deep wound as a defense against reopening it. When the man could retrench himself, and stop thinking, and hold tight, and win a code to live by, he could get along. It has already been argued that he held so tight so long that some of his functions and emotions atrophied, as will a limb if the pressure of the tourniquet is not released occasionally to let the blood flow freely past the barrier. If you are going to be your own therapist, and of course the hero will go it alone, then perhaps this is the only way. When Hemingway was at his best, describing the narrow, bare and limited world he allowed himself to see and for the most part mastered, the reader is aware of what is missing, because Hemingway was aware of it, and communicated his awareness. The fact that very many things are missing, and pitifully missing, is often his point. But this is a level of meaning that his imitators lack utterly. They are not aware of what is left out, or even that anything is. Their world is not barren because Catherine died, but because they never knew she existed. Their protagonists withdraw from their fellows, and assume the stances of the attacked—all where no man pursues. It is a pose, or worse, a disease. Against a background of "peace" in our time the virus finds ideal conditions, and spreads wildly. Hemingway's work has been a rich source for various kinds of faking that are popular and profitable. The gestures, attitudes and preoccupations which are meaningful and valid in him have become in his imitators a host of sounds and furies which signify nothing that we could not do without.

Of course his influence has extended to realms other than the subliterary. Many serious writers learned from him, among other things, the values of objectivity, of honesty (what you really felt, and not what you ought or had been taught to feel) and something of how to write a hard clean prose style. In such ways his influence was all to the good. He helped to purify our writing of sentimentality, literary embellishment, padding and a superficial artfulness. Almost singlehanded he vitalized the writing of dialogue.

Hemingway's prose is easy to mimic, but hard to reproduce; efforts to write a style like it become tedious. And at best it is not a style suitable for all kinds of writing. However, when Hemingway wrote it well it is full of meaning, is pure and clear and does not spoil. In some ways a leader bears a responsibility for the excesses and defects of his followers, but we seldom weigh it against him. If we did, the greatest man in history, whoever he might be, would find it hard to survive the atrocities committed in his name.

It is of course as a stylist that Hemingway commands the most respect, and has had his widest and deepest effect on serious writers. When he was at his best we had no better, as even his detractors will occasionally and reluctantly admit. There is no need to describe the style at any great length, so well is it known. It is for the most part a colloquial and, apparently, a nonliterary prose, characterized by a conscientious simplicity of diction and sentence structure. The words are chiefly short and common ones, and there is a severe and austere economy in their use. The typical sentence is a simple declarative sentence, or a couple of these joined by a conjunction; there is very little subordination of clauses. The rhythms are simple and direct, and the effect is of crispness, cleanness and clarity, and sometimes of a monotony that the author does little to relieve.

It is a style which normally keeps out of sight the intelligence behind it. The sequence in which events are described is strictly the sequence in which they occurred; no mind reorders or analyzes them. Perceptions come direct to the reader, unmixed with comment. Consequently the impression is of an intense and disciplined objectivity, a matter-of-fact offering of whatever details are chosen to build in the reader the response for which the author has provided only the stimulus. Since the subject matter is most often violence and pain, the result of this tensely unemotional, "primitive" and "objective" presentation of experience is frequently a characteristic effect of irony and understatement. The vision which selects the details is narrow, and sharply focused. A great deal is not seen at all, but what is looked at is caught brilliantly, and the images strike the eye as if it had never caught them before.

Equally remarkable is the dialogue, which at its best shows Hemingway to have had an ear for the sound of human speech that was as sensitive as his nose for the smells of animals or as acute as the eyes of his father for birds. His ear picked up and recorded the accents and mannerisms of the characters that the speech is in the process of swiftly revealing. The conversation is as laconic and carefully controlled as the unspoken prose. The customary substitutes for the past of the verb "say" are scrupulously avoided; Roget's "assert, affirm, state, declare" go out the window in an effort to avoid the artful use of synonyms. Since the speech itself is normally eloquent of the way in which it is spoken, the crutch of verbs and adverbs which explain the manner of the speaking becomes unnecessary and is thrown away too. But for all the impression of authenticity Hemingway's dialogue gives, it was no simple reproduction of actual human talking. If it were, no particular credit would go to a writer who could turn the trick, for all he would need would be a portable home-recorder, a little meddlesome impudence and the services of a competent typist; few people would care to read much of the transcription. Instead, Hemingway's dialogue strips speech down to the essentials which are typical of the speaker. He built a pattern of mannerisms and responses which give an illusion of reality that, in its completeness, reality itself does not give.

This is of course a description of the style which made Hemingway famous—of his original and distinctive way of writing, the one by which he is still best known. It does not, however, accurately describe the style he had developed by 1940, say, when *For Whom the Bell Tolls* came out. In this novel, as in some of the work which he published later, there is still the same clean precision and freshness. It remained clear that this was Hemingway writing. But the prose, still very distinguished, called much less attention to itself. It is less tense, less austere, less behavioristic and impersonal, is more relaxed and orthodox. The sentences are longer and more graceful in their rhythms, as for example in the opening paragraph:

> He lay flat on the brown, pine-needled floor of the forest, his chin on his folded arms, and high overhead the wind blew in the tops of the pine trees. The mountainside sloped gently where he lay; but below it was steep and he could see the dark of the oiled road winding through the pass. There was a stream alongside the road and far down the pass he saw a mill beside the stream and the falling water of the dam, white in the summer sunlight.*

* Perhaps it is worth noting that one of the finest sentences Hemingway ever wrote (in *Green Hills of Africa*) is a highly atypical one, little known, and a full page-and-a-half in length. The last and best part of it runs:

> "... when, on the sea, you are alone with it and know that this Gulf Stream you are living with, knowing, learning about, and loving, has moved, as it moves, since before man, and that it has gone by the shoreline of that long, beautiful, unhappy island [Cuba] since before Columbus sighted it and that the things you find out about it, and those that have always lived in it are permanent and of value because that stream will flow, as it has flowed, after the Indians, after the Spaniards, after the British, after the Americans and after all the Cubans and all the systems of governments, the richness, the poverty, the martyrdom, the sacrifice and the venality and the cruelty are all gone as the high-piled scow of garbage, bright-colored, white-flecked, ill-smelling, now tilted on its side, spills off its load into the blue water, turning it a pale green to a depth of four or five fathoms as the load spreads across the surface, the sinkable part going down and the flotsam of palm fronds, corks, bottles, and used electric light globes, seasoned with an occasional condom or a deep floating corset, the torn leaves of a student's exercise book, a well-inflated dog, the occasional rat, the no-longer-distinguished cat; all this well shepherded by the boats of the garbage pickers who pluck their prizes with long

Whichever style one might prefer—the earlier one was more striking and the later might be called more "mature"—the earlier writing is of more interest and more importance, for it was this prose which established Hemingway's innovations and brilliance, and which had such an influence on other writers. Nothing in the account given here of that original style, the "Hemingway style," should seem very surprising. But not understood as well as they might be are the purposes, implications, and ultimate meanings of that manner of writing which people for years have recognized without much difficulty.

A style has its own content, the manner of prose its own meanings, and there have been two or three fairly incisive attempts to figure out what Hemingway's prose style adds up to, what it does and says. It has been shown, for instance, that the style itself is very suggestive of the dislocated and disunified world which it reflects. Mark Schorer has argued that the bareness of the prose suggests the bareness of life, which is Hemingway's "subject." He also showed that the style was itself an expression of the novelist's stiff-lipped morality.

But the things that Hemingway's style most suggests are the very things that he was trying also to say directly

---

poles, as interested, as intelligent, and as accurate as historians; they have the viewpoint; the stream, with no visible flow, takes five loads of this a day when things are going well in La Habana and in ten miles along the coast it is as clear and blue and unimpressed as it was ever before the tug hauled out the scow; and the palm fronds of our victories, the worn lightbulbs of our discoveries and the empty condoms of our great loves float with no significance against one single, lasting thing— the stream."

Nelson Algren has apparently been in orbit ever since Hemingway some years ago called him "a man," and he remarks of the same sentence (part of which he "quotes," committing only six errors): "Call that babytalk."

and outright. His style is as eloquent of his content as the content itself; the style is a large part of the content. The strictly disciplined controls which he exerted over his hero and his "bad nerves" are precise parallels to the strictly disciplined sentences he wrote. Understatement, abbreviated statement and lack of statement reflect without the slightest distortion the rigid restraint the man felt he must practice if he were to survive. The "mindlessness" of the style is the result of the need to "stop thinking," and is the purest reflection of that need. The intense simplicity of the prose is a means by which the man said, Things must be *made* simple, or I am lost, in a way you'll never be. There is no rearrangement and reordering of the material because the mind operates no more than it has to. And all these things are communicated by the manner of the presentation.

The "impersonal tone" speaks the need to escape personality. The "objectivity" exists because subjectivity could mean that the brain could get to "racing like a flywheel with the weight gone." The "directness" and "immediacy" with which objects are seen convey the necessity for seeing for one's self, straight and anew, when so much of what others have said they saw seems false. The "economy" of the prose masters the little it can control cleanly. The style is "unemotional" and "primitive" because it has to be, and it says so. It is "tense" because that is the atmosphere in which the struggle for control takes place, and the tension expresses the fact. The prose gives an impression of "bareness" because, as Schorer said, so much of life is barren for the hero. But that was not really Hemingway's "subject." His subject was violence and pain, and their effects, and recovery from the effects in the face of and partly through more of the same. The style which expresses this subject matter is itself perfectly expressive of these things, and of the message: life, which is the material, must be constantly forced under the most intense and rigorous control, and held in the tightest of rein, for it is savage and can get out of hand.

An argument for this view of the implications and meaning of Hemingway's famous style is fortified by the fact that the style was developed and perfected in precisely the same period when Hemingway was grimly reorganizing his whole personality after the scattering of his forces in Italy. The fact that the two efforts came together chronologically has nothing to do with coincidence: they came together because they were inseparable aspects of one effort. The man learned to hold tight, not think, and let in the little at a time that he could control. It was a big part of his partial recuperation that he learned also to write a prose in which he could write things out the way he let them in. When it got a little better, when Robert Jordan won a kind of mastery over his difficulties, then in corresponding fashion the writing is less rigidly controlled.

He wrote it so that he could get rid of it, Hemingway said. What he did not say was that he wrote it in the style that would get rid of it. The mastery was not only a purpose for the writing, it was also an explanation for the way in which the writing was written. After the war had climaxed the process under which the hero became an emotional cripple, he built a careful, new self, walled in against a world that seemed to have been murderously faking in that war, a world of brutality against which he seemed otherwise unprotected and wholly vulnerable. He moved with caution, his guard up, his feelings hidden low, and began to learn how to write. All he wanted, he said, was to know how to live. Later he said that all he wanted was to write well. Any discrepancy which might appear to exist between the two statements is illusory. Learning to write well was a way of learning defense.

"If he wrote it he could get rid of it" might just as well have read, "If he wrote it he could live with it." He could not live with it without controlling it, and the place where it could best be mastered was under the disciplined pen.

Hemingway reproduced on paper the life he had seen through the eyes which his experiences made distinctive. What was muddy and messy became ordered and clear. The large part of it that was unpleasant was repeated, mastered, exorcised. The discipline that made the new personality made the new prose style, which developed as a crucial part of the personality that developed it, and which bespoke the personality. Hemingway's style is the perfect voice of his content. That style, moreover, is the end, or aim, of the man. It is the means of being the man. An old commonplace takes on new force: the style *is* the man.

Whatever his faults and limitations, Hemingway was a marvelous unity of man and writer, and of matter and manner, who wrote as his hero must live. His attitudes, personality, preoccupations and subjects had complex origins, like those of other writers. But it is clear that in him all of these things traced more than anywhere else to a series of blows which began to take up in Michigan, and then took "finally and for good" at Fossalta. It seems very strange, but his style—shaped into a new thing from the materials of so many other styles, and itself the source of so much that we read and hear—was, like a great deal else in Hemingway, a direct result of trauma. And this, finally, is the message the style has to give.

| # ADVENTURES OF HUCKLEBERRY FINN

It made me so sick I most fell out of the tree. I ain't a-going to tell all that happened. . . . I wished I hadn't ever come ashore that night to see such things. I ain't ever going to get shut of them—lots of times I dream about them.

HUCK FINN

In the last analysis, what a man says cannot be separated from the way he says it. But the fact remains that the things Hemingway had to say are by no means so highly regarded as his way of putting them. A good many people admire Hemingway's prose, and have little use for the rest of him. Some of them object particularly that as with many other modern writers there is too much bitterness and violence. One diagnosis is that he wandered too far from the traditions of his own country, and got lost. And one suggestion has been that, along with the others who are astray, he should find a way home to some such American traditions as are to be found in a novel like *Huckleberry Finn*. This is of course the novel that Hemingway says modern American writing comes from: somebody is mixed up.

One reason for the confusion may be that *Adventures of Huckleberry Finn* * is a very rich book, and offers several aspects which could conceivably sponsor American traditions that modern writers might get in line with. The book has among other things a wealth of life, a morality, a great deal of first-rate comedy, a sense of mystery and myth, some marvelous prose and a wonderful boy. Despite a nearly universal admiration, there is very little agreement as to what exactly it is that makes the novel a great and truly native one. No one has ever fully explained why the book is so popular, and the popular views of what it is all about, what it finally "means," are confused and sometimes demonstrably false. This would not be the proper place to discuss such matters, however, except for the fact that a consideration of them provides some striking insights into Ernest Hemingway, and into his significance for our civilization. There are times when you can see a man better by tightly and abruptly closing your eyes on him for a while, to think back. This is one of them, and for a few moments we can forget all about Hemingway to our eventual profit.

Huck Finn's prenatal experiences were mostly in the nature of misadventures which date back to the moment of his conception by a curiously indifferent parent. The novel was written as a sequel to *The Adventures of Tom Sawyer,* at the completion of which Twain had said, "By

---

* Like *Green Hills of Africa, Adventures of Huckleberry Finn* has no definite article in its title, though one is usually put there. Tom Sawyer's adventures were *The Adventures* . . . but they were completed, while Huck ends his book with anticipations (never fulfilled) of further goings-on in the West. For this reason, very likely, Twain hesitated to call the job he had done definitive.

and by I shall take a boy of twelve and run him through life in the first person." He began the book, got about half through it, disliked it, lost interest, and put it aside for several years. Then a visit to the Mississippi River restimulated him and he returned to the manuscript, finishing it at a speed which amazed even him.* Involved all the while, however, in a thousand other projects, he then went off lecturing, quite uninterested in his book, his biographer tells us glumly, except as to its sales, and quite unaware that he had written what is by far his best novel.**

A lot of publicity was provided to the end that Huck should make a lot of money, though. The best move in this direction was taken shortly after publication in 1884, not by Twain, but by a Concord (Massachusetts) Library Committee which found the book morally dangerous for youngsters and banished it from the shelves. This aroused a considerable furor, most of the combatants favoring the Concord view, and some even to the point of finding an exposure to the boy "vicious" for adults. Other public institutions followed New England's lead, and it was in the present century that a Brooklyn library removed the novel from its children's department on the unimpeachable ground that the boy told lies, itched, scratched and said "sweat."

Today, of course, the book is permitted the young and is even forced on them. Not that an interest in the morals is past: they are now approved. Various people have made a good deal of this. They praise Huck as a "child of nature" who has lived close to the simple facts of life, and is "unperverted by the tyrannies of the village

* Or so the story used to be. See, however, Walter Blair's *Mark Twain and Huck Finn*, Berkeley, 1962.

** Two years before he died Clemens wrote out a statement and signed it: "I like the Joan of Arc best of all my books; and it *is* the best. . . ."

that would make a good boy of him." This approach naturally makes much of the conflict in the boy over what to do with the runaway Jim. This is a conflict between the village code and the human code which is climaxed by Huck's decision to protect the slave in his escape, and which climaxes the whole book with Huck's "I studied a minute, sort of holding my breath, and then says to myself: 'All right, then, I'll *go* to hell!' " Of course if Huck were the child of nature alone, and were really unperverted by the village tyrannies, there would have been no conflict. But he is not. Life in a household dominated by women, and adventures with the relatively bourgeois Tom Sawyer, have complicated his early empty-barrel existence. He gets his moral stature not because he is "scornful of everything but himself and what he regards as right," but because he has an uneasy and courageous struggle with the values of St. Petersburg, and wins.

He is really a wonderful boy in many ways, and the pleasure of getting to know him as a person has certainly had a lot to do with the book's popularity. Very colorful and yet very real, Huck is about as attractive a character as one will meet in print. And while he never loses his identity as a particular and unforgettable youngster, he has for some people taken on epic size as a symbol. Just as American life can be seen as a continual debate between the legendary figures of Paul Bunyan and Rip Van Winkle, so the arguments are epitomized by Tom Sawyer and Huck Finn. Paul Bunyan is the man who gets things done. He expresses our drive for power and leadership. But if we love power we also despise drudgery, and so we are partly Rip, who hated exertion although he'd walk all day hunting. Victories accomplished in Bunyan's name mean hard work and self-denial, repressions and frustrations. A vicarious rebellion against thrift and labor results, and in a rather wistful way we love Van Winkle. No less a personage than Winston Churchill (once with T. S. Eliot, Santayana and Charles de Gaulle a staunch member of the International Mark Twain Society) testified that Tom Sawyer and Huck Finn "represent America" to him. This is because the Bunyan—Van Winkle dichotomy is repeated in them. Tom like Paul is bold in spirit and inventive of mind. He is a doer, the idol of free enterprise. Huck is a loafer. Faced with material problems petty or vast he slips away in the night. There are no figures to show how many daydreaming victims of respectability have climbed aboard the raft with him.

Since it has often been claimed that the book's popularity results from the fact that it cooperates with an American desire to play hooky, some might not think it the ideal classroom favorite it has become. But the editors of one edition of the novel "for high school use" merely reinforce the point by capitalizing on this subversive aspect, and in Some Teaching Suggestions forgo the usual discussions of Style, Plot and Characterization to remark: "In order to quicken the curiosity of boys and girls, it may be sufficient . . . to suggest that anyone who has ever longed to run away from home and civilizing influences . . . to be a tramp . . . should read the story of Huck's wanderings." There is a kind of finality here that defeats all criticism, and it is also to be found in a letter Clemens himself once received from a little girl:

> I am eleven years old, and we live on a farm near Rockville, Maryland. Once this winter we had a boy to work for us named John. We lent him "Huck Finn" to read, and one night he let his clothes out of the window and left in the night. The last we heard from him he was out in Ohio. . . .

Huck's journey seems a kind of national dream. It keeps cropping up. There is, for instance, the newspaper columnist who testifies for himself and "about a million other guys" that "maybe a thousand times, as boy and man," he has resolved: "So help me, someday I'm going to take a boat clear down the Mississippi. . . . Gosh, just think of shoving off . . . where the river begins to give promise of being wide and long, sort of lazying all the way. . . ." *

Huckleberry Finn is one of the most widely read and reread novels in America, and a perennial wish for escape in the boy's image is based on the book about him in the firmest sort of way. Huck is forever lighting out. He was on the loose in *Tom Sawyer*. He was taken in by the Widow Douglas, but "when I couldn't take it no longer I lit out" again. Tom talked him into returning to the proper and pious widow's, but even during his incarceration he slipped out nights and slept in the woods. In the novel that bears his name he is always taking off— not only from St. Petersburg but also from most of the other places where he has been involved. He is returned once more to respectability at the end, only to determine that pretty soon he will make for the "territory." Tom Blankenship, a boy Sam Clemens knew and in part based his runaway on, is said (though it is doubtful) to have settled down, finally, in the West. But for Huck himself the escape seems permanent.

Apparently there is something vastly suggestive about this boy's escapism. Whatever it is seems to start in the novel when Huck—trapped by his father in an isolated cabin, abandoned at one point for three days, and "all over welts" from the blows of a hickory stick—makes an

* In *Dark Laughter*, the novel Hemingway burlesqued, the protagonist goes down the same river, and Anderson writes: "Since he was a kid and had read Huckleberry Finn, he had kept some such notion in mind. Nearly every man who had lived long in the Mississippi Valley had that notion tucked away in him somewhere."

epic decision that has a little of the tone and motion and a bit of the appeal of something very like "myth." He has got to get out, and he is going:

> I thought it all over, and I reckoned I would walk off with the gun and some lines, and take to the woods when I run away. I guessed I wouldn't stay in one place, but just tramp right across the country, mostly nighttimes, and hunt and fish to keep alive, and so get so far away that the old man nor the widow couldn't ever find me any more.

The river changed all this, of course, when the June rise provided first a canoe and next a raft. Then finally Huck and Nigger Jim escape together down a river that is beautiful, powerful, solemn and full of wonder. Most people sense that the Mississippi has something to do with the way the novel holds and stays with them and draws them back. Some of them have spoken of "poetry" in this connection—of a "wilderness of moving water . . . the mysteries of fog and night and current," of Twain's having given to the river its "elementary place in the American experience" and even of the mighty stream as a "source of spiritual power." A movie called "Huckleberry Finn" was produced in 1939 with a bungling Mickey Rooney as impersonator, and there was one startling moment in the script when Mickey, in a tight spot, looked piously at the river and began to pray to it. It is hard to believe that T. S. Eliot, who like Clemens grew up beside the Mississippi, brought Mr. Rooney into the large circle of the men who have influenced him, but he was soon to begin some lines on the same river with the same perception: "I do not know much about gods; but I think that the river/Is a strong brown god. . . ." *

* Quoted from Eliot's "The Dry Salvages," in *Collected Poems 1909–1962*, with the permission of Harcourt, Brace and World, Inc.

It was D. H. Lawrence who once said: "You *must* look through the surface of American art, and see the inner diabolism of the symbolic meaning. Otherwise it is all mere childishness." This is a hopped-up remark, characteristic of Lawrence, and it contains as usual a kernel of truth worth more than the usual expositions of several sober writers. It seems pretty clear that *Huckleberry Finn* is to Lawrence's point—that something or other lies beneath its surface. Whatever it is that lies there speaks richly to people, whether of dreamy rebellions from the everyday concerns of their ordinary lives, or of gods, in a language strange to the ear which needs translating to be fully understood. Some symbol lies beneath this surface. People speak of "levels of meaning" in the novel—of a "legend," of something "forever true," of something "mythic" and of a night journey which "the whole world shares." Bernard De Voto, for one, was especially sensitive to this quality in the book. He wrote that "Huck sleeping under stars, or wakefully drifting through an immensity dotted only by far lights . . . satisfies blind gropings of the mind"—that there is something here which lies "beyond awareness."

Of course this is not the most precise way in the world of speaking. But when people use words like "legend" and "myth" here, they are trying to describe their reactions to something about which it is very difficult, if not impossible, to speak clearly. Some scholars believe that the word "myth" comes from the word "mü," which is imitative of the lowing of a cow and therefore inscrutable in denotation. But there is something about Huck's journey by water that moves his friends deeply, and even if it is a mystery we can talk about it.

Somehow the mythic or legendary quality of the novel, its glamour and escape value, and the invocations of the gods, and the deepest of all its levels must be bound up together. The basic appeal of the book is surely not accounted for with Huck as just a latter-day Van Winkle. This would be Huck without the river, and a land-locked version of the story would drain off with the water a good deal of the magic. In the same way the Mississippi loses meaning if we subtract from it a boy and a raft. The symbol is of Huck on a river.

The Mississippi was in point of fact a pretty glamorous place a century ago. Twain deleted from the picture the floating brothels he calls "steamboats," but he did not have to betray his desire to be honest about the giant stream in order to make it seem a wonderful and amazing body of water—a whole mile broad, and "awful still and grand," with logs drifting by black and silent, with everything dead quiet, and looking late and smelling late, and Jackson's Island standing up out of the middle of the stream big, dark and solid, like a steamboat without lights. It was a different but still haunting place when the heat lightning was "squirting around low in the sky," and the leaves were beginning to shiver; or by real lightning "bright as glory," with the treetops "a-plunging about away off yonder in the storm," and a glare lighting up the white caps for a half mile around, the islands "looking dusty in the rain." The river is a very strange place, too. The June rise goes so high that Huck and Jim find themselves paddling among the animal-crowded treetops of the island they had been living on. A house goes past, and in it all over the walls were "the ignorantist kind" of words and pictures made with charcoal, and a naked man shot in the back and dead for days. There is nothing unnatural about a steamboat at night: "she would turn a corner and her lights would wink out and her pow-wow shut off and leave the river still again; and by and by her waves would get to us, a long time after she was gone, and joggle the raft a bit." But it made you "feel crawly," as again when in a fog the rafts with the men beating tin pans to avoid collisions go by invisible but loud.

Yet the river counts for most with us when Huck is riding it under the conditions which are more normal to him, and it is here that we should go searching the symbolic meaning, buried deep and yet most compelling, and perhaps even diabolical. The normal mode of Huck's existence is escape, and the flight downstream starts when— having got loose from his father—he shoves off in the dead of the moonlight for Jackson's Island. Here he joins Jim, and gets a raft, and then one night, fearing capture, they

> got out the raft and slipped along down in the shade, past the foot of the island dead still—never saying a word.

There might seem to be nothing very remarkable or suggestive about that by itself. But this is only the first of a series of almost identical departures which, gradually, begin to add up. Three things characterize each one of them: ease, silence, and darkness. After a while these things begin to grow on you. The escapes become a consistent symbol, and here lies the key to the novel's least accessible compartment.

The escape after the fraud of "The Royal Nonesuch," for example, is described as briefly as the departure from the island, and in exactly the same terms:

> We struck the raft at the same time, and in less than two seconds we was gliding downstream, all dark and still, and edging towards the middle of the river, nobody saying a word.

Once again: gliding, dark, still.

When you are on a river and untied there is nothing to it. There is no rowing, downstream on a river. There is no machinery to start or tend and listen to. There are not even sails to set and trim: you just let go and you move away. Twice all that is involved is the cutting of a rope, as for instance when the two companions flee the victims of another attempted fraud. Huck reaching the raft in a very great hurry yells to Jim,

"Cut loose and let her slide!"
So in two seconds away we went a-sliding down the river, and it *did* seem so good to be free again. . . .

There are appeals in this recurring process beyond the obvious ones. There is of course escape for Huck and Jim, and escape for the reader, which mingles with all the other escapes in the book. But here too there is a deeper appeal, the deepest of the novel. This strange journey, blurred and mythic down a glamorous river, becomes a very special and supremely effortless flight into a dark and silent unknown: we escape more than we are aware of and to something from which—if this were not vicarious—we could not return.

There are more brightly lit passages in the novel about the way Huck and Jim spend their more relaxed hours that are wondrously attractive, and the source for many day-dreams. Mornings the runaways would hide and watch the daylight come—"not a sound anywhere—perfectly still—just like the whole world was asleep." They watch the river's "lonesomeness," and by and by lazy off to sleep. The night's running has the same quality of drowsiness, of nothing much happening. This works to break off the sharp edges of Huck's perception, to smooth the thing, to make it vague, general, magical, in some way portentous and in some sense "mythic":

It was kind of solemn, drifting down the big still river, laying on our backs looking up at the stars, and we didn't ever feel like talking aloud, and it

warn't often that we laughed . . . nothing ever happened to us at all—that night, nor the next nor
the next.

In this atmosphere of forgetfulness, we relax our
defenses. We are without care, and the river is beautiful.
We go ashore, occasionally, and when fleeing what invariably turns out to be some difficulty there we are relieved to
return to the water, and ready to experience symbolically
the process which takes us with such dreamy ease into
the black and breathless silence. There must be Freudians
who, with a suggestion of knowing smiles on their lips,
would leap to explain this "mystery": These gliding escapes
into the silent darkness are simply lyrical expressions of
the "death instinct," or of that desire to "return to the
womb" which is about the same thing as dying, with an
added advantage in the possibility of being reborn. Water
metaphors frequently have to do with birth, and we believe
that the first life on land actually did come from the sea;
we still come into the world from a kind of salt water called
amniotic; the French have variations of the same word,
mer and *mère,* for sea and mother. And there are notable
precedents for this symbolism right in American literature.
It is as a substitute for suicide that Ishmael takes to the sea
in *Moby-Dick,* he specifically says; the ocean is really a
death-symbol in that novel, and the Pequod offers a temporary passage out of human existence. When the sea
spoke to Whitman it was the "delicious" word "death"
that it whispered over and over. Here then in another
masterpiece Twain has all unawares drawn up from his
subconscious a metaphor for dying. It moves us because,
diabolically, we do not wholly wish to live.

There must also be Jungians who would be quick to
explain what is going on in this flight, for here seems to be
a perfect example of a psychic reaction in readers which is
out of proportion to its exciting cause, and must therefore

—according to Carl Jung—lead us to suspect the presence of an "archetype," a pattern in the "collective unconscious" of the race, which has been stirred. Huck's escapes by water are vastly more suggestive than some of the *Archetypal Patterns in Poetry* investigated by Maude Bodkin. Here is one of those downward movements "toward quiescence or toward disintegration and death" that she wrote about. Or, not much different, here is a repetition of the archetype of rebirth, which she found in night journeys.

Of course there is no conclusive evidence for such claims as these. And yet the responses of countless modern readers to some "mythic," unknown quality in Twain's story of a boy escaping down a river keep one from closing his ears utterly to the "depth psychologists." There is no more need to accept the existence of a collective unconscious than of a death instinct in order to understand that the dream of a final flight from a very imperfect life could powerfully attract us. We do participate with Huck in a series of escapes made glamorous by a mighty river. Repeated over and over in the same terms, the process compels, and does establish itself as symbolic. This time the raft has broken loose from a wrecked ship. Huck plunges into a rowboat, and

> I out with my knife and cut the rope, and away we went!
>
> We didn't touch an oar, and we didn't speak nor whisper, nor hardly even breathe. We went gliding swift along, dead silent, past the tip of the paddle-box, and past the stern; then in a second or two more we was a hundred yards below the wreck, and the darkness soaked her up, every last sign of her, and we was safe, and knowed it.

Or ever the silver cord be loosed—cut with a knife. We too are released again from a noisy and difficult life. In a second we are free, and do not lift a finger. Motionless ourselves, the black stream moves us mutely and endlessly down. Darkness, silence and ease overwhelm us: we are safe, and we know it, in the shadow of the last escape of all.

It is even easier to understand the magnetism of this event if the life one flees is sufficiently frustrating, disgusting and shocking. It is well known how the successful Clemens steamed under the pressures of the very respectability he sought and gained, and well known that by 1884 a corrosive despair for humanity, full of evil and duplicity, was beginning to oppress him. In writing Huck's adventures he expressed, among other things, his impatience with the middle-class status he had attained. But it is seldom remarked that in re-creating Hannibal and the river which flowed by it he was extraordinarily conscious of the facts of hideous violence and death, and expressed a horror of them that he had learned as a boy and had never forgot.

Adventures of Huckleberry Finn has so much about it that is hilarious or idyllic that our attention is easily diverted from the spill of blood that seeps through its pages, giving them a large part of their meaning. Life on the Mississippi around 1845 could be gory: Twain based the novel largely on experiences he himself had undergone as a boy or had known intimately of, and had never quite got over. We are often disinclined to consider how peaceful and restricted, aside from television, is the average recent American childhood compared to childhoods of other times and of other places today. Many people have become adults without ever having seen "live" a human being killed. Plenty of boys have never looked at a corpse, and very few of them have witnessed a murder.

Things were different with young Clemens and thus with Huck. The difference is profoundly important to the novel. Sam often looked hard at slaves chained together flat on the dirt in the baking summer sun, awaiting shipment to the market. He was a boy in Hannibal during a time when that town was terrorized by a lynching, murderous gang ludicrously called "The Black Avengers of the Spanish Main." A cave near Hannibal contained as a public amusement the body of a young girl preserved in alcohol; it was arranged so that one could seize the corpse by the hair, and drag it to the surface in order to study the face. When he was ten years old the boy saw a man take a lump of iron and crush a Negro's skull with it; then Sam spent an hour in fascinated horror watching the slave die. One night he heard a drunk announce that he was going to the house of a certain widow for the express purpose of raping her daughter, and Sam followed him, lurking close by while he bellowed his intentions outside the girl's house. The widow approached the man with defiance, counted ten, and then gave the swaying fellow a musket charge full in the chest. At this point the townspeople collected like ants, but Sam had had enough. He went home to dream of the murder and was not disappointed, he says.

One night it was not a dream. Trying to sleep in his father's office he became aware of some awful presence, and shortly the moon revealed a naked corpse with a hole in the middle of its chest. On another occasion he was playing near the spot where a runaway slave had drowned days before, and by accident he jarred loose the body, which had not been located, but which now popped up at him head first half out of the water, and seemed certainly to be chasing him as he fled. He watched knife fights in Hannibal, and at the end of one of them the loser fell dead at the feet of the boy who had wormed his way in for a good look. He was also witness, at noon on Main Street, to the murder of a man named Smarr. Kind persons placed a large Bible on the chest of the dying man. As he wrote years later, Sam "gasped and struggled for breath under the crush of that vast book for many a night."

The murders of Mr. Smarr and of the drunkard who was shot in the chest by the contemptuous widow are the direct sources for the murder of a man named Boggs in *Huckleberry Finn.* Of the shocks young Clemens was exposed to as a boy, many others found their way, years later, into the novel. These facts help explain what might otherwise seem a very curious thing: that with no exceptions but the rather irrelevant Tom Sawyer scenes which open and close *Huckleberry Finn,* every major episode in the novel ends in violence, in physical brutality, and usually in death. All along the way there is bloodshed and pain. There are thirteen separate corpses. All this despite the fact that Twain, in planning his book, made many notes for similar episodes which he did not use.

He used enough. There is a woman drowned so long her face is a face no longer, and there is Pap's face, which is not much of an improvement—"white; not like another man's white, but a white to make a body sick, a white to make a body's flesh crawl,—a tree-toad white, a fish-belly white." Until he escapes this face Huck is constantly being beaten. He is twice caught and thrashed on his way to school, and when Pap locks him in the log hut he is worked over whenever the man comes in drunk. Huck likes the hunting and fishing they do to stay alive, but after two months of regular pounding he cannot stand it any more. Before he is able to escape, however, he spends one night with a father who has at last drunk himself into delirium, who hammers the floor, feels snakes crawling across his face, and tries to kill the boy with a knife.

Then there is the naked man, shot in the back, with a face Jim describes as too ghastly to look at, and another man who is tied to the floor of a sinking boat, "sort of blubbering" for his life while his companions leave him to go down with the wreck. Still more brutal is the murder of Boggs, a harmless drunkard, "the best-natured old fool in Arkansaw." Boggs is shot down in cold blood in the middle of a town street by a contemptuous man whom he has been exuberantly insulting. He comes out of his alcoholic haze long enough to yell in terror, "Lord, don't shoot!" and his daughter runs to help him. But Colonel Sherburn shoots anyway, a Bible is placed on the dying man's chest ("they tore open his shirt first, and I seen where one of the bullets went in"), and the screaming girl is pulled off him, and taken away. Then (in one of the great moments in fiction) a long, lanky man in the street re-enacts the event to the intense satisfaction of all those who have assembled at the scene, and a dozen people offer him a drink. Not even the Duke and Dauphin depart in the humorous way that is so often taken to be the way of the book. The last time Huck sees them they are to be sure tarred, feathered, and astraddle a rail. But this, Huck makes clear, is not a funny picture as far as *he* is concerned: it is "a dreadful thing to see."

The most violent episode in the book is of course the Grangerford-Shepherdson feud. In all the novel, this is the horror Huck finds hardest to stomach. The Grangerford family takes him in, and soon all four of its males are killed, as well as two or three Shepherdsons. The death of Buck—Huck's young friend—is the worst. He and his cousin, both already shot, jump in the river and swim downstream as two Shepherdson men run along the bank, firing at the boys and yelling out, "Kill them, kill them!" Later Huck pulls the bodies from the river, and covers the faces. This is the most terrible experience in the novel for Huck, first because he so admired Buck and his relatives, and second because the slaughter comes on top of so much more of what sickens.

It is absolutely essential to an understanding of either this boy or the novel about him to see what the effect of all this brutality has been. It is also very easy to see: an over-exposure to violence has finally wounded the protagonist.

Each episode makes a mark: the conversation of the robbers on the "Walter Scott," with the man on the floor blubbering for his life, takes all the wind out of Huck; he cannot help thinking about the drowning; it is "dreadful." The swindle of the Wilks family also bothers him a great deal, and when the King sold the colored servants, and they were all crying together, "it most made me down sick to see it." The departure of the King and the Duke also "made me sick."

Each mark leaves a scar: these are not passing upsets for Huck. About the picture of the slaves who are being separated he says, "I can't get it out of my memory." And the sight of Buck Grangerford and his cousin being shot to death as they swam along in the water, already hurt:

> made me so sick I most fell out of the tree. I ain't a-going to tell *all* that happened—it would make me sick again to do that. I wished I hadn't ever come ashore that night to see such things. I ain't ever going to get shut of them—lots of times I dream about them.

The aspect of these brutal episodes that is most relevant to the main plot of a boy going down a river on a raft is quite simply this: that they serve to *wound* him. His experience of violence is tied together, and given its total meaning, by this result alone: violence has made him sick. Innumerable readers have tried it, but the plain truth is that Huckleberry Finn, boy or book, cannot really be understood without this clear perception. *Now* we may look at what has happened to this uncomplicated "child of nature." He may be still "unspoiled," but from having been knocked about so much he is very bruised. Better he had never come ashore that night to see such things, but he came. Now exposed to more bloodshed, drowning and sudden death than he can handle, he is himself their casualty. And Twain—working from his own bitter experience—could predict with unhappy confidence: he isn't ever going to get shut of them. Lots of times he dreams about them.

There are other things besides bad dreams which interfere with Huck's peace. Among them are a very active mind which he cannot put to rest, and a growing bitterness about human nature. He cannot sleep, he tells us: "I couldn't, somehow, for thinking." His encounter with the frauds called the Duke and the Dauphin is supposed to be funny. But Huck is not amused; they disgust him with mankind in general. He is wounded, and bitter, and suffering from both insomnia and nightmare, and he rebels. His rebellion brings the crisis of the novel when he, utterly perplexed and sickened by his experiences, tries to decide whether he will "steal a poor old woman's nigger" or protect him. He is all conflict, and tries to pray, but the words won't come. Finally, tortured, he decides. He will protect the slave, although to him this means taking up wickedness again, and eternal punishment in the hereafter. He has deserted the values of the society of his time.

This is of course his second desertion, really. Completely dissatisfied with his pious foster mother and the effeminate respectability which surrounded her, he had already run away from St. Petersburg. Now, off on his own, and exposed to the violence and evil of society as a whole, he renounces it. He goes on now outside its ways. If it is good, he is wicked. And if it aims for heaven, he will go elsewhere.

The fact that it is in the chapter immediately following this crisis that Mark Twain turns the story over to Tom Sawyer, abruptly transforming Huck into a simple narrator, a straight man who sets up jokes for the comedian, is not really so hard to explain. The rest of the novel is irrelevant to almost everything that has gone before, but the common explanation that Twain simply didn't know the difference is unacceptable. At this point in the story the boy is about as far from the carefree, laughing urchin he is almost universally mistaken for as it is possible to get. He is a wounded and damaged boy. He will never get over the terror he has seen and been through, is guilt-ridden and can't sleep at night for his thoughts. When he is able to sleep he is tortured with bad dreams. Wildly superstitious, his waking world is made fearful by the spirits that people it; he has broken with the morality he has been taught, and is so disgusted by the evil and duplicity of his fellows that he declares himself finally to be ashamed of them. This is a boy who has undergone an unhappy process of growing up—clean out of his creator's grasp. So cockily Twain was going to take a boy at twelve and run him through life in the first person, and so rapidly the boy got out of hand. Once Twain had planted in Huck the complications he suffered himself—they had seen the same horrors, dreamed the same nightmares, suffered blamelessly the same guilt and developed the same distaste for humanity—it was easier to write comedy, and revert to the Huck that Tom Sawyer thought he knew. Precisely as Clemens could never solve his own complications, save in the unmitigated but sophomoric pessimism of his last books, so he could not solve them for Huck, who had got too hot to handle and was dropped. What the man never realized was that in his journey by water he had been hinting at a solution all along: an excessive exposure to violence and death produced first a compulsive fascination with dying, and finally an ideal symbol for it.

* * *

There shouldn't be much need to point out that we

have here an elaborate pattern that we know rather well, having become fully acquainted with it in our own time. It is of course the pattern of the Hemingway hero who—up in Michigan and then in a war—was overexposed to violence and death, became preoccupied with these things in an unhealthy way, and finally in idealized terms envisaged his end, the only escape left him being in the image of the force escaped from. We even remember the part that rivers have played—the river that must be crossed before one rests in the shade of the trees, the river beside which the hero suffered his crucial wound, the river in which Frederic Henry was reborn, and carried into his long exile.

Nor is there perhaps much need to point out that in his writing career Hemingway has done very little if anything at all that is not sharply foreshadowed in the short space of Twain's novel. All we need do is recall the adventures of a boy named Adams, and place them beside certain adventures of a boy named Finn. In each case we have a boy dissatisfied with respectability, chiefly as represented by a Bible-quoting woman of the house, who runs away from home. St. Petersburg was a violent place, full of murder and body-snatching when Huck lived there and participated in *The Adventures of Tom Sawyer,* just as there had been violence and pain in northern Michigan. It was easy to flee respectability, but as for brutality both boys jumped the pan for the fire. Off on their own they came up against it hotter than ever. Then they were both hurt, and permanently scarred, and after that they both rebelled utterly against the ways of a society that sponsored horror. Nick's adventures are climaxed with his declaration that he is no patriot, and has made a separate peace with the enemy, Huck's with his decision to take up wickedness, and *go* to hell. In each case a sensitive, decent boy has been wounded by contact with a senselessly brutal society, and has disaffiliated. Now like the scars, the escapes seemed permanent: Huck to the "territory" and—since America has no longer a frontier, is "finished"—the hero to foreign lands. The stories are very nearly identical in structure.

The boys themselves, Nick and Huck, are very nearly twins. Both are sensitive, both rather passive, both quick with a lie when they need one but honest about important things; both are masculine and solitary and out-of-doors, being not quite housebroken, and fond of disreputable clothing, and of hunting and fishing and being off on their own. Both are humorless, and intensely serious; both are courageous despite their fears, nervous, and with a good deal of nerve. Each boy learns to think for himself, becomes perplexed, and comes then to reject a good deal of what he has been handed as true and false, right and wrong. Each has soured on people—the ones he meets on the fringes of society and the ordinary people whose ways he deserts. Deprived by their situations of many of the quiet pleasures of life, both take extreme pleasure in the life of the senses. Each delights in the food one can cook out-of-doors, each delights in cooking it, and each is placed in situations where this pleasure is increased by privation, or considerable physical exercise. And yet each of the boys is a great reader of literature who likes to discuss his reading. Each boy is attractive—a "good kid"—and each for the same reason.

Tom Sawyer, who revises the world around him in the images of his reading, is a real romantic. Huck, though his life is romantic, is by temperament a dogged realist. He is forever trying to see things as they are, beneath the lies people describe them with. He insists always on deglamorizing for himself Tom's fantasies. But he is also wonderfully superstitious, wide-eyed for omens, signs and portents. Ghosts, demons and witchcraft are all a part of his world; it is a strange, complex, ominous and primitive planet that he inhabits. And yet, though he cannot distinguish it from superstition, he is full of "know-how." He feigns his own murder masterfully, can make a brass quarter pass for silver by leaving it overnight in a raw potato, needs no clock in the darkness to tell him when morning approaches and can draw important conclusions from his knowledge of the difference between the floating habits of male and female corpses. He knows his way around, and that is what keeps him going. This sort of knowledge is of course what Hemingway's hero has cultivated for his survival and display, and it is only in the degree of sophistication that Nick's superstitions differ from Huck's. They both devote a large part of their time to complicated rituals for warding off the hostile spirits which pervade their lives and worlds.

Except chiefly that one boy makes us hurt, the other, laugh, what we have here are two nearly identical persons. The man fishing the Big Two-Hearted is Huck grown. His character is the same, and he has been through the same process. They covered Boggs' chest with a Bible, but not until Huck had seen where one of the bullets went in. They sent Nick from the cabin, but not until he had had a good view of the bunk and of the Indian's nearly severed head. Ernest Hemingway did something amazingly like what Mark Twain once announced he would do but did not: he took Clemens' boy, and "ran him through life," in *our* time.

Once you depart the society you had belonged to, you need new values to replace the old ones, and a logical place to sit is at the feet of those who opposed its way long before you did. As the hero struggled to learn from crooked gamblers and fixed prizefighters, so Huck learned from an outlaw. Courage was a product of his own nature, for the most part; despite his fears he is usually able to function. But honor is a thing he learned from a runaway slave. Before he learned it he made some bad mistakes, and it took a crushing remonstration from Jim—after the boy had tricked his companion—to awaken him to a real sense of what is "not done." There was a lot to be learned from a man who had been outside the going-concerns of the society he was born into from the day he was born into it.

The parallel is pretty complete. For twenty-five years Hemingway went on telling Twain's story, as it was lived by Twain's protagonist, as both heroes came up against the vices and false values of their societies, were struck down and limped off. There are only a couple more differences worth remarking. The chief one is that at the very point where Twain found his boy too complex and let him go, Hemingway exploited the condition and raised him to complicated manhood. And after the hero became a man he felt as men do, and not as boys, about women. But except for the humor, which is in Twain and not in Huck, these are the only important changes. The adventures of the generic Nick Adams are the adventures of Huckleberry Finn in our time. Hemingway's remark that all American writing comes from this one book would mean more if he had gone on to say, "Well, make it that maybe *mine* does." And if he had gone on that way it seems impossible that he could have known how close to dead center his shot had hit the bull's-eye.*

* In recent years other critics have pointed out that J. D. Salinger has extended the line drawn here from Huck to Nick to Holden Caulfield, whose stature in many minds is comparable to that of the precedents for him. Parallels between *The Catcher in the Rye* (1951) and *Huckleberry Finn* are indeed striking. Each book is written in a flawless boyish vernacular (one urban, the other rural) of its period. Both protagonists are archetypally in the American tradition of the Good "Bad Boy" who longs to escape "sivilization" for a state of natural innocence; both face a brutally corrupt adult world against which their uncorrupted hearts rebel, and on

The affinity between Hemingway's work and Twain's novel is often as close in small ways as in large. There is, as an instance, the scene in *For Whom the Bell Tolls* where Robert Jordan remembers seeing as a boy a Negro being hanged from a lamppost for burning. Something broke, the man fell to the ground, and that was the end of the story. It was a pointless thing—unless one saw the point, as Pilar and Maria did. The incident was not about the Negro, really, but about Robert. So the murder of Boggs was not about Boggs, primarily, but about the boy who saw where the bullet entered his body. The objectivity with which Hemingway and Twain alike customarily present such episodes has obscured their ultimate meaning. The Negro-burning scene could have come straight from Clemens' boyhood, and have gone straight into *Huckleberry Finn* as a perfect fit with an identical purpose. This is because the parts of Twain's story and of Hemingway's are standard parts and interchangeable. This is because they are telling the same story.

It is to be sure the same story with significant extensions and intensifications that we read in Hemingway. The essential meaning of these variations is clear in a story like "The Battler." This was the story about the Nick who had run away from home and met with strangers who travel along the fringes of society, as Huck did, and who—like Huck again—was profoundly impressed by the encounter. Hemingway's first substitution is of the railroad for the river. Twain himself remarked the appropriateness of this change when in 1882, after returning from his visit to the

which their comment is devastating; both are wonderfully honest—and most clever liars when the need arises; both are very funny, yet both also psychologically wounded (though many people have missed the fact that Holden has suffered some sort of "nervous breakdown"). Nick Adams will not fit this pattern at all points—it is obvious that he is usually very *un*funny—but that does not destroy the pattern.

Mississippi, he wrote in his notebook: "The romance of boating is gone. . . . The youth don't talk river slang any more. Their pride is apparently railways." The boy who in earlier days would wander down a river, and in more recent years would hitchhike on the highway, would in between these periods ride the rods, if he had the nerve. Naturally Nick has.

Life along the tracks, as on the Mississippi, is colorful, tough and eventful for a boy off on his own. The tracks have most of the river's strangeness, too, appearing "ghostly in the rising mist," as the atmosphere and isolation prepare for experience uncommon to Oak Park or Hannibal. And then, just as Huck ran into two men who pass in Twain for the "scum of society," so Nick meets two of the same. Huck's Duke and Dauphin are Nick's Ad and Bugs, who present just as odd appearances, and probably exist in part by means as illegal. One of Huck's acquaintances claimed to be the Lost Dauphin of France; Ad says he was a world champion, and his situation is a bit more disturbing than the Frenchman's since he is telling the truth. This, in a minor way, is of a piece with what is changing all through Hemingway's story: what was unpleasant about Huck's acquaints, and his experiences with them, is made greatly more so for Nick and his. While the Dauphin was a little "crazy," Ad Francis is often completely so; while the two river tramps were only moderately—and often amusingly—sinister, the railroad hoboes are intensely so, and they are not funny. Where Huck's pair was seldom more than he could handle, Nick needs help to avoid what would have been a very bad beating.

But Huck was only figuratively alone on his voyage; there was the Negro Jim, too, who also had to deal with human flotsam. It is in the way that Hemingway has condensed his cast of characters from four to three that truly makes sinister what was once amusing, or affectionate and even touching. The Negro Bugs has taken over Jim's role, and what Hemingway has done to the slave, whose manner occasionally crossed the border into nobility, should not happen, as they say, to a dog. But Jim is completely recognizable in the short story. It is easy to forget, but we had seen before, for example, the very discomforting and oily courtesy which Bugs shows Ad. We have heard before the unctuousness with which he addresses "Mister Francis," waiting on him with obsequious, ironic servility. We saw and heard all that on the raft, when royalty received such treatment as befitted its former status, and Jim attended the Dauphin's needs, addressing him as "your Highness," and asking "Will yo' Grace have some o' dis or some o' dat?" What was innocent play in Twain has become something else in Hemingway, just as what was innocent affection in Jim is something else again in Bugs. Jim was a very fine and motherly soul. He used to console Huck; he used to "pet" him, habitually called him "honey," and went naked with him, Twain says, "most of the time." These overtones, anticipated by the relationship of Melville's Ishmael and the "colored" Queequeg, Hemingway has borrowed for his own purposes. What was innocence —because unconscious and unintentional—in the novel is not at all that in the short story, and that Nick may be thoroughly shaken Hemingway has significantly intensified Huck's misadventures in a later generation.

But the changes are only matters of degree, after all. Huck's Battler did not sit so easy with him, either. Of Nick we learn only that he was struck deep by what he had seen and half sensed. The effect of the Duke and Dauphin was profound enough on Huck. He was disgusted by them. As a matter of fact he said that they were "enough to make a body ashamed of the human race."

It makes little difference whether you take him as a

whole or in part: there is little in Hemingway—and next to nothing of ultimate importance—that has not its precedents where we have been reading them. As we shall see, this fact in no way diminishes his accomplishment. But it does among other things, as in his affinity with Stephen Crane, align Hemingway in the strictest sort of fashion with the culture of his own country. And, as in the case of Crane again, the chief clue to the reason for the close connection seems to lie in the relationship of the authors as human beings. It would be ridiculous to look at the resemblance of Hemingway to Twain's novel as a matter of literary derivation alone, even if we could ever know exactly to what extent, conscious and otherwise, Hemingway has shaped his work in its image. At bottom, the continuity must be psychological and biographical. A similarity of experiences must ultimately be responsible for the similarities of story and characterization. Both men did undergo similar experiences, and both have written autobiographically.

The boyhoods of Clemens and Hemingway show a remarkable likeness. The environments—upper Michigan and frontier Missouri, to say nothing of Oak Park and the quieter side of Hannibal—match. The struggle between a religious and feminized respectability on one hand, and the lure of the out-of-doors and a more masculine freedom on the other, is the same. Huck, Nick and Ernest as boys all ran away from what they found stultifying and troublesome, and Clemens at eighteen impatiently left his own home for good, and set out to see the world. So did Hemingway at precisely the same age. Both men were "educated by life": Twain did not have very much formal schooling and Hemingway is the only prominent American novelist of his time, excepting only O'Hara, who never went to college. Both men were especially educated by journalism, and by the travel that profession can afford, as well as by their own undisciplined reading. Both roamed widely, and both were expatriated for substantial periods, as their disgust for America led them to look kindly on Europe. Both men became pessimists. Twain has been called our "first consistent preacher of futility," and for twenty years Hemingway could have qualified as our outstanding literary exponent in that role.

There are many parallels. A curious one involves the problem of "obscenity." We have changed quite a bit since the Gilded Age, and it is no longer likely that Huck will be banished for saying "sweat." But the Hemingway hero has been attacked for saying something that sounds very like that, and books he has appeared in have been dismissed as "trash" for their impropriety. Both Hemingway and Twain have been banned in Boston; the step we had in those days taken forward was a short one. Yet there is an irony here, and it must have been the result of a similar quirk in both writers that indeed they did feel compelled to write what might still be called "obscenity" by healthy people. The nature of the crimes centers alike on a coprolalial pre-occupation with words of four letters relating primarily to processes of excretion and flatulence. Twain's notorious, funny *1601* is still unacceptable to many readers, and some of Hemingway's early poetry—which certainly would have got him in trouble if published in this country—he himself called "obscene."

But all similarities between these two men fade before their parallel exposures and responses to violence and pain. The death symbolism in *Huckleberry Finn* and the fascination with death in most of Hemingway, combined with the corpses that litter all the pages, seem to offer at least some sort of argument for the view that there is a force in men which compels them to visit such scenes as were the places of their injuring. There is no question about this in Hemingway, and we know at least of Clemens that despite his notoriously poor memory he long held in his mind, in a most literal, accurate way, the horrors of his boyhood. This is particularly true of the violence which was the source of the Boggs episode in the novel. After the lapse of a whole half century he not only remembered clearly, but could still recall the nightmares he had suffered, and how he "gasped and struggled for breath . . . for many a night."

He remembered another even worse thing just as vividly. In 1847 his father, John Marshall Clemens, died. The family doctor performed a post-mortem on the body of that stern man, and watching the whole hideous procedure through a keyhole was an eleven-year-old boy, his son. Writing in his notebook of this experience after a lapse of fifty-seven years of the time that heals all wounds, Samuel Clemens was still so shaken that he pretended the corpse had been really his uncle's.

As we have seen, the term "traumatic" is a relative one, and experiences a lot less shocking than such as these will result in difficulty if the individual is properly constituted for it. Surely the generic Nick had a high potential, and so, it must be, had Huck. He was a projection of a part of Mark Twain, and an extremely sensitive boy. In addition, there is at least one unforgettable image of him which is much to the point. It is registered when he is at a circus, and a "drunk" nearly comes to grief on the back of a prancing horse. Everyone in the place was delighted, and stood up "shouting and laughing till tears rolled down." Everyone, that is, but one white-faced boy: "It warn't funny to me. . . . I was all of a tremble to see his danger." It is also true, according to contemporary psychoanalytic theory, that Twain's adult rages, his tantrums and his "Eruption," can be seen as symptoms of the trouble that can result from the kind of overexposure to horror he underwent as a boy, just as his nightmares and insomnia can. It seems very likely that a part of

Twain's trouble was the same as afflicted Ernest Hemingway.

There is one further item of interest here, if only a curiosity. If Nick Adams is Huck Finn, and if he is also Hemingway, and if this were a proposition in logic instead of a study in continuity of pattern and character from one century to another, then we should be stuck with the conclusion that, *ergo,* Ernest Hemingway is Huckleberry Finn. This is less embarrassing than it might seem, for there is available as "evidence" at least one goose-pimpling snapshot. This is a picture of Hemingway as a boy (printed here opposite page 55), and it looks more like our image of Huck than any painting Norman Rockwell or Thomas Hart Benton has done or will do. Out from under the brim of a peaked and dilapidated straw hat grins the fresh, sensitive face of a boy we had thought to be not of this world.

No other photograph of Hemingway is as revealing as this one, and nothing can ever say more about him than one novel of Twain's can do, for the origin of his long story lies not only in his own experience but as well in a book that prefigured it half a generation before he was born. It is in the light of this understanding that we might return to the notion that the trouble with Hemingway was that he broke from American traditions. Particularly we might turn to a book like J. Donald Adams' *The Shape of Books to Come* (1945), where the critic offered as an instrument for mending this severance a return to the virtues of our earlier days. Adams, in the shape of a critic to go, recommended with a solemnity momentarily radiant that writers like Ernest Hemingway get their bearings, and go back to books like *Huckleberry Finn.*

7 | THE WORLD AND AN AMERICAN MYTH

An obsession with evil, early sorrow and death appears astonishingly native to the American muse. "Whatever the American men of genius are," an English critic observed, "they are not young gods making a young world."

MATTHEW JOSEPHSON

Every true novelist has a "world" of some kind, an imaginary vision of some sphere or scene of life and action which his individual experience has caused him to see, and which he re-creates in fiction. This is his equivalent for what, if he wrote philosophy, would be a system of ideas. He sees a kind of life going against some background, and he tries to make it coherent and dramatic. He induces us to see it all through his eyes, and after we have done this we ask ourselves questions about the breadth of his vision and the depth of his perspective. We ask if this is a "real" world, one we can recognize and accept as true.

The pattern of Hemingway's coherence is plain and for the most part dramatic. His vision and its texture make up his world. This world is the world of Missouri transformed first into the world of northern Michigan. Indians replace Negroes as primitives who exist outside the bounds of middle-class ways, where life is in the raw, and feuds and jackknife Caesareans are possible. It is a place overlaid with a distorting respectability that forces an escape, which is an escape to pain. And then this place is itself transformed to a European battleground, where violence is organized on a grand scale into the formalized brutality of war.

Hemingway's world is ultimately a world at war—war either in the literal sense of armed and calculated conflict, or figuratively as marked everywhere with violence, potential or present, and a general hostility. In his view of it the hillside is pocked with shell holes, the branch of the tree is shattered, the highway is clogged with soldiers, trucks, refugees and carts, and the daughter of the innkeeper has been raped.

The people of this world operate under such conditions—desperation, apprehension, emergency, stiff-lipped fear and pleasure seized in haste—as are imposed by war. Their ordeals are by fire; manhood is attained under it, and womanhood is tested by its courageous acceptance. The old are scarred and have the wisdom of their wounds; the young are off somewhere learning, awaiting their turn. The brave are the fair. In the background are the walking wounded, the special figures of those who have survived their ordeals and come to some adjustment—the matadors and gamblers and fighters and deep-sea fishermen. Behind them are those who did not survive and readjust—the physical, intellectual and moral cripples, the stretcher cases; the bereaved, the doped and the queer. Emerging from them are the hero: a soldier, struck down but returned to duty, gear packed, ready to move. And the heroine: the girl the soldier can meet, love and part from forever in a space of days spent in some foreign city. They leave no children behind them. They leave nothing behind them but empty bottles and the signature in the register; when they are gone they exist only in the short memories of the tipped—the desk clerk, the waiter and the elevator boy. They are going to lose and they know it, but they can delay what is inevitable with the special knowledge that hazard teaches and by a decent respect for mystery. A shadow envelops them, which is the shadow of death, the essential preoccupation of those who live close to the front.

Restricted grimly by the urgencies of war, their morality is harshly pragmatic: what's moral is what you feel good after. Related to this is their code, which summarizes the virtues of the soldier. It is tested by conduct in the face of death; it is the ethic of wartime. And it operates, in a way, off–duty, for when the soldier is not at war he is in escape of it—on leave or, at the very least, in the reserve. And escaping this world is but to imitate it: one kills, instead of other soldiers, ducks, marlin, kudu, lions, bulls and horses. This escape functions to keep alive the conditions escaped, until the real thing comes back. In despite of alcohol, the muscles stay hard, the reflexes quick and the eye clear against the day when once more it is not in fun, and the target shoots back. The activities of escape go according to the rules of sport, which make up the code of the armistice, the temporary, peacetime modification of the rules of war.

As the exigencies of warfare obliterate the niceties of moral considerations, so a state of war limits the soldier pretty much to those pleasures which the senses communicate. Peril heightens his awareness of his senses, and privation enhances their gratification. The pleasures of taste and touch predominate, and the hero is like all soldiers in that women, food and drink supply all that he values beyond the code.

Hemingway's world is one in which things do not grow and bear fruit, but explode, break, decompose, or are eaten away. It is saved from total misery by visions of endurance, by what happiness the body can give when it does not hurt, by interludes of love which cannot outlast the furlough and by a pleasure in the landscapes of countries and cafés one can visit. A man has dignity only as he can walk with a courage that has no purpose beyond itself among the fellow wounded, with an ear alert for the sound of the shell that really has his number on it. It is a barren world of fragments which lies before us like a land of bad dreams, where a few pathetic idylls and partial triumphs relieve the diet of nightmare. It has neither light nor love that lasts nor certitude nor peace nor much help for pain. It is swept with the actualities of struggle and flight, and up ahead in the darkness the armies are engaged.

Of course it is easy to protest this world. It is a world seen through a crack in a wall by a man who is pinned down by gunfire, who can move outside to look around only on penalty of the death he seeks but also seeks to stay. Missing from it is a very large part of what our own eyes have also seen. There is a farmhouse down the road. The farmer was born there and has lived there all his life. His daughter, who was never raped, has married, had children and moved to town. Most of these people will never see a kudu or a bullfight, and war for them is a thing to be wholly avoided or, failing that, forgot with the discharge papers. Hemingway's world is a narrow one, which is real to us in a limited and partial way only, for he has left out of it a great deal of what many people would quite simply call "life." And his view of his world is not much less restricted. Nowhere in this writer can you find the mature, brooding intelligence, the sense of the past, the grown-up relationships of adult people, and many of the other things we normally ask of a first-rate novelist. Only battles, or their preludes or aftermaths, and Hemingway hypnotized by the one note he sounds. Only a tiny cast of characters, who change their names, but never represent more than a tiny minority of the people we have known. This vision is eccentric and verges on psychosis. It is violence-obsessed. The gaze is a glassy-eyed stare at what is or soon will be a corpse. It insists that we honor a stubborn and nearly hysterical preoccupation with the profound significance of violence in our time.

We do not do badly to protest Hemingway's world. It is not the one we wish to live in, and we usually believe that indeed we do not live in it. It is not a world, ultimately, in which some of us are even very interested. But if we should look back over our time, what facts could we choose to stack against the facts of violence, evil and death? We remember countless "minor" wars, and two major slaughters, and prepare for a third holocaust beyond which we cannot see anything or at all. We count casualties by the millions and run out of fingers, appropriate billions and can see no end to it. We may argue the utter inadequacy of the world Hemingway refracted and re-created. It is a hell of a world, and we should protest it. But on the other hand we should be hard pressed to prove that it is not the one we inhabit.

It is still too early to know which of all the worlds our writers offer will be the ones we shall turn out to have lived in. It all depends on what happens, and you never know at the time. But it is not too early to make predictions on the basis of the evidence that is already available, and there is enough of that to back Hemingway's world as strongly as the world constructed by any other twentieth-century American. It is a gloomy guess, but what we call a "good" one, that while other writers were watching the side acts,

Hemingway's eyes were from the start riveted on the main show. "Peace in our time" was an obscure and ironic prophecy. But it was stated at the very beginning and stuck to, and it was a brilliant prophecy, as our bad luck would have it.

Our bad luck is not necessarily a writer's, who has an iron in the fire that we do not, a future that passes over his death as if it did not matter. Among other people, this kind of future belongs to writers who have written prose which will still be "valid in a year or in ten years or, with luck and if you stated it purely enough, always." It is hard to think that some things could be stated more purely than Hemingway stated them; there are passages in him which, given his purposes and preconceptions, cannot be improved. It is harder to know about "luck," or even what it means. Still, there are ways in which Hemingway may be said to have often had it. He frequently showed a kind of sixth sense for relevance, for seizing on the exact mood of the moment and expressing it. But more striking is the stroke of his wounding, which fixed his attention permanently on his subject. The series of accidents which began up in Michigan and was climaxed at Fossalta restricted Hemingway to a world that a rational choice might never have hit on.

It was not long ago that we thought other worlds than Hemingway's were the true ones. These worlds were, speaking loosely, "social" or "psychological." They were built of Main Streets and "the American scene" for a while, and then of cities and factory towns and their workers. Or they were built on insights provided by a new psychology, and investigated the complexities of human personality. As far as both groups were concerned, war was an utter tragedy, yes, but it was a thing we knew better than to get involved in any more. Once a hatred for it had been firmly expressed, it became really a kind of

THE WORLD AND AN AMERICAN MYTH | *247*

bore, and to write about it was juvenile or cheap. War was a kind of odd irrelevance to the serious concerns of the age.

But we have lived to see all this look silly when set for significance beside the breakdown of peace in our century. It is quite possible that Hemingway, with all his obvious limitations, has been saying the truest things of our age truly, and these are materials for the building of permanent reputations. The early up-in-Michigan stories bespoke a vision of the public future that was chillingly accurate. It would be simple timidity not to predict that the private visions of "Kilimanjaro" and *The Old Man* were just as clear.

*   *   *

Prose fiction has characters, a style, a setting and a story to tell. Hemingway's characters we have met. His style and its origins and effects we have had a look at. We have abstracted and judged his world, and retold his story. There is nothing superficial about his vision, however narrow it may be. But when the adventures of his hero are placed as they ought to be beside those of Huck Finn, they may be made to say something profound. When a story is told in such a way as Twain told his, and it sticks and we return to it to find it always fresh and moving, we may be pretty sure that something is being said that we have an interest in hearing. When the story is told again, in a way befitting its own time, and literate Americans follow it and are moved again, we can be positive that it has more than a passing significance for us. The story of Huck and the Hemingway hero says some very basic things about what it is like to live in America.

First of all we can see that the ordeals of Mark Twain and Ernest Hemingway and their protagonists are excellent examples for the anonymous Englishman who wished to point out that our men of genius have assuredly not been young gods making a young world. And yet this is the reverse of what we often assume. We have a long tradition that prepares that assumption, and *Huckleberry Finn* has often been thought a part of it. Vachel Lindsay once wrote that Huck is the "American race," and that race the "new childhood of the world." We frequently think of this country as being still in the spring of life.

In a way it is true. Some years ago, during an investigation of Communist activity in Hollywood, Mrs. Leila Rogers testified in Washington that a movie called "None but the Lonely Heart" was un-American because it was "gloomy." This lady was the mother of a movie star named Ginger Rogers, and many did not think that she was peculiarly qualified to define, however negatively, the nature of American experience. But the fact is that this was one of those bungling insights like the one Mickey Rooney communicated when, dressed as Huck, he prayed to the Mississippi River. Mr. Rooney has been backed by T. S. Eliot, and Mrs. Rogers was also in excellent company.

The classic statement of her point of view was one made by William Dean Howells, who put it better, and also located the origin of the trouble in the place where the investigating committee expected to find it. "It is one of the reflections suggested by Dostoievsky's novel, *The Crime and the Punishment,*" Howells wrote, "that whoever struck a note so profoundly tragic in American fiction would do a false and mistaken thing. . . ." Here life is not so bad: "Our novelists, therefore, concern themselves with the more smiling aspects of life, which are the more American. . . ." It is "the large, cheerful average of health and success and happy life" which is "peculiarly American."

This opinion was later reinforced by Robert Frost in verse:

It makes the guild of novel writers sick
To be expected to be Dostoievskis
On nothing worse than too much luck and comfort.

THE WORLD AND AN AMERICAN MYTH | *249*

Just before this Frost had asked:

How are we to write
The Russian novel in America
As long as life goes so unterribly? *

The Howells view of American experience is not the ignorant error it is often taken for. It is a half-truth or a partial truth. But there is an impressive body of evidence in our literature which presents the other part, contradicting cheer, health, success and happiness. Commencing with our first Puritan writers, and coursing down through Poe, Hawthorne and Melville, say, and spreading widely in our own time, this literature often testifies for gloom indeed, and often for sickness, failure and misery. And we have seen how even Mark Twain contributed in *Huckleberry Finn* bitterness, introversion, nightmare and death.

Hemingway was not alone, in contemporary literature, in presenting a picture of misery and sickness. It was long a common complaint against modern writing in general that it "refused to look on the good side." In a way there is sense in the observation, for although pessimism was by no means born with our century it is nevertheless an obvious feature of contemporary literature. This literature has many beginnings; in American fiction books like Crane's *Maggie* (1893) and Norris's *McTeague* (1899) stand out as landmarks. But often overlooked in our literary history is one particular moment at which something we recognize as more or less "modern" in our fiction —its frequent insistence on looking "only at the bad side" —may be said to have begun. This insistence, which writers of our time generally, and Hemingway specifically,

* From "New Hampshire" from *Complete Poems of Robert Frost*. Copyright 1923 by Holt, Rinehart and Winston, Inc. Copyright 1951 by Robert Frost. Reprinted by permission of Holt, Rinehart and Winston, Inc.

have been charged with, had a kind of beginning one day in the mid-Nineties when Theodore Dreiser sat down and began "examining the current magazines." His dissatisfaction with what he found, recorded in *A Book About Myself* (1922), was epochal:

> I was never more confounded than by the discrepancy existing between my own observations and those displayed here, the beauty and peace and charm to be found in everything, the almost complete absence of any reference to the coarse and the vulgar and the cruel and the terrible.... Love was almost invariably rewarded... dreams came true... with such an air of assurance, omniscience and condescension, that I was quite put out by my own lacks and defects. They... wrote of nobility of character and sacrifice and the greatness of ideals and joy in simple things.... I had no such tales to tell, and, however much I tried, I could not think of any.

It happens that one of the writers Dreiser had been reading in the magazines was Howells himself. The disgust the younger man shows for a life in literature which he could not find elsewhere was a very large part of the motivation for his own work. It lasted him the better part of a writing lifetime, and it has survived him. Surrounded today by magazine fiction and movies, radio and television dramas, advertisements and the like, serious writers are driven to their insistence that cruelty and vulgarity exist, that love and dreams go sour. They are driven to it, as was Dreiser, because all about them is a world of "fiction" in the sense that it is "false." Part of their preoccupation with the darker sides of things comes from a completely human perversity that reacts in disgust from the piety and cant our people are fed commercially. For those who cannot accept the desperately censored pictures of life, with their fake satisfactions and sentimental sorrows, which "the current magazines" present, it is as though the statement of thesis brought with it the compulsion to antithesis. The serious writer who does nothing today to contradict or qualify "the greatness of ideals, and joy in simple things" becomes party to a conspiracy to ignore a good deal of what we all know to be real. Since the eighteenth century we have had a literature which reflects the health and happiness which American life affords, and it is quite proper that we should have too a literature which reflects and expresses the sickness and misery life in America also offers its people. And so we have novelists like Hemingway who help to right a balance which would otherwise weigh crazily on Howells' side.

Robert Frost—through no particular fault of his own the darling of the critics who most deplore Hemingway, and the recipient of four Pulitzer prizes and any number of honorary degrees—wrote of common sense, of wood smoke and apple orchards. Hemingway saw hysteria, and the smoke gunpowder makes, and knew the dull-green distillate of wormwood. Even through his melancholy— even in occasional desperation—Frost saw the eternal fields of New England, stitched together with stone walls, and in the distance the birches and the pine woods; Hemingway painted an American Guérnica. One takes sides in these matters, and thinks his opposition leaves out significant facts. But the argument as to which picture is American and which is not is misleading and premature. We do not know how things are going to come out, and to date both pictures reflect the nature of our experience, or neither does. We have had many years of peace and many wars. The face of America neither smiles with Howells nor twitches with Hemingway. Or it does both, and even at once.

Hemingway's principal opposition has come from

those who have attacked him for emphasizing the twitches, and for being pessimistic. Placing him in the flattering company of Joyce, Eliot and others, they complain passionately of his bitterness. Van Wyck Brooks, for example, demanded that modern writers have faith, faith in the goodness of human nature, for great literature has always had it, and had also health, will and courage. Hemingway, he protests, seems "bent on proving that life is a dark little pocket," and that "only the ugly is real." Brooks argues persuasively for the value of faith, but does not establish its basis. Other critics, too, have wanted Hemingway to write about "the good life."

These are familiar sounds, and even if *The Old Man and the Sea* had not come along to mock them, rather hollow do they ring if one listens closely to the terms. The "goodness of human nature" is a phrase to give any man who reads his paper pause; "health" and "will" are words of barbed complexity for any thoughtful modern. As for "courage," it is the chief virtue in Hemingway's hierarchy of values, and certainly he tried very hard to show that many things beside the ugly—many women and many countries and their peoples—are real. It might be, though, that he would not have known exactly what is meant by "the good life" for never having lived enough of it.

No writer can write well about what he has not lived, known and found real for himself. One of the silliest minor spectacles our time affords with any regularity is that of critics telling writers what they should write about. It is hard to know precisely what the result of such counsel would be, because there are few clear-cut cases where anyone has paid much attention to such advice. But it would be a safe bet that capitulation would mean the end of any work that would outlast the moment. *Huckleberry Finn* is full of brutality and disgust, as well as of peace and content, because these are the things Clemens had known and felt and remembered. We should have forgot the book long ago, or never have read it, had this been otherwise. Hemingway's world is full of pain, and of moral, mental and physical wreck—and love and endurance and courage—because these are the things that were real to Ernest Hemingway. The critics make a mistake. You can tell a writer to go to hell, or stop reading him, or read him and tear him up, in private or in print. But you can't tell him what to write. If he is any good he writes what he knows and feels and that is the end of it as far as he is concerned.

It is a vague feeling of some critics, which is articulated by Brooks again, that the trouble with Hemingway came from his expatriation, which is the cardinal sin for nationalists. "When we leave our country," Brooks wrote in his *On Literature Today* (1941), "we are apt to leave our roots behind us, and we fail to develop roots in any other country." If anything at all has become clear by now it should be that if Hemingway had a hundred troubles this was not among them. Superficially, of course, his work did come to us by way of 27 rue de Fleurus, the Deux Magots, and the various hotels of Paris, Madrid, Havana and Venice where he labored. But at bottom the analysis is as mistaken as any single one could be, for although we can never know precisely what Hemingway learned abroad, we do know that he did not learn much of any great significance there that was not already available to him in the experience and traditions of his own country.

In its purely literary aspects, this is rather *like* the case of Robert Frost, who is supposed to have learned in England how to make poetry, instead of literary prose, out of the words and rhythms of ordinary American speech. It might be true; maybe Wilfred Gibson taught him all he knew. But Frost brought back from England a "new" kind of writing which in its rural New England diction is very like Thoreau, in its rural description very like the best of Whittier and in its sentiments and speech rhythms is like nothing so much as a well-known experimental poem of Emerson's called "Hamatreya." We are in the process of developing our own literary traditions, or rather of discovering that we have them. And while it would be suicidal to cut ourselves off from the sources of things we require or can use, it does not hurt to know what are the things we no longer have any need to import.*

It is even harder to know how Hemingway may be said to have left his roots behind him when we were able to find the basic, permeating pattern of his entire output with its source so deep in one of the most native of all our books. The fact that for Huck and for Nick the same experiences had identical results means among other things that the smiling, sun-tanned mask which hides a pallor that no smile brightens is an American mask for an American pallor. If Huck is truly American—and this has yet to be denied—then so is the bitter, insomniacal, death-driven hero American, and wholly so. Two of our most prominent heroes are casualties whom the "knowledge of evil" we are commonly said to lack has made sick. We are trying to get out of something when we attempt to pin the blame for what we might not like in Hemingway on his expatriation. It will not do, for he was aboriginal and the product was home-grown.

America is a lucky country, and it is not surprising or unjust that a great deal of our literature should reflect the smiling aspects of our present and our past. But not every prospect pleases. To keep a balance, and because

* As result of this passage Frost was once asked what else, in his opinion, American writers had no need to import. He promptly answered "bourbon."

many writers do not feel at all like smiling, we get in the midst of healthy growth, death in the spring. In the case of Hemingway we get it in a form and manner that are made indigenous by his experience as a boy of life in this country and by the clear and complete precedent of one of the greatest and most compelling of all our native tales.

This theme of the boy shattered by the violence of the world he grows up in is a variation on one of the most ancient of all stories, and the greatest of all American stories, which relates the meeting of innocence and experience. This was a theme of our first professional man of letters, Charles Brockden Brown, and in one way or another it seems now to have been at the very least the greatest theme of the second half of our nineteenth century. Here it was chiefly related at the very poles of our national experience—on the frontier and in Europe—as if tendencies are clearest when carried to their extremes. With a steady flow of travelers abroad at this time, it was primarily in Europe that the drama of the meeting of youth and age was enacted.

The story of the American in Europe had two rather separate developments. There was a crude, comic one, as the foremost humorists of the age—Artemus Ward, Mark Twain and Petroleum V. Nasby—each in turn wrote his account of innocents abroad. This version can be traced at home back to Seba Smith and the "stage Yankee" before it fades into its folk origins, where various rural native types confront city slickers or foreign aristocrats. But the theme was potentially rich in many other ways, as the European fiction of Nathaniel Hawthorne, William Dean Howells and Henry James shows. It is of course in James, on the European end, that the matter gets its fullest development. Inclined to simplify the two sides of the conflict himself (though of course less than this), James' picture of the American visitor under the impact of the

European social order was a picture of simplicity, benevolence, naïveté and virtue struggling with complexity, sophistication, and even corruption and evil.

This story of innocence leaving its home and coming up against things which are not innocent is a great American story because it is based not only on the experience of every man as he grows up but also on the particular and peculiar historical experience of this nation. Once the country was fully discovered and established, we began after the Civil War to rediscover the world, and this adventure resulted in our defining ourselves in the light of people who did not seem, to us or to them, quite like us. In one way the definitions came back alike from both the frontier and the European poles, and the ways in which the definitions were changed by experience were similar. Huck's simplicity is complicated; *The American* Christopher Newman is a lot less naïve at the end than he was at the start; and by the end of "Daisy Miller" the girl is dead.

The Huck-Nick story shares this theme, for again it tells what happens when a spontaneous virtue meets with something that is not at all itself. But it is a variant, because there are differences here which change everything. Despite the fact that the traveling comedians made spectacles of their ignorance, they usually had the last laugh. And though in their contact with Europe the more serious pilgrims were usually enriched at their pain, more often than not they had showed up well in the process, by virtue of a kind of power that comes from purity. But there is nothing subtle about the force that confronts the natural goodness of Huck and Nick. It is violence, which is an essential experience of the frontier and also—in our time, which is a war time—of the American in Europe. And this time there is nothing in any way triumphant about the beating which innocence takes, or about what happens to it after it is beaten.

The repetition of Twain's story by Hemingway establishes a continuity of American experience from one century to another, and vastly reinforces the meaning of either story taken separately. When across the generations we take twice to ourselves the same pattern we should know that it has more to say to us than we heard at first. When a story is repeated it is sanctified by tradition. It proves too that it has a vitality that may not have been immediately evident, and a significance that is not apparent on the surface. And when the tale also explains something, in an imaginary and narrative way, we call it a "myth."

Myths are stories which have something about them that we clumsily call "magic." They have a special quality, an aura of portent. They deal, normally, with some critical phase of life, some crisis. The figures who undergo the adventures of the tale take on a symbolic air because we begin to recognize some aspect of our own. In an imaginative way we participate in myths, and the more we are able to do this, the more meaning they have for us. Of course we know that myths are false, as matters of fact. But they can be so profound as matters of metaphor that they make the facts seem superficial, and even accidental.

The story of the adventures of Huck Finn and the Hemingway hero is such a myth, which relates once more the Fall of Man, the loss of Paradise. But it is a myth for Americans, which speaks to the people of the country from whose experience it springs, saying: We start out smiling, and well disposed toward the world and our fellows. We are made in the image of this naturally good, simple, innocent boy, eager and expectant. But in the process of our going out, and when we meet with life, we are struck down, and afterward nothing in the kingdom can put us all the way back together again.

The boy was bright-eyed at first. But then, soon, on

one side of him were the twisting inhibitions and distortions of domestic life, and on the other a brutality and pain he had no reason under heaven to expect in a world of men who should be as goodhearted as he. In a tight and tortured place, he lights out in rebellion from the life of the world his elders have made and thrust on him. And then it is that he is really smashed, for the small world opens on a greater one that is much worse. His adventures there disqualify him from ever returning to the life he has deserted, and the world he has run away to becomes more and more a land of horror until finally he is hit hard and for good. Broken now, and pale and sick at heart, he rebels wholly. He can never be completely reconciled, and he has a permanent need for defense and escape.

The epic, national hero, call him Huck or Hemingway's, is virile and all-outdoors, but he is sick. He is told that as an American he does not "think," he has no "mind." But after what he has been through, mind and thought mean misery; his simplicity is forced on him and he dares not let it go.

This myth says something about us that is rather wistful. But it is as eloquent as any voice we can speak with of an innocent desire for a decent life on the one hand, and a sense of terrible betrayal on the other. We would do justly and be kind, it says. We wished no evil. But as we grew up it was everywhere, and all our expectations were sold out. This is as deep, and as great and beautiful, as any myth we have. It tries to explain us to ourselves and to a world that does not comprehend—and understandably does not, since it sees not our morning wishes but the mess that has been made of them by afternoon. It also tries to explain why it is that despite all our other, opposing myths—of success, progress, the certain beneficence of technical advance and the like—we are neither happy nor whole, nor, for the most part, kind and completely decent ourselves. It says with overwhelming poignance: We *would* have been, we *could* have been, but we were crippled before we were grown by the world we were given to grow in and now it is too late.

It was a lovely world for Huck and Nick, with its rivers and woods at first unspoiled. But the natural beauty of the land was a part of the betrayal, by which they were lulled into letting down defenses and misled into expecting only the best. The original beauty of the country and a breathless anticipation of the possibilities of life here in what seemed the newest and most promising world since Eden were part of a seduction that went bad and should have ended at the doctor's.

Thus we try to explain our experience. We believed all the visions were true and went abroad. But they were false. Someone stuck his head out and smiled and it was smashed. He asked only that others be as honest and as well disposed as he, but they were not and the damage is done and for good. It was treason, and the response must be extreme. It is. Finally there is only one defense left. It is an escape which is the same escape either way, down or across the river. It is a flight from violence and evil which Mark Twain once dreamed, and which Hemingway's life and Hemingway's work eternally rehearsed.

AFTERWORD | TOUCHING DOWN AND OUT

In my beginning is my end. . . .
*In my end is my beginning.**

The story called "Indian Camp" represents a number of "firsts" in Hemingway. From the standpoint of the boy's probable age it is very likely the first Nick Adams story. It was the first story in the author's first book of stories, *In Our Time,* and that was his first significant book of any kind. Attendance at Dr. Adams' jackknife delivery of the unanesthetized Indian woman's baby, and on her unanesthetized husband who razored his throat from ear to ear, was the marked beginning of a very great deal for Nick. It was a piece of unhappy preparation for his climactic wounding in Italy and, because he is the generic hero, an important clue to the meaning of Hemingway's work as a whole. "Indian Camp"

---

* T. S. Eliot, "East Coker," in *Collected Poems 1909–1962.* Quoted with permission of the publishers, Harcourt, Brace and World, Inc.

comes, however, to a subdued conclusion, as father rows son home across the bay:

> "Why did he kill himself, Daddy?"
> "I don't know, Nick. He couldn't stand things, I guess."
> "Do many men kill themselves, Daddy?"
> "Not very many, Nick."
> "Do many women?"
> "Hardly ever."
> "Don't they ever?"
> "Oh, yes. They do sometimes."
> "Daddy?"
> "Yes. . . ."
> "Is dying hard, Daddy?"
> "No, I think it's pretty easy, Nick. It all depends."
>
> They were seated in the boat, Nick in the stern, his father rowing. . . .
>
> In the early morning on the lake sitting in the stern of the boat with his father rowing, he felt quite sure he would never die.

Now from a purely esthetic point of view it is perfectly irrelevant, but from a human point of view perfectly irresistible, to remark the uncanny fact that the originals of both these characters, doctor and son, who make their first appearances here, were to die in the fashion they discuss in the story. Dr. Hemingway, depressed and in ill health, shot himself in the head on the morning of December 6, 1928, with a Smith and Wesson revolver, a relic of the Civil War that had belonged to his father (which his widow was to send to Ernest at his urgent request). The son, in much worse health and more deeply depressed, blew most of his head off with a double-barreled, 12-gauge shotgun on the morning of July 2, 1961. He couldn't stand things, I guess.

Thus Hemingway's life ended where his fiction had begun—had begun with a "forecast" so unintentional and obscure that only hindsight has chillingly felt it as an omen. So Hemingway's career came full circle, from early wounds around to a final one. With the sketches of *A Moveable Feast,* a record of the brilliant apprenticeship days in Paris, even the writing to date ends where it began.

If one learned anything at all from the New Criticism, provision of biographical data is a feeble dodge in the discussion of an esthetic object. But the human mind lacks power to suppress forbidden information voluntarily, and will it or nill it what it knows will surface. Hemingway would not have liked that and was right in not liking it—at times, anyway, wishing mightily for a disassociation of his biography from his books. But the public personality was too colorful to erase (indeed he often did the coloring himself), and the personal element in the fiction is too strong to ignore. Thus even if future generations can read his work in relative ignorance of its author the intense individuality of style and vision, hence of a personality behind it, will still provide a powerful sense of him. And so it is probable that even a reasonable separation of the man from his writing never will in this case be possible.

Shortly following his death, and once the belief that it might have been accidental had gone to rest too, there was a certain amount of puzzling, which faced a mystery: how could a man who had so convincingly bespoken courage, endurance and indomitability commit suicide? The answer was there for any who cared to search for it as far as the newspapers: the Hemingway who celebrated those virtues was not the man who pulled the triggers. At the end, and for some time before it, he was "not himself." Not that he was unrelated; he was the shadow of himself. To ask for grace under the pressure of being a very sick old man, particularly if prematurely old, is a little lacking in humility. Further, the worst of all his illnesses was a severe depression of the spirit that provides the will to endure. A man who is seriously depressed is always a suicide-risk; a man who is severely depressed is a risk more severe. The mysteries of suicide are not questions of value or virtue or coherence but the mysteries of mental health and disease. Not entirely mysterious or unknown, however, are the years that led slowly and then much faster downhill to the way out.

*   *   *

The declination of Hemingway's powers—physical, mental, hence literary—is also clearer by hindsight than it was at the time. He did seem in all those photographs to be moving very rapidly through middle age, and there was a suspicion that he felt rather close to Santiago, his Cuban fisherman: embattled and pretty old for his vocation. But for quite a while he maintained the illusion, perhaps even with himself, that he was still going strong. He gave the impression that he was writing as much as ever, and that he thought of his manuscripts as heirlooms to be passed on to survivors, properly stored for safekeeping in the vault of a bank whenever he left Cuba. Posthumous accounts of what he left behind appeared to bear him out that he wrote many pages, if less than he tended to claim, but not that the gilt edges were so thick as to require safe-deposit boxes and time locks where in his prime he had abandoned manuscript in the basement of a hotel and the back room of a saloon. A novel based on his Caribbean experiences with German submarines in World War II, called *The Sea-Chase,* has been reported complete, but no eagerness to publish it has been as yet detected. The little that did find its way into print over his last years—parts, only, of *The Dangerous Summer,* a couple of stories and two poems in the *Atlantic*—did nothing to enhance or even help retain the reputation he had generally reacquired with *The Old Man and the Sea* and was concerned to keep. He had been ten long years between books when the disappointing *Across the River and Into the Trees* appeared. *A Moveable Feast* turned out to have solid gold edges, but twelve years were to pass after *The Old Man and the Sea,* and Hemingway was to die, before the profits from it, in reputation and cash, were to be realized.

Perhaps himself uncertain of the confidence that he displayed like a good athlete, his no longer nearly so creative mind began to look back, as Santiago's had done, to the days of his great strength and equally to the settings in which he had enjoyed them. In 1953 he happily planned a great journey in remembrance of things past, or in search of time lost, to those locations: Spain, Africa, Paris. Ambitious literary projects eventually grew out of touching down at all three places. But this looking backward was a bad sign, and only the most conservative of these investments of time and depleted energy, the recollections of Paris, was to pay off.

Things started well enough, and if he had not now been—yet once more like Santiago—close to "definitely and finally *salao,* which is the worst form of unlucky," it is at least conceivable that he might have brought off a successful trilogy of revisitation. He and Mrs. Hemingway had a splendid time at the Pamplona fiesta; since he had made it famous in *The Sun Also Rises* he was treated, he said, "like local boy makes good." He came to know well the great new matador Ordóñez, son of the original for Pedro Romero of the novel; he also showed his wife the scenes where "in real life," as we say, *For Whom the Bell Tolls* was enacted. And for quite a while things went well in Africa. His old British hunting guide, Philip Percival (apparently his guide "Pop" in *Green Hills of Africa,* and probably the model for Francis Macomber's guide,

Wilson), was induced out of retirement to come along. Another son of a fondly remembered "blood brother"— his previous African gunbearer, by then dead—now amply filled his father's old capacity. It was a simple wish to make Mrs. Hemingway the somewhat belated Christmas present of a flight to the Belgian Congo in mid-January of 1954 that brought disaster.

While banking so that his special passengers could photograph some spectacular falls in Uganda, their pilot hit a defunct telegraph line with a wing and crash-landed the plane in the brush. Mrs. Hemingway was badly but not dangerously hurt. Her husband was damaged dangerously: *

> Hemingway's injuries, which might have killed a lesser man, included yet another full-scale concussion, complete, as he said, "with solid gold handles," as well as a ruptured liver, a ruptured kidney, complete stoppage of peristalsis in the intestines, damage to the lower vertebrae and the sphincter muscle, and severe sprains in the right arm and shoulder and the left leg. According to his wife Mary, both his scalp and his skull were laid open, and cerebral fluid oozed from the wound. Indeed, as Hemingway later put it, blood and water flowed from all the bodily orifices; for some time he was afflicted with double vision, and the concussion caused the temporary loss of hearing in one of his ears.

After a night spent near the Victoria Nile, close by elephants and crocodiles and with Mrs. Hemingway in

* Already too closely identified with such lists, the critic prefers to borrow one this time, gratefully, from Hemingway's authorized biographer, Carlos Baker, who composed it for the third edition of his *Hemingway: The Writer as Artist*.

shock, the crippled party was at least lucky enough to get the attention of a launch, which took them where another plane and pilot could fly to decent medical facilities. Almost incredibly they crashed again. This time, as not before, the plane caught fire, and Hemingway was badly burned. But he and Mrs. Hemingway did eventually make it alive to Venice.

On his previous trip to Africa he had needed to be flown out of the Kilimanjaro region because of amoebic dysentery (not, as the experience is refracted in "The Snows of Kilimanjaro," gangrene). The last time he had been to Venice, in residence at the Gritti, he had nearly died of a form of streptococcus infection (not, like his Col. Cantwell, of a heart attack). Now it was in the Gritti where despite considerable pain he read the obituaries of himself printed at the time of the crashes. And read them with pleasure; the notices were favorable. But the punishment he had taken seems sufficient indeed to have killed a lesser man, and it permanently injured a strong one.

Out of the airplane misfortunes came an amusing account of the experience called "The Christmas Gift," which appeared in *Look;* and out of the epic contests between the great modern matadors Antonio Ordóñez and Luis Dominguín were to come the extracts from *The Dangerous Summer* which were published in *Life.* But greater plans for a new book on Africa, whetted by the memory of writing *Green Hills of Africa,* aborted; and the notion of publishing a new sort of *Death in the Afternoon* on the modern bullfighters also went down the drain when it was decided that no more of the completed book on that famous competition than had already been printed in *Life* was to appear.

Winning the Nobel Prize in 1954 had provided a considerable lift, however. Given his opinion of several compatriots who had previously won it, the award must have seemed tardy, and he was not well enough to go to Stockholm to accept it in person. But his aversion to public speaking was such that his inability to attend the ceremonies may have been an unexpected boon; he composed a short statement of gratitude, and a few characteristic sentences about the problems of being a writer, which our ambassador to Sweden read for him.

This was a happy interlude and for a while it looked as if he was really on the mend. For the first time he took an active interest in the filming of one of his works, *The Old Man and the Sea,* his special concern being the boating of a proper marlin for it. After the Caribbean failed to produce one he took a camera crew into the Pacific where, off Peru, he eventually caught four very big but not truly enormous fish. So it was necessary to rely on Hollywood, and on other film, for the illusion of a giant specimen. This was naturally a small blow, but to a nonprofessional eye, anyway, the final results were satisfactory, and he himself was encouraged that his back had stood up well during the protracted fighting of some very large marlin.

It seems that after every recovery he could stage, and each was a more modest one than the one before, more trouble was waiting in the wings. This time it was new difficulties, discovered in Madrid, with his heart. But if alarming they were not extreme, and during most of 1958–1960 he moved without great difficulty between Spain, Paris, Cuba, Idaho, and on brief occasions New York. He was often writing again. There was a novel which has been described only as "set in southern France in the Twenties," and there were the Paris sketches which became *A Moveable Feast.* Some of the time, moreover, he seems to have been enjoying life as much as ever; there were some notable, noted parties. Indeed there appears to have been quite a bit of drinking in violation of doctor's orders; his blood pressure had gone high enough to give real concern; and he struck some friends as being "sad."

Then there was a new and serious frustration—not the tired one that said you can't go home again; home is the place where, when you go there, they have to take you in. But there was no such place. In the early days of the Cuban revolution Hemingway, like so many others, had strongly favored Castro; he was even to get into a spot where he was forced to award the man a prize in a fishing contest. But the disastrous nature of the new government began to become apparent, and in late July, 1960, the Hemingways quietly left Finca Vigia with thirty-two pieces of luggage for Idaho, but expecting to return. Looking back, the move has all the appearance of a retreat. So does an earlier departure from Spain in the fall of 1960, when he made for New York, where he and his wife had leased an apartment, only quickly to take off for Ketchum, Idaho, where they had bought a house.

Retreats they turned out to be, for by now it was entirely clear that he was in serious trouble. Under the name of his nearby Sun Valley doctor he soon checked in at the reknowned Mayo Clinic of Rochester, Minnesota. He had the remnants of a case of hepatitis, the old hypertension, diabetes (like his father) and perhaps a rare disorder called hemochromatosis. Hardest of all to dominate, however, was a deep depression for which he received fifteen electroshock treatments. But the treatments seemed to be working; by the start of 1961 he had improved. His weight and blood pressure were down and his spirits up. He was not well enough to accept an invitation to the inauguration of President Kennedy, but he watched it all on television, experiencing great satisfaction, hope and pride in Kennedy's courage and in his wife's beauty. Soon he was well enough to go back to Ketchum. By spring, however, he had to return to the Clinic, where he had ten more shock treatments.

Released in late June he was driven by car back to Idaho. The trip was slow and, for him, anxiety-ridden; he followed the progress town by town on a large map. His weight was now down to 155. On July 1, a Saturday, he was well enough to go out to dinner at an inn with his wife and an old friend, his erstwhile chauffeur. It is said that he seemed preoccupied. But back at the house Mrs. Hemingway felt that his morale was gratifyingly high. If so, it was to prove a tragic and violent intensification of an old and banal story: Saturday night and Sunday morning.

One morning a few days later I was phoned by a reporter for the Minneapolis *Tribune,* Victor Cohn, who had discovered that Hemingway had been hospitalized less for hypertension as announced to the papers than for an "emotional disturbance." The reporter asked what, in view of this book, I had to say. I answered that I saw no reason to go back on what I had written, but I took care to point out that "whatever bothered him at the end may have been unrelated. I don't know." I also told him how to locate Leslie Fiedler and Seymour Betsky, probably the last literary people to visit the writer. Cohn interviewed both, and the story appeared all over the country. Fiedler told of being shocked by Hemingway's uncertainty that he had ever written *anything* good, and Betsky remarked especially the psychological complications which left him unable to speak more than a few words of a sentence at a time. After a while, embarrassed for him, Betsky said, "we wanted to get out of there. . . . The man we saw was something of a ghost." Judging from these remarks and the occasional photographs, it struck me that all those years of hard living, fighting, drinking (and working) had ganged up and climbed all over Hemingway in a rush. One certainly felt for him. It was a shocking portrait, etched in dorian grays.

*   *   *

Following the death of the author there were two principal reactions, one critical, the other popular, which sped off unsurprisingly in opposite directions. The critics tried for some estimate of his value that history would verify. In effect if not intention this attempt came pretty much to an attack on all his "recent" work (not including *A Moveable Feast,* which had not been published) as of inferior vintage. Perhaps the clearest statement of this position was Dwight Macdonald's: "After 1930" Hemingway "just didn't have it any more," he wrote. He was "fast and stylish in the hundred-yard dash but he didn't have the wind for the long stuff." He made "one big, original stylistic discovery" but he "was unable . . . to invent anything else," and even the invention became a "slack, fake-biblical style which retains the mannerisms and omits the virtues." *

There is no doubt that Macdonald is himself both imitative *and* inventive: "he went to Stockholm and the King of Sweden put the medal around his neck and they shook hands." It would also seem that a few of the short stories Macdonald wants to praise were written after 1930. But one recognizes the position all right, and John Aldridge, re-experiencing *The Old Man and the Sea,* put some of it a little differently, in the best capsulization ever of what I have tried to describe in Hemingway's prose: "That whole, vital Hemingway dimension of simplicity forced under enormous pressure out of complexity" is absent from the book. ("Nothing is at stake except the profes-

---

* Macdonald's opinions appeared in *Encounter* for January, 1962; Aldridge's, below, in *Book Week,* June 20, 1965.

sional obligation to sound as much like Hemingway as possible.")

But if the critics bore down, the popular reaction to Hemingway's death amounted to a revitalization of the whole legend that had got started some thirty-five years before. There was intense curiosity about left-over manuscript, the creation of a Hemingway museum, and a whole flight of trash in book form, which circled like vultures round a choice bit of prey. As for future publication, available comment has been confusing and occasionally contradictory; best to say now that there will probably be more but the Estate is in no hurry. As for the rest of his papers, Mrs. Hemingway early announced that in view of her husband's admiration for the assassinated President they would go (was this the first important contribution?) to the proposed Kennedy Library. Of all recent books about the writer the only ones of popular interest to have any value were the sibling biographies—one by his brother Leicester, one by his sister Marcelline—and even they are of very restricted use.

The popular enterprise that is thriving would seem to be the "museum" (it has more the atmosphere of a shrine) that to our national embarrassment Fidel Castro had made of La Vigía, Hemingway's Cuban finca. (To deepen the blush the Russians promptly donated a bust of the author.) The grounds are being restored, the garage is to be remodeled for the display of innumerable photographs. The table is set for dinner, clothes are hanging in the closets, the writer's glasses lie on a bedside table. Lodged about the house are still 9,039 books, which are being catalogued, and carefully preserved on the wall of his bathroom is the cryptic: "212½ lb. Oct. 7 after NY. 17 days off diet and 5 drinking." Ordinary visitors arrive in large quantity, though they are allowed only to peek in at the windows, but if Americans were free to come and go in Cuba as they used to one suspects that the place would be as crowded as any memorial to an American outside the area of Washington, D.C.

The people who make the pilgrimage to the Kennedy grave in Arlington Cemetery are motivated by much the same sort of fascinated devotion to a charismatic figure as those who visit the Hemingway museum.* A question urges itself: will history that is not going to forget the assassinated President in a hurry remember the writer as well? Best to lead up to that one with a simpler question: what, if one were rewriting instead of revising this book, would he change in it?

For one thing he would deal at much more length with the writer's parents, who turn out to have been much more interesting and formidable people than their famous

---

* There was a remarkable affinity between the writer and the President. Both were serious but not solemn, witty, realistic men who determined to go to the top and did. Omniverous readers, insatiably curious, both were men of "style" and admirers of courage who wrote many profiles of it; indeed as definition of the term on the first page of his book Kennedy borrowed Hemingway's phrase, "grace under pressure." (For the lone epigraph to his book *on* Kennedy, Arthur Schlesinger, Jr., chose the passage in *A Farewell to Arms* from which this book took its epigraph for Chapter Three.) Curiously, a list of Hemingway's injuries could nearly be matched by a list of Kennedy's illnesses. (Four times before his son's actual death his father stood by his bed and said good-bye to him.) It is good to learn, furthermore, that the writer's admiration for the President was reciprocated. According to a letter from Schlesinger, Kennedy "obviously" felt some sort of affinity with Hemingway, and at one time or another had read "most of" his work. He was deeply distressed by the suicide, and had been particularly touched by a message Hemingway had sent him from the hospital following the inauguration, in which the writer put down in unaccustomed language how each day after it he had renewed his faith, and also said how lucky we were, in times so difficult for us and for the world, to have so brave a man in the White House.

son made them out to be, in fiction or elsewhere. Their Victorianism was so preposterous—so, too, their lack of understanding—that as a context for his general rebellion the family now looks bigger than the war.

For another, and in line with critics already cited, he would greatly tone down the praise for *The Old Man and the Sea,* with which he went out farther than Santiago. (One critic, Marvin Mudrick, wrote recently that I treated it as if it were one of Beethoven's last quartettes.) The feeling is now that although the tale is here and there exciting it is itself drawn out a little far. Even the title seems an affectation of simplicity, and the realization that Hemingway was now trading on and no longer inventing the style that made him famous came just too late. Redolent of self-admiration, Manolin's boyish worship of the old man is harder than ever to take. The boy himself once seemed a "substitute heroine," but the book by brother Leicester Hemingway supplied a better insight:

> Ernest was never very content with life unless he had a spiritual kid brother nearby . . . someone he could show off to as well as teach. He needed uncritical admiration. . . . A little worshipful awe was a distinct aid. . . . I made a good kid brother when I was around.

Heroine or kid brother, this need was almost always part of the trouble when Hemingway was around in the novels; self-praise is always most embarrassing. And, this time, identifying with his "code hero" brought on confusion as well. Thick as a "pencil," and set out with more care than the opposition's, Hemingway was thinking more of his own lines than Santiago's; allegory overwhelms reality when we are told that the young boy carries this fishing line—three-quarters of a mile of it—plus a harpoon and the gaff to the boat. (A gaffe indeed, unless, as we are not told, the lad was actually a giant.) Similarly it does not make very much sense to say that *Santiago* "went out too far": he did after all boat his fish out there, and the sharks that took it away from him are not confined to waters distant from land. It is not so much that Santiago was a fisherman in whom the writer saw himself; rather that Hemingway was a writer who thought he could disguise himself as Santiago. The autobiographical element unfortunately triumphs again: it wasn't Into the Caribbean but *Across the River* where somebody felt he went out too far. Hemingway, taking a view of that failed novel which occasionally overrode his concern for his sea story, went way out and hooked his great prize, a book to keep a man all winter, but then the critics ate away at it until there was nothing left. Not as strong as he had been once, he felt that he was still the master of many tricks and still up to bringing in the big one—which, in his opinion, may have been the same small book that was the allegory of his vicissitudes.

Hemingway remarked somewhere of his chewed-up *Across the River and Into the Trees* that having been through algebra and geometry and trigonometry he had now moved into calculus. It is not safe to dismiss such a statement as simply pretentious. Years before when he wrote of "the fourth and fifth dimensions that can be gotten" in prose it turned out that he had something in mind. Perhaps someday it can be shown how the calculus, which is often described as a symbolic means of "grasping the fleeting instant," throws a more attractive light on the novel than has yet been observed.

That doesn't really seem likely, but if it is ever accomplished the man who turns the trick will probably also discover such things Hemingway referred to in his Nobel Prize address as are "not immediately discernible in what a man writes." In the same speech the author appears to contradict himself, and argues that "going out too far" is not only not a fault, but precisely what if he is any good a writer must always do. Calling Santiago immediately to mind he says that "a writer is driven far out past where he can go, out to where no one can help him" —and to where, presumably, the critics cannot follow.

When William Faulkner was awarded the same prize in 1949 he responded with a widely-admired and grandly-rhetorical speech in which he said that a writer must stand for "the old verities and truths of the heart . . . love and honor and pity and pride and compassion and sacrifice." These sentiments made some of the people who admired them uncomfortable: wasn't *Faulkner,* they asked nervously aside, one of those who refused to face and write about these truths? It has long been clear that the people the question occurred to had been fooled by the wild indirection with which that novelist embodied abstract virtues in the most implausible of characters—the cowlike Lena, a bag of bones, Dilsey—and had never read "The Bear," regarded by many as his masterpiece, where alas he spoke the virtues almost directly.

When Hemingway received the prize in 1954, it is virtually certain that the combatant in him had a fist for Faulkner as he began: "Having no facility for speech making nor any domination of rhetoric. . . ." Then he said: "For a true writer each book should be a new beginning where he tries again for something that is beyond attainment . . . something that has never been done. . . ." Consternation once more!—it being almost a cliché that Hemingway, once established, took only very small chances. In various ways on various occasions Faulkner said it himself: that having discovered very early how to do one thing well, Hemingway was content to keep repeating it. The unavoidable question is: are we misreading Hemingway as badly as we once did Faulkner?—which is to ask: are there important things not yet discernible in some of his books that make them truly new attempts at the unattainable?

If that seems extraordinarily doubtful, we must consider the alternatives. Perhaps he was faking us. (This is unacceptable; as someone once said, he was "hopelessly sincere.") Possibly he was fooling himself, or attempted things that failed so badly they cannot be said to be really there. (Much more likely.) At any rate, in the same address Hemingway expressed his belief that things which are not immediately apparent in a writer are "eventually quite clear and by these and the degree of alchemy that he possesses he will endure or be forgotten." About that he was surely right. If there is time and alchemy, they decide it.

To speculate about writing that will endure in a world that is changing as fast as this one, and could transform itself out of existence, is just a little presumptuous. But most of us do it, and may be obliged to. Alchemy, the "magic" of Hemingway's prose at its best, will preserve him even if nothing really important, new and different is ever found in him. For this was a poet—surely not in his verse, nor because he wrote "poetic prose." Rather because his stylistic gifts are commonly found in a genre where there are fewer words as a rule and more attention paid them. The process whereby base language is converted to gold, and worked into brilliant patterns charged and disciplined against chaos, is not easily discovered, but when he was in top form Hemingway had the formula. The language of many poets who knew other things, but not precisely that, has survived a long time, and so should his. He was not the competitor, as he once suggested, but the antithesis of Tolstoi, whom he seems to have regarded with the rest of us as the greatest novelist of all. Style in Tolstoi—even in Russian, we are told—is fairly inconsequential, so that we may indeed need a new prosaics for dealing with him, and many others. But in Hemingway style is foremost, and the new poetics will do until better ones come along.

Readers who still find him crude and unsubtle are not reading the man under discussion, or are reading him through different lenses. Giving the devil his considerable due in the attack mentioned before, Dwight Macdonald remarked that Hemingway was "stylistically sophisticated to the point of decadence." This is a perception calculated to astonish many, and it calls to mind adjectives—like "rarefied," or "exquisite"—of such incongruity as to strike the many as ridiculous. But "a perfection in workmanship or design that appeals only to very sensitive taste" (the dictionary on "exquisite") is there. Macdonald calls the general "absence of subordinate clauses" in Hemingway "beautiful"—another word that will seem extreme or precious to unbelievers. But the part of Hemingway's audience that holds its breath watching him go unsupported way out there on a tightrope to see if he can make it safely to the end of the line knows what is meant. Esthetic snobbery is not the point. Rather that Hemingway has long appealed to more than one audience and continues to attract more. No modern writer capable of "rarefied" or "exquisite" effects in prose has ever in our time enjoyed so large a following as Hemingway has had for some thirty-five years.

With such things said one is willing to extend himself, peering ahead to the judgment of time. My prediction falls about halfway between that of the critics who dismiss the novels and want to cut the stories back to 1930, and those who will not admit that he ever published a really bad book: Hemingway wrote two very good early novels, several very good stories and a few great ones (to name them might raise a debate that would obscure the claim), and an excellent if quite small book of reminiscence. That's all it takes. This is such stuff as immortalities are made on.

*   *   *

A Moveable Feast (1964) has been saved for last so that we may finish as is proper with the cognac, and on an elegiac note; like him may end in Paris where as a writer he began. And may for the final time face the matter of the imitative and creative styles, which is become truly curious, since the most surprising thing about the *Feast* is that it is written not in the manner of the last two novels but of his best prose of nearly forty years before. How this recovery came about in the face of so many difficulties, if it did, is a mystery. If it didn't it is because what Hemingway wrote far back in the Paris days was not notes later worked into these sketches, which is the impression we have been given, but to some substantial degree was the sketches themselves. Nothing but a reading of some decades-old notebooks, if they have not been destroyed, will tell. Meanwhile they should not be bad to read about.

Most of us can remember without much trouble the discovery Hawthorne imagined having made in the storeroom of "The Custom-House." Among "aged cobwebs," "bundles of official documents," "musty papers" and "similar rubbish" he came upon a "small package . . . done up in . . . ancient yellow parchment" and tied with "faded red tape." The package contained "the record of other doings and sufferings," "the groundwork of a tale" that became, after the author had allowed himself "much license" with the record, *The Scarlet Letter*. (He thought eventually to deposit the package with the Essex Historical Society.)

Now, as related by Mary Hemingway, we have had a sort of counterpart to that happy event. This is in the discovery of some notebooks, packed away in two old trunks recovered from the storage basement of the Paris Ritz, where they had rested for some thirty years. The "trunks" were "two small, fabric-covered, rectangular boxes, both opening at the seams," wherein were found, amidst "ancient newspaper cuttings . . . a few cracked and faded books, some musty sweatshirts and withered sandals," several "blue-and-yellow covered penciled notebooks." After Hemingway had transformed them into what he says "may be regarded as fiction," these notebooks became *A Moveable Feast.* (One hopes they survive and are destined for final disposition in the Kennedy Library with the rest of his papers.)

There is a little more to this. Just as Hawthorne remarks in his sketch that he was happier in the composition of this work than at any time since he left the Old Manse (where of course he spent the early years of his marriage), so may Hemingway have found some happiness in writing sketches about places and events in the early years of *his* married lives. Lastly, with Hemingway's first posthumous work before us, it is a little awesome to hear Hawthorne, referring to a political "decapitation" that lost him his job in customs, conclude the passage: "the sketch which I am now bringing to a close, if too autobiographical for a modest person to publish in his lifetime, will readily be excused in a gentleman who writes from beyond the grave."

And so Hemingway's book appeared in the year and very month of the centenary of Hawthorne's actual demise. It is probably gratuitous to mention a "movable festival" (May Day) in the *Blithedale Romance,* but an additional afterthought is harder to resist—that this is not the first time these two unlikelies have been hitched together. For the chief point of his *Across the River and Into the Trees,* 1950, the notion of a person's sense of identification with a place most painful to him, had its classic American expression in this same introductory "Custom-House" in 1850. Time and literature are playing tricks on us.

Though his words, themselves astonishingly alive, surely came to us from beyond the grave, how readily will Hemingway be excused? (Hawthorne caught hell for his little sketch.) In life Hemingway maintained where he could a pretty steady vigilance against the slightest injury to his reputation. And though he often let down the bars himself he was quick to take offense at any uninvited invasion of his privacy. Whatever principles lurked in these attitudes seem to have applied only to the living, and to have existed chiefly for the benefit of himself alive. But reputations do not end with the death of writers, as he was ever well aware, and several suffer from the holes fired into them here. So descendants of the dead live on, and a few people at least have been hurt. What Fitzgerald confided to Hemingway after lunch at Michaud's, the dialogue with Ford Madox Ford in the Closerie des Lilas, what Hemingway overheard in Miss Stein's apartment one spring morning—these bullets are likely to keep on hitting home as long as the targets are up. In each of these cases Hemingway was promptly taken severely to task for telling tales out of school.

All the jokes in *A Moveable Feast* are on other people; Hemingway comes out—steadily, effortlessly—smelling like a *vin rosé*. Underneath his well-known openness and generosity there was a mean, wary streak. He couldn't have been all that good nor they, perhaps, all that vulnerable. It is possible to make exactly the same objection to this book that Hemingway made to Lillian Ross's once-notorious profile of him (which, incidentally, some of his chapters rather resemble). This objection would be that the sketches do not give much sense that the writers attacked were, much of the time anyway, serious and hard-working people. If his cruelty is to be excused, and it will be as Miss Ross has been, it will have to be with reference to the fierceness of competitive spirit without which he, at least, could not have been champion at all or ever and to the *éclat* with which these people are shot down. This was the fighter he said he was and, considering the infirmities of the late years, this is perhaps his most remarkable comeback, following as it does on the abortive *Dangerous Summer,* which he himself did not think well enough of to publish in full, and on *The Old Man and the Sea,* which has suffered a demotion. We will eventually forget the belligerence and arrogance, along with a lot of other things, by summoning up the same "strange excuse" with which Auden let off Yeats: "Time . . . Worships language and forgives/Everyone by whom it lives."

Hemingway shared in this devotion, and his success is with language. It is the shock of immediacy, the sense of our own presence on the streets he walks or in the cafés where he writes, talks, or drinks, that makes the book. When he is hungry so are we. And when, for instance, a small check enables him to break the fast at Lipp's, thought then as now to have the best beer in Paris, and he orders a great one, a *distingué,* and *pommes à l'huile* and a large sausage, this reader, who was only reading (it's not all *that* immediate), was driven ravenous. Or take the first little sketch in the book. It is too cold to write in his room so he goes to a café, sees a pretty girl there, works on a story, drinks a *café au lait* and decides to go where there will be snow instead of rain. Nothing has happened, the girl is wholly anonymous, the story is not named. But the scene is etched in the reader as if a diamond had scratched glass.

There are flaws in the diamond. Some of the dialogue with Hadley—his first wife, who now becomes the first "Hemingway heroine"—is unreal and a little embarrassing in the now-familiar way; sometimes the borders of sentimentality are skirted if not transgressed. But for the most part the prose glitters, warms, and delights. Hemingway is not remembering but re-experiencing; not describing, making. In several cases the results are comparable to his fiction. So much have things changed that he could have invented names for the characters and called the sketches stories, reversing the process whereby editors once rejected the stories as sketches. Then the book would seem like a book of stories, but a little like a novel, too, as does *Winesburg,* which he once called his first pattern, or *In Our Time.* And the novel would pick up a little more than the unity of place from the sense of irretrievable loss that haunts it—loss of the spirit of youth, innocence and springtime, soon to pass.

This sense of melancholy is present from the start. The keynote sounds faintly on page six: "all Paris belongs to me and I belong to this notebook and this pencil. . . . I felt . . . both sad and happy, as though I had made love. . . ." But it is amplified in reminiscence and by hindsight. "We're always lucky," he said to Hadley, "and like a fool I did not knock on wood." Later we are told that for luck he carried in his pocket a chestnut and a nearly worn-out rabbit's foot, so precarious was his happiness.

> Life had seemed so simple that morning when I had awakened and found the false spring and heard the pipes of the man with his herd of goats and gone out and bought the racing paper.
> But [Cold Pastoral!] Paris was a very old city and we were young and nothing was simple there, not even poverty, nor sudden money, nor the moonlight, nor right and wrong nor the breathing of someone who lay beside you in the moonlight.

This is by no means the best of it, but if, as already remarked, the style that had years ago begun to seem self-conscious and *faux-simple* came back to life toward the end, it must itself have helped sustain him for a while. A few excursions into self-imitation aside, most of *A Moveable Feast* is either witty (this was always his most under-rated virtue) or hardhitting, or moving and evocative.

Just as the book is well written it is good on the subject of writing—Hemingway's writing, that is. When once the last Mrs. Hemingway commented that the manuscript was not much about him he objected that it was—"by *remate*," a term in jai-lai which she translates "by reflection." And this is true; even when the focus, as so often, is on someone else there is an unflagging sense of his presence, of himself. But the largest part of the book's biographical value lies in what he has to say about the writing. The deep well-spring was there, and he explains how he tapped it and kept it flowing. He speaks much more directly than before about the "dimensions" he was trying to put in his stories, though at the time "it was a secret." He explains specifically how he did not put a "real life" suicide into the story called "Out of Season" "on my new theory that you could omit anything if you knew that you omitted and the omitted part would strengthen the story and make people feel something more than they understood." This passage goes on very nicely:

> Well, I thought, now I have them so they do not understand them. There cannot be much doubt about that. There is most certainly no demand for them. . . . And as long as they do not understand it you are ahead of them. Oh sure, I thought, I'm so far ahead of them now that I can't afford to eat regularly. It would not be bad if they caught up a little.

The theory worked eventually; people did catch up, more

or less. It only took time and it only needed confidence, as he said.*

The book contains many pleasant shocks of recognition for *aficionados,* particularly in those parts of it which serve as a partial gloss on the flashbacks in the familiar "Snows of Kilimanjaro." In the story the protagonist, Harry, about to die, thinks back to the opening scene of *A Moveable Feast*—the Place Contrescarpe, the Café des Amateurs and the drunkards, the hotel where Verlaine died, the Boucherie Chevaline and the Bal Musette—regretting that "he had never written a line about Paris. Not the Paris that he cared about." But now his maker has, and later Hemingway tells an uncomprehending Ford about his connection with the proprietor of the Bal, which is the same connection Harry remembered. In another flashback Harry thinks back to the Vorarlberg, Schruns and the skiing; the Madlener-Haus and the card games with Herr Lent when they were snowbound; "he had never written a line of that." But now he does, extensively and with the

---

* There is a pretty good game here for burgeoning scholars. Try to find out exactly what was left out of other stories written according to this theory. (We have the answer to "Out of Season"; we have long been in a position to know that another suicide—the father's—was left out of "Fathers and Sons"; further it might be argued, feebly, that when he leaves himself pretty much out of some of the tales in this book his felt presence adds an enhancing dimension.) But there would be few winners. It took twenty-five years for someone to see and say in print what was missing, and not understood but felt, in "Big Two-Hearted River"—that, as we have seen, the protagonist on his fishing trip was back and in bad shape from the war. But unfortunately this example, cleared up well over a decade ago, is the only other one Hemingway, cannily, gives away here; it is just after thinking over his new theory that he finishes the beer, leaves Lipp's, goes elsewhere for coffee and begins to write that same story, which is easily identified by the presence of the trout, the river, and the statement: "The story was about coming back from the war but there was no mention of the war in it."

same names and settings. He also writes it now with the same fierce resentment of the "rich bitch" and rich people generally that helped animate the story; in addition he gives an account of his first marriage, and how his connection with the rich was the beginning of the end of it —things only touched on in the story. In short Hemingway lived to write in *A Moveable Feast* at least part of the book Harry did not live to write in "The Snows of Kilimanjaro."

It is also possible for the knowing to identify such things as the story Hemingway was writing in the opening sketch of the book (though critics generally misidentified it as "Up in Michigan"); it is clearly the early Nick Adams item called "The Three-Day Blow." The same people can play guessing games about various "so and so's" who are insulted along the way (Cocteau? Harold Loeb? Wyndham Lewis?). And sometimes they will not need to guess. For instance when Fitzgerald speaks of "those absolutely bloody British" in a café—especially of "that girl with the phoney title who was so rude and that silly drunk with her. They said they were friends of yours." "They are"—it seems likely that the drunk is Mike Campbell, *né* Pat Swazey. And it seems much more than likely that the woman is our old friend and his fiancée, Lady Brett Ashley, in life Lady Duff Twysden (though it does not hurt to know that Fitzgerald's *Letters* confirm his dislike of her).*

* Has anyone noticed how Fitzgerald seems to have countered Hemingway's portrait of the lady with his own toward the end of *Tender Is the Night?* Here Brett appears to reappear as Lady Caroline Sibley-Biers, who has been arrested for disguising herself as a sailor and picking up a girl. And thinking of such an aberrant escapade, doesn't a touch of Zelda's Paris behavior—making Scott "jealous with other women"—put one in mind of both Lady Caroline's little lark and that neglected Hemingway story called "The Sea Change"? How about an episode involving Zelda's husband and a centigrade thermometer? Isn't this the germ of another story called "A Day's Wait"?

But enough of that. The book was not written for specialists so much as for the many who paid the price of it. They may have been overcharged for so small a volume, but they were not cheated by privacy, for the best things in it are completely public. As in the novels, for instance, anyone can divide the good guys from the bad. The good, beside the wife, Hadley, are Pascin, Joyce, Sylvia Beach, Ezra Pound and Evan Shipman. The bad are Ford, an aspiring critic and arrived homosexual named Hal, Zelda Fitzgerald, Wyndham Lewis and Ernest Walsh. However the two persons who get most space, Gertrude Stein and Scott Fitzgerald, are not so easily classified. Miss Stein evolves from good to bad; Fitzgerald dangles somewhere in between.

The sketch of Ford, prominently described as a "thin and stupid anecdote," is a malicious little masterpiece, deft, controlled and an absolute joy—even if it is also, as it may be, a largely invented private joke. Hemingway just got his subject to talk, which was easy, and then put it down with a lancet. At the end poor huffy-puffy Ford no longer needs piercing. The section on Ezra Pound and his Bel Esprit, a society he had helped to found "to provide a fund to get Mr. Eliot out of the bank so he would have money to write poetry," is very fine. ("This seemed like a good idea to me and after we had got Mr. Eliot out of the bank Ezra figured we would go right along and fix up everybody.") Another nice little piece concerns an obscure poet and opium eater, Ralph Cheever Dunning. In Pound's absence he was briefly in Hemingway's charge, and one Sunday morning Pound's concierge shouted up at Hemingway's window a sentence that gave happiness to Evan Shipman and can give happiness to all: *"Monsieur Dunning est monté sur le toit et refuse catégoriquement de descendre."*

But Stein and the Fitzgeralds get three sketches apiece, and these sections—by turns funny, sad and horrible—probably overshadow anything in the book but the *remate* presence of the author of it. The portrait of Miss Stein is not a painting, but an evolving story which starts in friendship, moves to a qualified affection, and explodes at the end in a scene as shocking as any in Hemingway, once famous as a shocker.* The pictures of the Fitzgeralds, especially a wildly funny account of a trip from Lyon to Paris in a car from which Zelda has had the top cut off, are also merciless and sobering. This story of the trip reaches its peak in a scene where Fitzgerald is dying, without symptoms, of congestion of the lungs in a hotel, and insists that Hemingway take his temperature, which he does, employing *faute de mieux* an absolutely unaffected bath thermometer "with a wooden back and enough metal to sink it in the bath." ("I shook the thermometer down professionally and said, 'You're lucky it's not a rectal thermometer.' ") The second installment, which argues that out of jealousy Zelda set about to destroy her husband, is not at all funny but rings true. The last sketch of Fitzgerald may indeed, however, "be regarded as fiction." In this one Hemingway tries to relieve Scott of worry inspired by Zelda about the size of his personal equipment. The conversation is plausible, even convincing, but two trips, first to *le water* to check the proportions, then another to the Louvre for the purpose of comparing them with the statues, have the look of invention. Despite doubt, however, the episode is funny, awful and sad all at once, and the ending of this recital is sad and a little cruel in a different way. Many years later Georges, the bar chief of the Ritz, where Fitzgerald in his fame is supposed to have been a center of attraction, asks Papa "who was this Monsieur Fitzgerald

* The last word on the vexed Stein-Hemingway relationship has surely not been said. One expert has remarked that the portrait of Miss Stein in this book is "selective to the point of real distortion."

that everyone asks me about? . . . You write about him as you remember him and then if he came here I will remember him."

In part the appeal of this little, almost trivial book lies in the fact of Hemingway's active and communicated presence in the great years of Americans in Paris, an ideal expatriation that thousands of literary people born too late have dreamed ever since. There was never for us anything like it; never such a sense that the arts were being born anew or such exhilaration at having escaped this country. The wine was nearly free, the food was excellent and cheap, it was a good place to work or not work; a couple could live well in this then-finest of cities on $25.00 a week. Many have tried to re-establish it all in Paris or Rome or elsewhere, but the arts are not being born anew, things have come to cost as much in many places as they do at home, and now we are teaching them how to drink.

But if it were simply a matter of time, place and nostalgia other writers would have been able to turn the trick, which they have notably failed to do. The difference is that this little collection of anecdotes and reminiscences is a minor work of art. The principles and particulars of poverty, the pleasures of food and drink disciplined by the shortage of cash, always how the weather was—these things and others are the texture of the book functioning almost thematically under the word-by-word spell of the style. This gentle effort toward unity is climaxed in the last scene, "There Is Never Any End to Paris," which is set mainly in Austria and has mostly to do with the skiing there: the magician has moved the activity so far to the side that you are not watching what else he is up to and do not see how he does it when suddenly there is the book, wrapped up and ending on the same sad loving note with which it began.

Then the tones of malice and superiority ring fainter,

and one remembers the terrible need for reassurance that caught Hemingway up during the months of acute depression in his last two years, when he felt that after all he had been knocked out and nothing he had ever written was worth a damn. As George Plimpton guessed in an early review, one function of this book was probably therapeutic. It was as if by "touching down" at these places and times, and even specific bottles and meals, the author could bring back the serenity and order that were failing him so badly. We know he had done this sort of thing before, as in "Big Two-Hearted River." And now he must touch down once more, with the same fanatical precision. We know, again via Mrs. Hemingway, how she and her husband walked over and over the routes he walks in this book, partly to check their accuracy. Everything must be absolutely and exactly right. Many months later she got a friend to recheck the itinerary. Finally she herself "flew over and retraced all the steps Ernest wrote he took, first by myself and then with my friend. . . ." It turned out that Hemingway had misspelled the names of two streets. They found nothing else amiss (though a couple of trivial misses remained to be found). But it was a loyal, worthy thing for her to do. She honored the therapy even though the patient was deceased.

INDEX

292 | INDEX

Fitzgerald, F. Scott, 13n, 15, 75, 80, 141, 174, 178, 186, 186n, 197, 201, 281, 286, 286n, 288–89
Fitzgerald, Zelda, 160, 286n, 287, 288
Flaubert, Gustave, 174, 188, 198
For Whom the Bell Tolls, 34, 61, 80, 82, 103–14, 119, 132, 136, 142, 150, 155, 205, 235, 265
Ford, Ford Madox, 85, 181, 185, 193, 281, 285, 287
Freud, Sigmund, 16–7, 81, 165–67, 222
Frost, Robert, 184, 249–50, 252, 254–5, 255n

Gable, Clark, 149
"Gambler, the Nun and the Radio, The," 66–8
Gellhorn, Martha, 142
Gibson, Wilfred, 254
Gibson, William M., 7
Gide, André, 152
Green Hills of Africa, 6, 42, 58, 66, 70–1, 74, 76, 95, 97–8, 108, 119, 140, 146, 186, 187, 194, 196, 197, 206n, 212n, 265, 267
Greppie, Count, 89n
Gris, Juan, 146
Groth, John, 151–52
Guthrie, Pat, 85

Hamlet, 183
Hammett, Dashiell, 201
Hawthorne, Nathaniel, 120, 121n, 188, 250, 256, 279–81

Hemingway, Clarence E., 60–1, 135–36, 262
Hemingway, Ernest,
the "code," 63–74, 96–7, 99–101, 119, 121–27
the "hero," 30–63, 74–8, 82–5, 90–1, 102–14, 115–18, 120–21, 125–27
the "heroine," 91, 108–09, 116, 125, 282
and Huck Finn, 211–40
as a legend, 134, 147–59, 272–74
life of, 135–47, 159–64, 261–70, 272
as "myth," 248–60
opposition to this book, 2–5, 6, 9–23, 26–8
place in literary history, 271–72, 274–79
and psychoanalysis, 16–21, 164–71
style, analysis of, 204–10, 271–72, 274, 277–79
derivation of, 172–200
influence of, 200–03
"world" of, 242–48
see also individual titles
Hemingway, Grace Hall, 135–36
Hemingway, Gregory, 140
Hemingway, John, 138
Hemingway, Leicester, 89n, 137n, 272
Hemingway, Mary Welsh, 2, 13, 124n, 142, 145, 153, 176n, 266–67, 270, 272, 279–80, 284, 290
Hemingway, Patrick, 140
Hernandez, Anselmo, 124n
Heyward, Leland, 124n
"Hills Like White Elephants," 178
Hobbs, Ranald, 12, 21